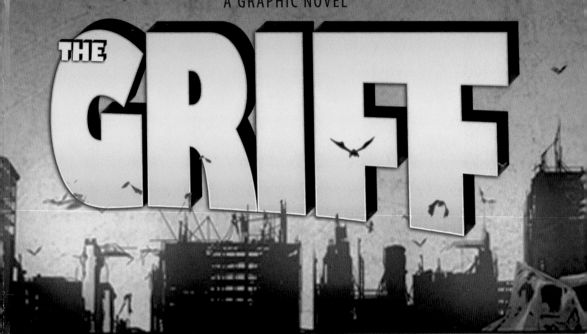

A GRAPHIC NOVEL

THE GRIFF

CHRISTOPHER MOORE and IAN CORSON

with JENNYSON ROSERO

WILLIAM MORROW

An Imprint of HarperCollins*Publishers*

THE GRIFF. Copyright © 2011 by Christopher Moore and Ian Corson. Illustrations copyright © 2011 by HarperCollins Publishers. All rights reserved. Printed in the United States of America. No part of this book may be used or reproduced in any manner whatsoever without written permission except in the case of brief quotations embodied in critical articles and reviews. For information address HarperCollins Publishers, 10 East 53rd Street, New York, NY 10022.

HarperCollins books may be purchased for educational, business, or sales promotional use. For information please write: Special Markets Department, HarperCollins Publishers, 10 East 53rd Street, New York, NY 10022.

FIRST EDITION

Designed by Dabel Brothers Productions, LLC
Ernst Dabel
Les Dabel
Derek Ruiz

Special Thanks:
Kevin Spent
Jennyson Rosero
Nelson Cosentino De Oliveira
Siya Oum
Cirque Studios
Andre Siregar
Dave Lanphear

ISBN 978-0-06-197752-7

11 12 13 14 15 QCT 10 9 8 7 6 5 4 3 2 1

This one is dedicated to Rachel Spradlin,

who has always wanted to be a dragon from outer space.

—C. M.

For my brother Jay,

who changed my writing forever when he first suggested I use verbs.

—I. C.

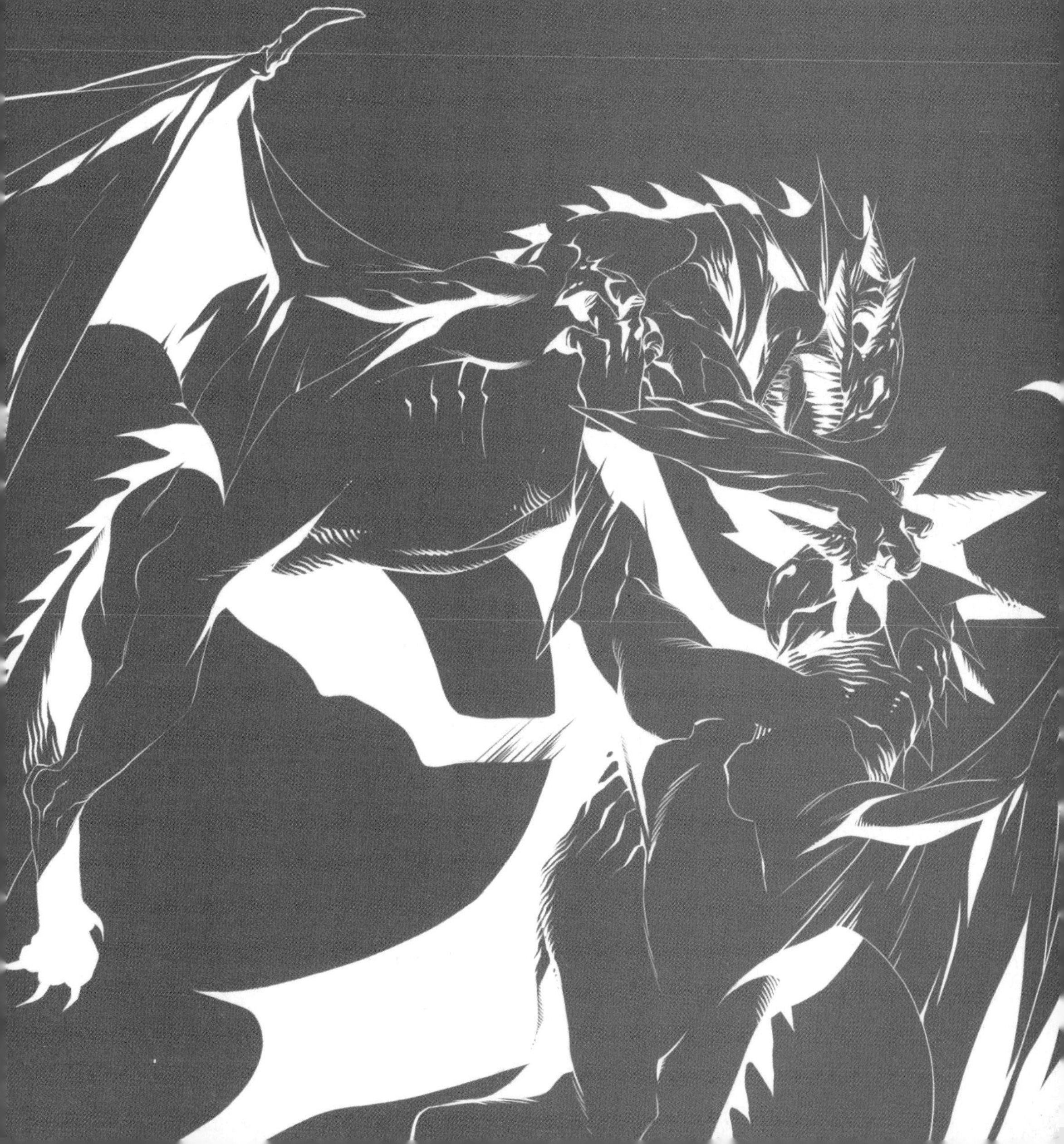

Acknowledgments

Thanks to Jen Brehl, Lynn Grady, Liate Stehlik, and the whole terrific team at William Morrow who brought this together.

—C. M.

Thanks to Glenn German, Mark Bacci, Lynn Hirshfield, Nana Greenwald, Kevin Richards, Jessica Sada, Jim Davidson, Lindsay Arn, Harlee McBride, Leigh Andersen, Viia Beaumanis, Suzanne Boyd, Stacy Ruppel, Sarah Dolgen, Eric Feig, Caren Bohrman, Nick Ellison, Jennifer Brehl, Lynn Grady, Les Dabel, Derek Ruiz, Vince Evans, Jennyson Rosero, Jim Krueger, Danny Miki, Simon Green, Christopher Moore, Jay Corson, and the rest of my family.

—I. C.

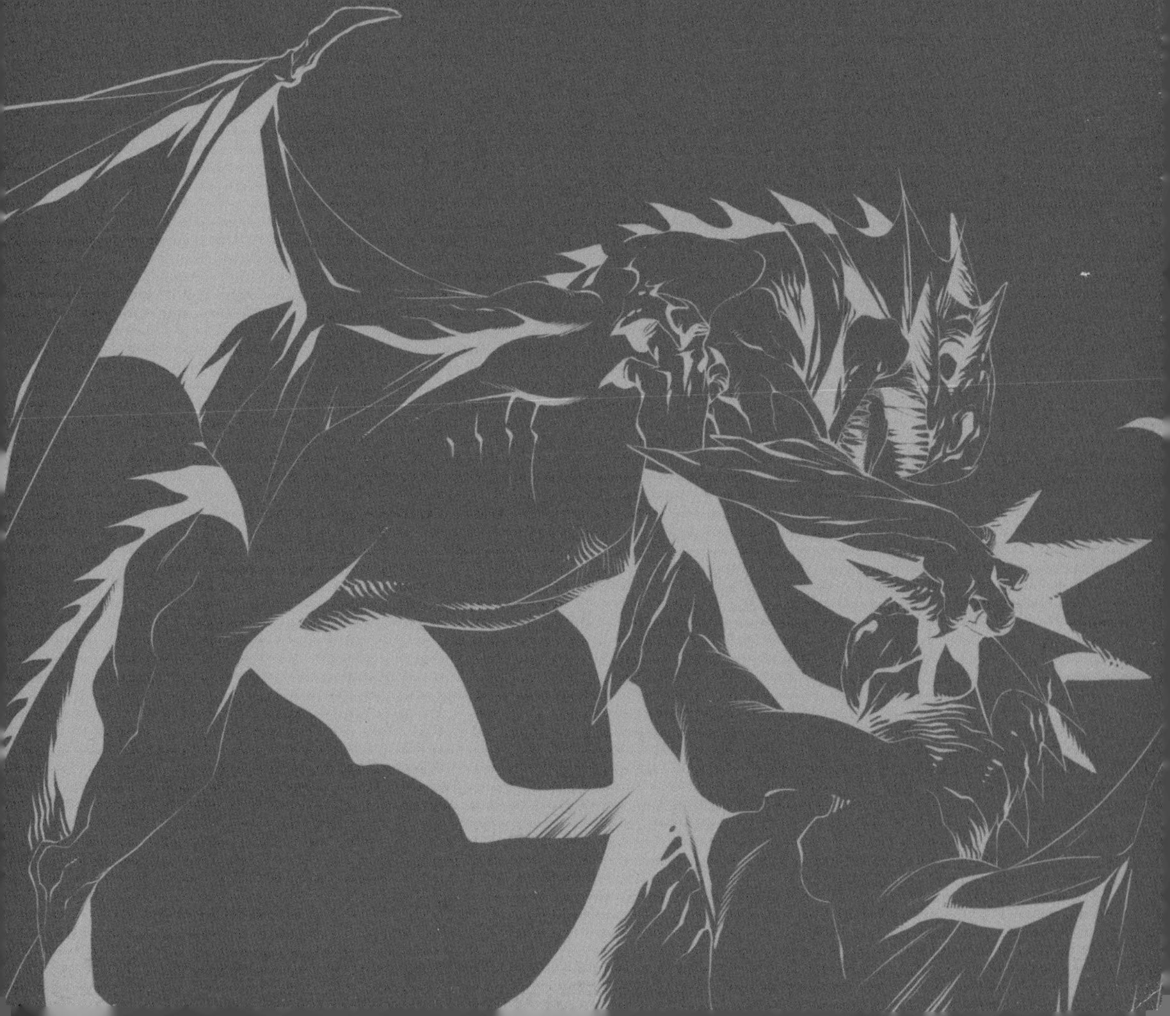

Foreword

So, I know what you're saying. You're saying, "How and why did Christopher Moore, a man allegedly known for writing novels of profound goofiness, come to write a graphic novel?"

Well, I'll tell you. It was like this: About ten years ago I was reading a story by my friend Catherine Ryan Hyde (in her story collection, *Earthquake Weather*) about a kid who has a nightmare of being chased by a giant bird of prey. The description was so vivid, and so frightening, that I started thinking about a story in which giant creatures came out of the sky to hunt humans. I ended up outlining the better part of a story that was just not a Christopher Moore book. It was too much material for a short story, and very visual, which would mean more description than I'm normally comfortable with. If it was going to breathe, it definitely needed to be a movie.

Meanwhile, another friend, Ian Corson, who is a director and who had written a script for my novel *Coyote Blue*, was visiting for a weekend so we could put a comic polish on the *Coyote* script. (Don't worry, that movie didn't get made, but that's only because people are horrible and they lie, not because of any flaw in Ian's script.) Anyway, I told him the idea for *The Griff*, a movie about giant dragonlike things that drop out of outer space for no particular reason and attack Earth. He thought, as I did, that it would never get made, and would cost a zillion dollars to make anyway, but it would be fun to write.

So, a few months later, I'm working on a book that would become my novel *Lamb*, and having a little trouble with it, and Ian calls me and says, "Hey, let's write *The Griff*. Of course it will never get made, but you could use it to avoid working on your book."

Well, I was sold. Over the next few months we worked by e-mail and phone and came up with the movie script, which we promptly put in a drawer and sort of forgot about because we were doing other stuff and because the movie would never get made because people are weasels and they lie.

So, fast-forward to a couple of years ago, and I start getting contacted by people who do comics. You know, THE people who do comics, both of them, as well as some people with a smaller THE. "Everyone is doing them and you should do one and if you want to write about guys with 'Super' or 'Spider' in their names that would be fine with us." And that would have been awesome, but I was kind of busy with another book, and I didn't know that I could follow through with a whole comic script at the time because I tend to think in terms of characters I create. And besides, I had a deadline and I'd be learning the form as I went along. So I sort of passed. But they were very nice about it and said, "Hey, if you ever get an idea that doesn't fit in a book, give us a call or, you know, flash a searchlight in the sky with your logo on it, because we monitor everything." So I started thinking about stories that really didn't lend themselves to books, and I remembered *The Griff*.

About that time I was talking to my publishers about what I was going to be locked in a room doing for the next couple of years, because they like to know when to send me notes telling me that I need to turn something in if I ever want to see sunlight or eat toast again, and I said, "And I'm also thinking about a graphic novel."

And they were like, "We'll do a graphic novel with you."

And I was like, "It's about dragons from outer space, and I wrote it with a partner."

And they were like, "You're still going to write novels, right?"

And I was all, "Sure."

And they were all, "Okeydokey, fire up the blender, let's make a furry-flurry smoothie out of that squirrel!" (Those may not have been their exact words.)

So I called Ian and I was like, "Hey, I know you're busy dating actresses and psychopaths, but you know that movie we wrote that no one is ever going to make?"

And he was like, "Who is this? I have an attorney and I watch mixed martial arts, so do not mess with me."

And I was all, "It's Chris. I have another book I need to avoid working on. Do you want to make *The Griff* into a graphic novel?"

And he was like, "Why not? Let's bat that nun out of the dog park!" (Those may not have been his exact words. He's Canadian, so it may have been something like "Let's high-stick that moose in the fun bags," because Canadians are very patriotic.)

So we did, and there was some drawing and stuff and here it is. I should probably say up front that this is a little different than one of my books, but if you are confused, here's a good guide to go by: If you like what you're reading, I probably wrote it, but if you don't, then Ian probably wrote it. If you like the art, then it's all Jennyson Rosero, but if you don't like it, that is not any of our faults because people are douche bags. Many people. Not all. But you know, most.

Which is why we destroyed the world.

Have fun.

—Christopher Moore

THE GRIFF

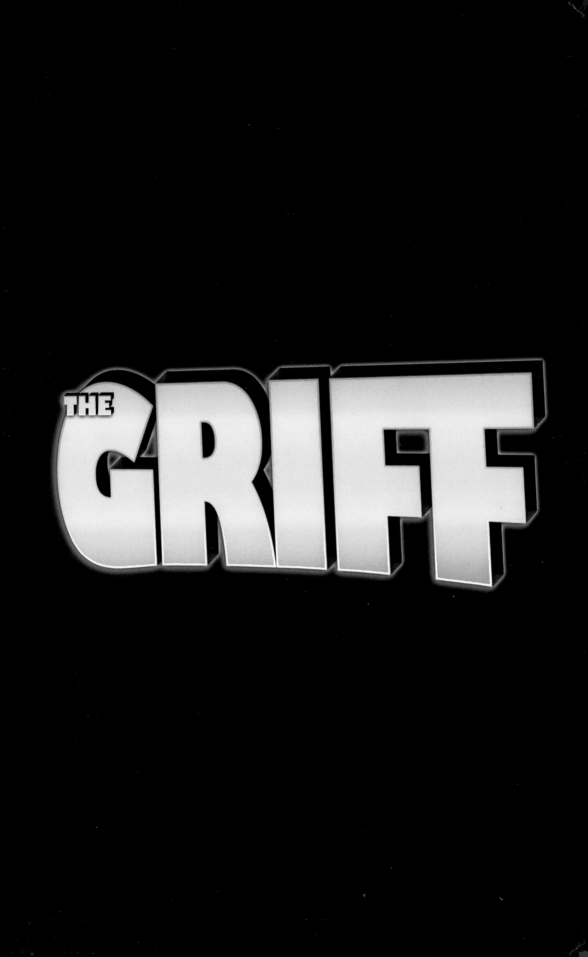

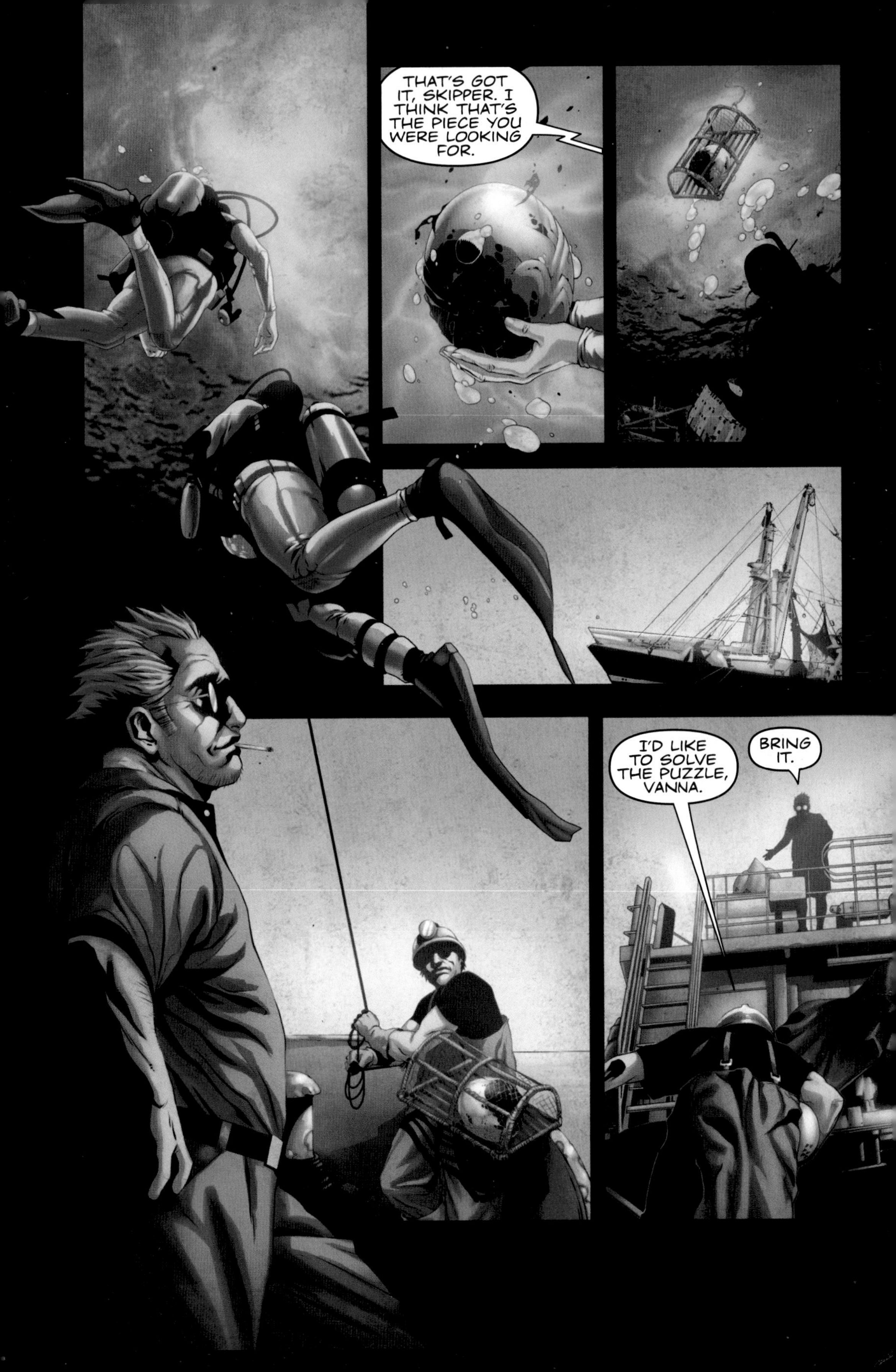
THAT'S GOT IT, SKIPPER. I THINK THAT'S THE PIECE YOU WERE LOOKING FOR.
I'D LIKE TO SOLVE THE PUZZLE, VANNA.
BRING IT.

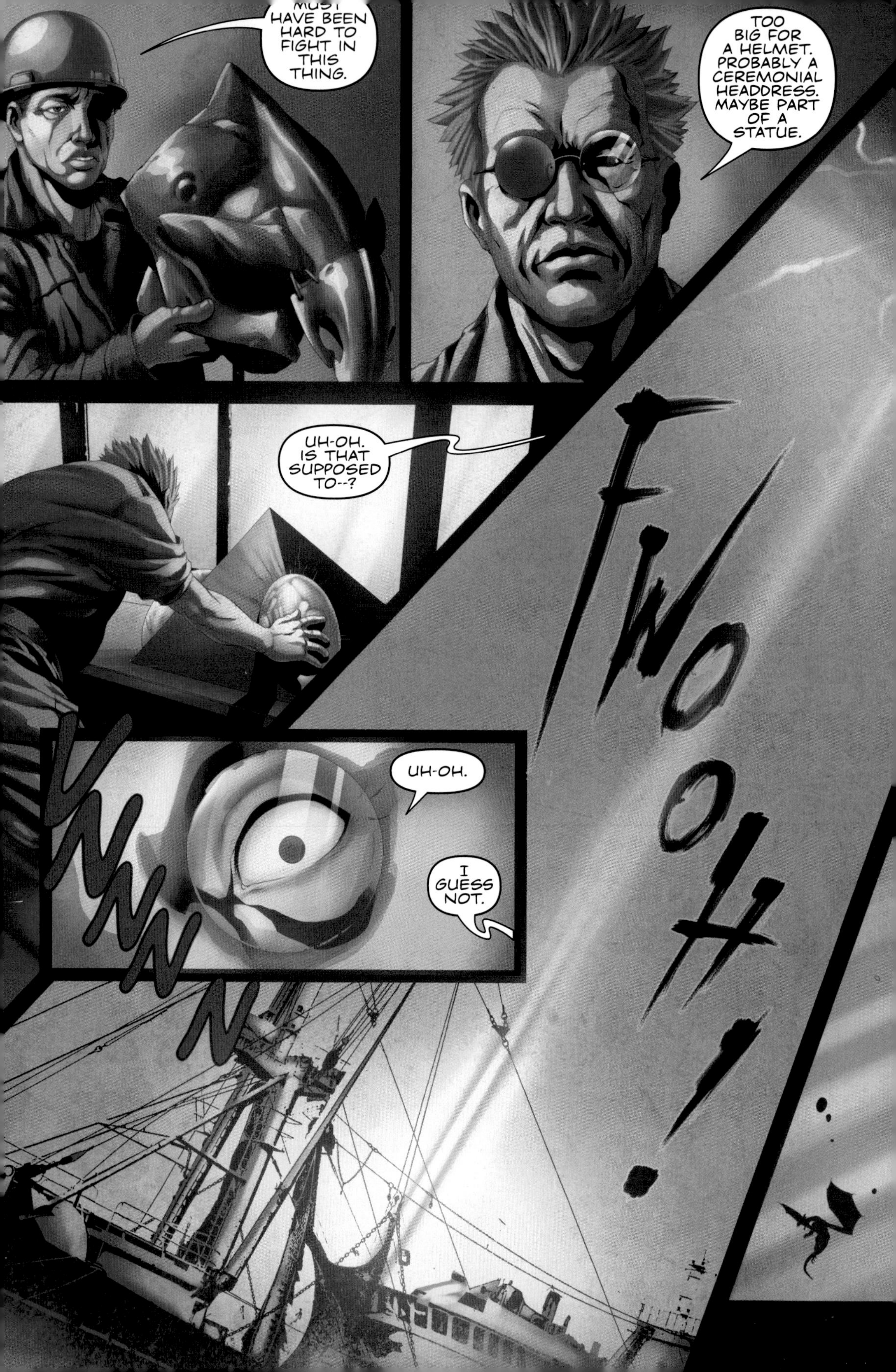
MUST HAVE BEEN HARD TO FIGHT IN THIS THING.
TOO BIG FOR A HELMET. PROBABLY A CEREMONIAL HEADDRESS. MAYBE PART OF A STATUE.
UH-OH. IS THAT SUPPOSED TO--?
FWOOH!
UH-OH.
I GUESS NOT.
VNNNN

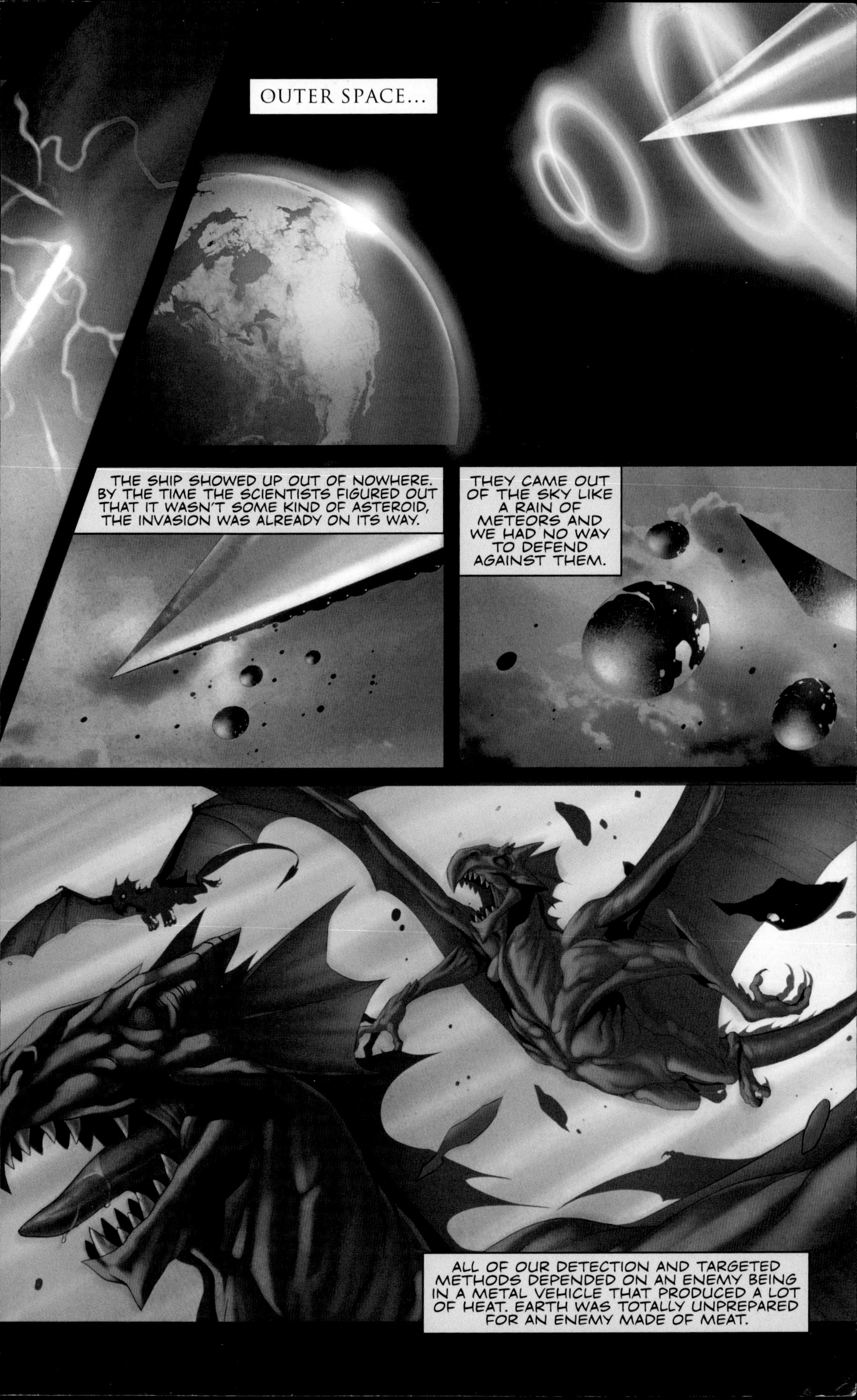
OUTER SPACE...
THE SHIP SHOWED UP OUT OF NOWHERE. BY THE TIME THE SCIENTISTS FIGURED OUT THAT IT WASN'T SOME KIND OF ASTEROID, THE INVASION WAS ALREADY ON ITS WAY.
THEY CAME OUT OF THE SKY LIKE A RAIN OF METEORS AND WE HAD NO WAY TO DEFEND AGAINST THEM.
ALL OF OUR DETECTION AND TARGETED METHODS DEPENDED ON AN ENEMY BEING IN A METAL VEHICLE THAT PRODUCED A LOT OF HEAT. EARTH WAS TOTALLY UNPREPARED FOR AN ENEMY MADE OF MEAT.

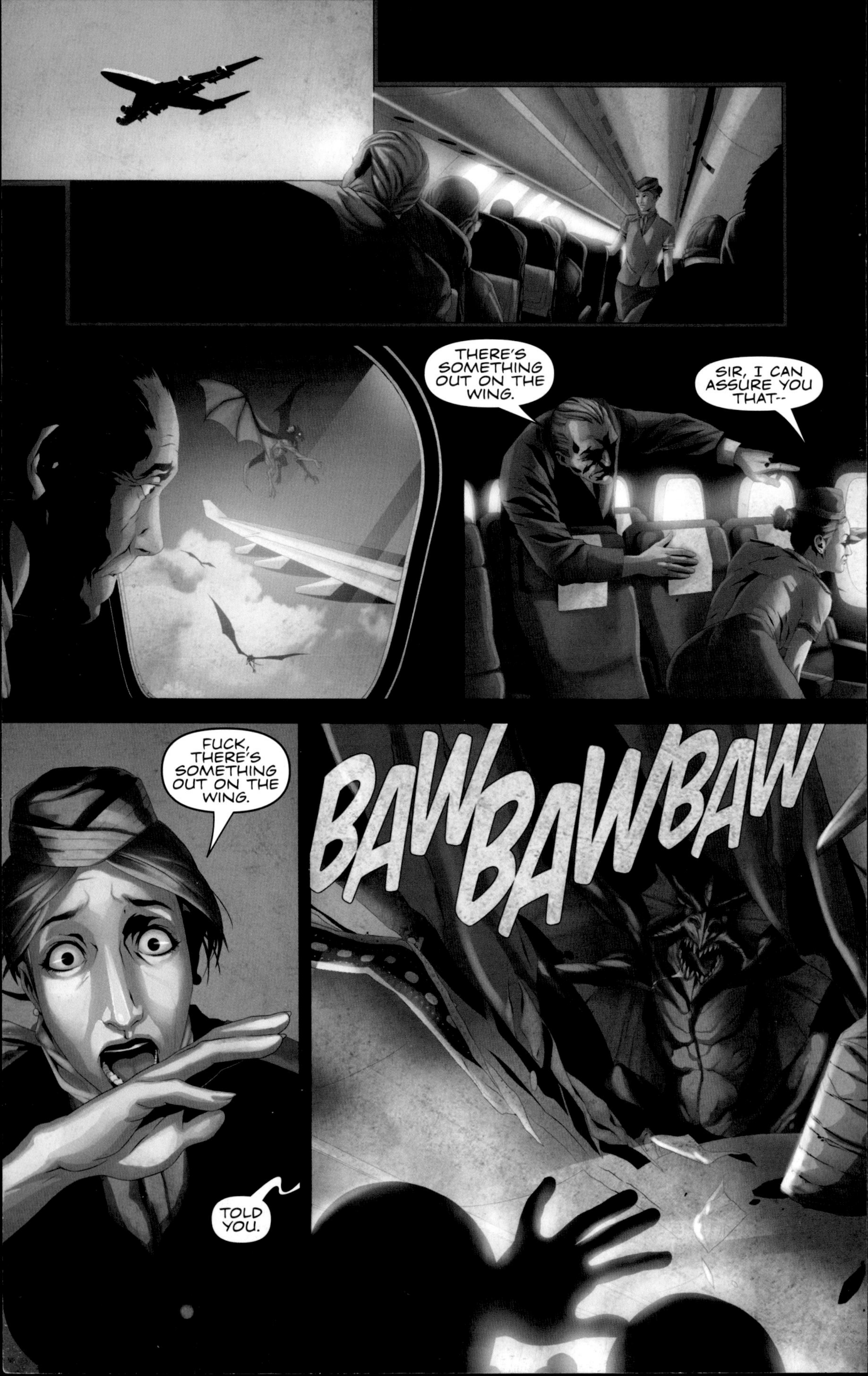
THERE'S SOMETHING OUT ON THE WING.
SIR, I CAN ASSURE YOU THAT--
FUCK, THERE'S SOMETHING OUT ON THE WING.
TOLD YOU.
BAW BAW BAW BAW

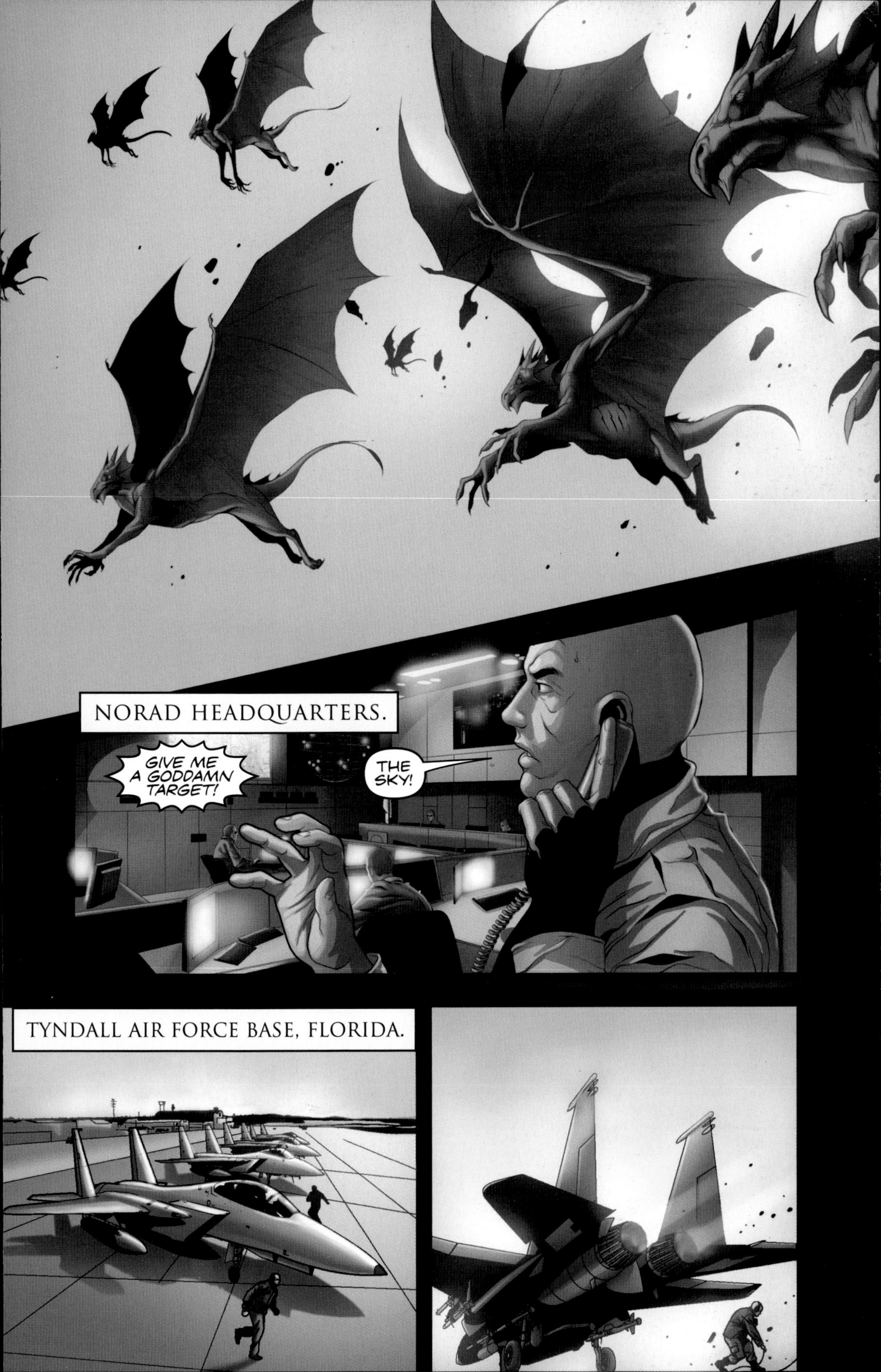

NORAD HEADQUARTERS.
GIVE ME A GODDAMN TARGET!
THE SKY!
TYNDALL AIR FORCE BASE, FLORIDA.

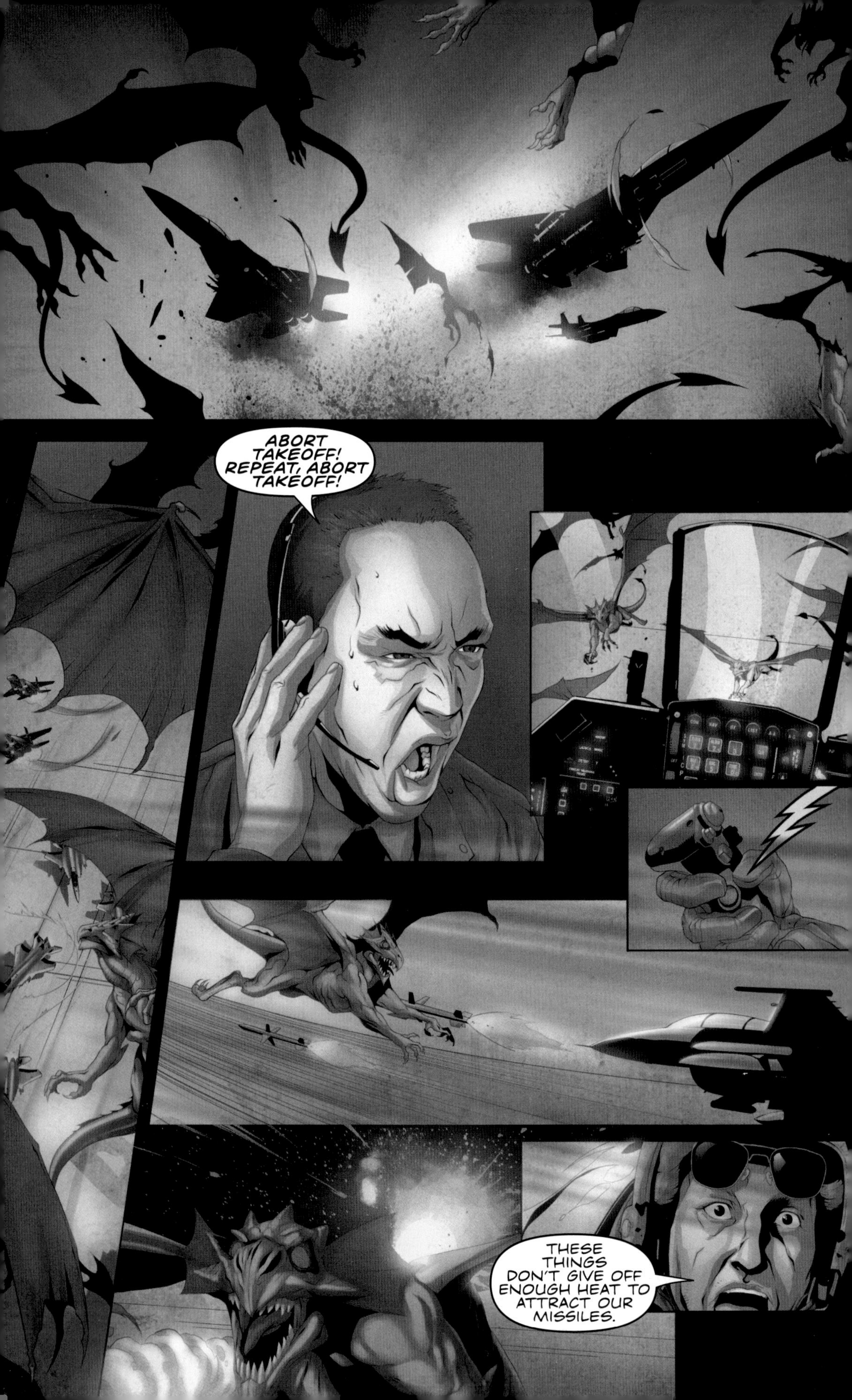
ABORT TAKEOFF! REPEAT, ABORT TAKEOFF!
THESE THINGS DON'T GIVE OFF ENOUGH HEAT TO ATTRACT OUR MISSILES.

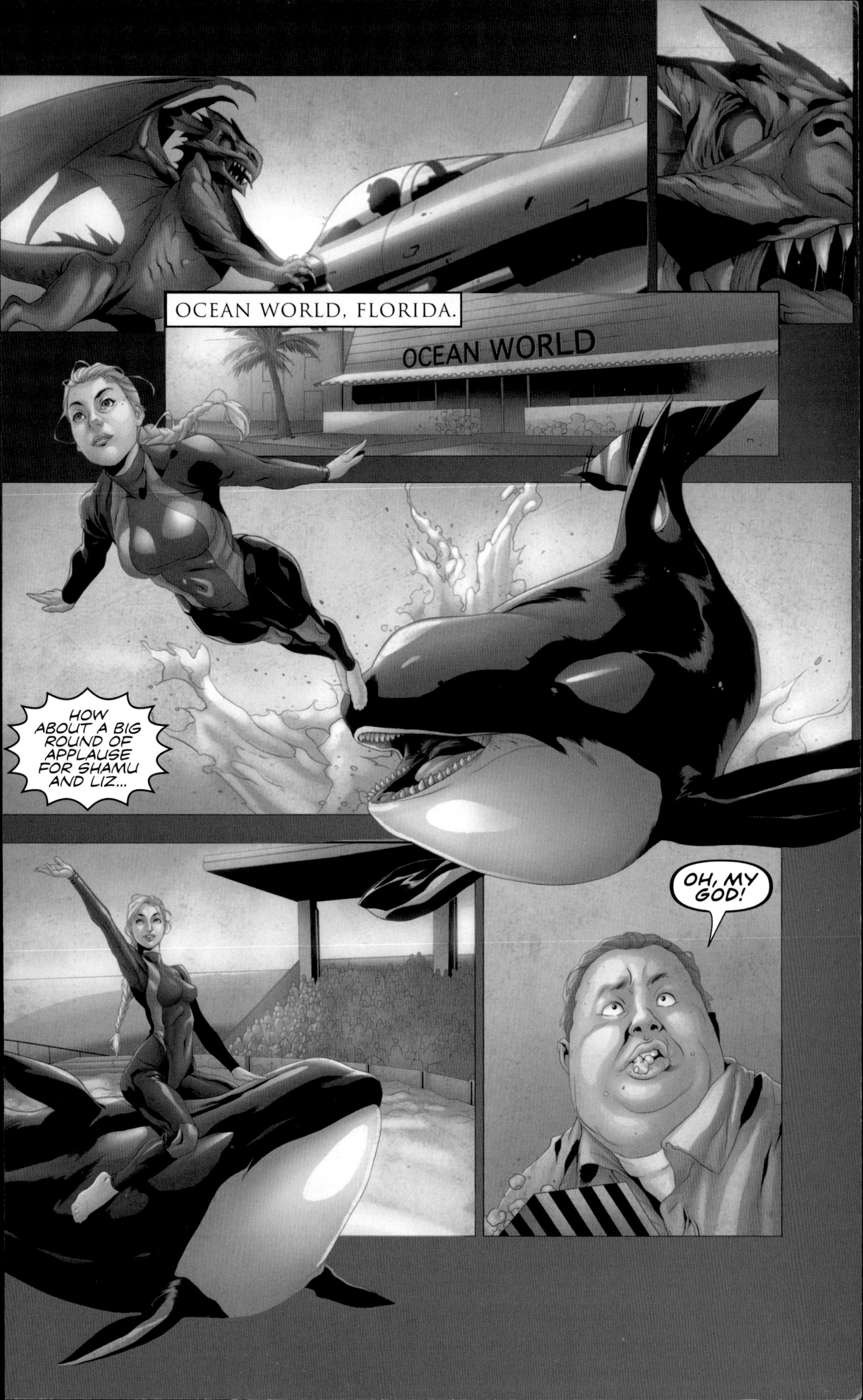
OCEAN WORLD, FLORIDA.
OCEAN WORLD
HOW ABOUT A BIG ROUND OF APPLAUSE FOR SHAMU AND LIZ...
OH, MY GOD!

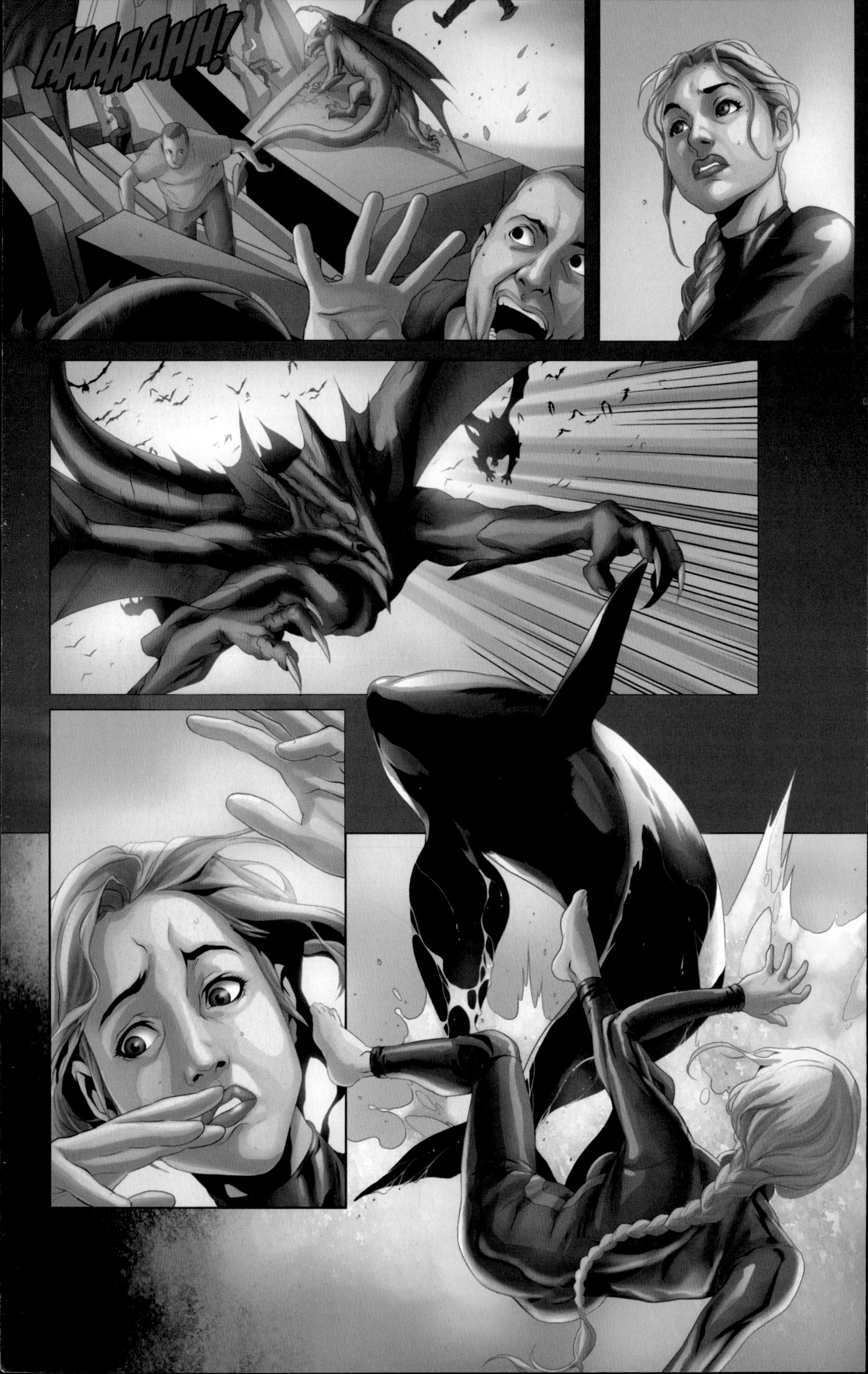
AAAAAHH!

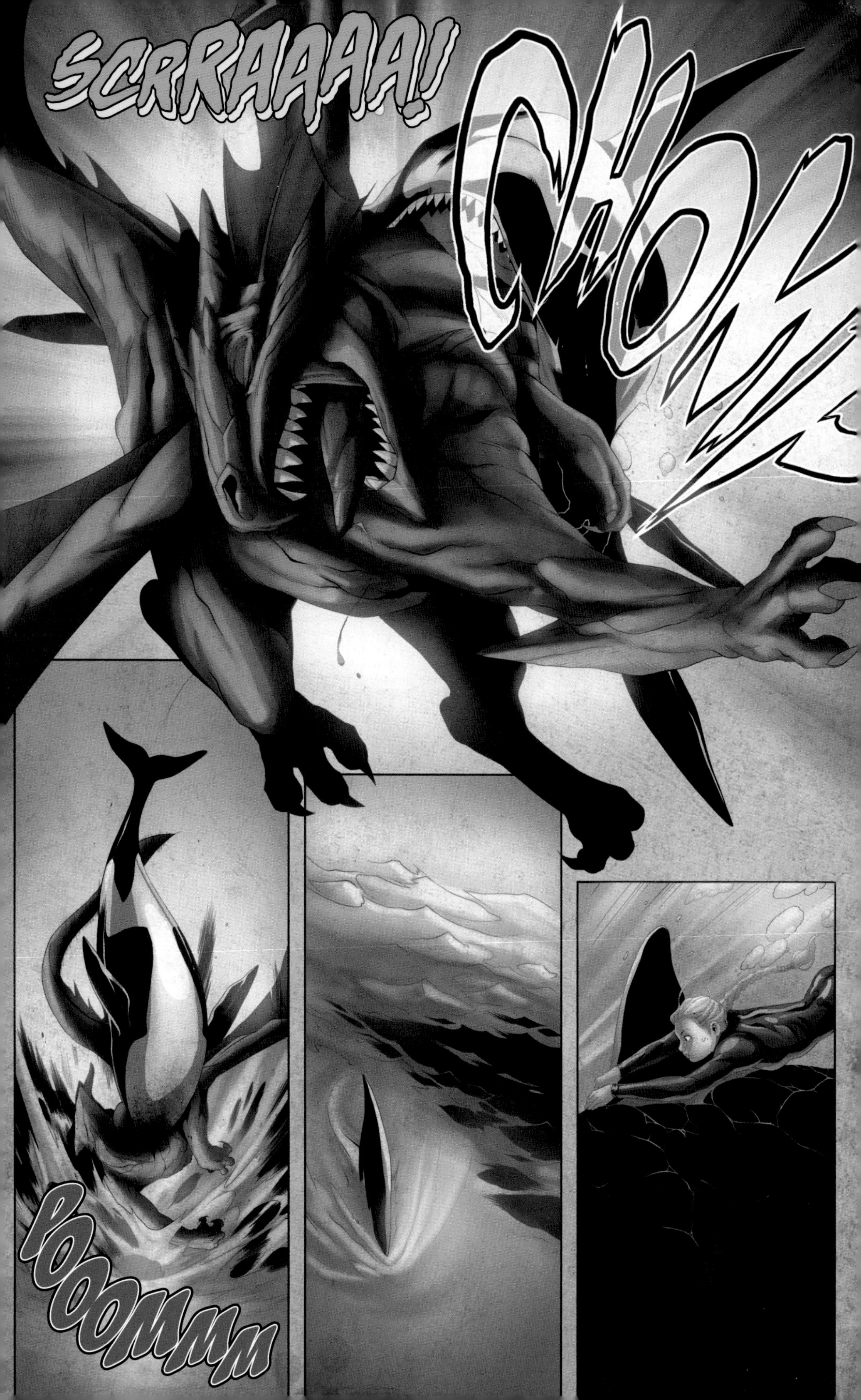
SCRRAAAAA!
BOOOMMM

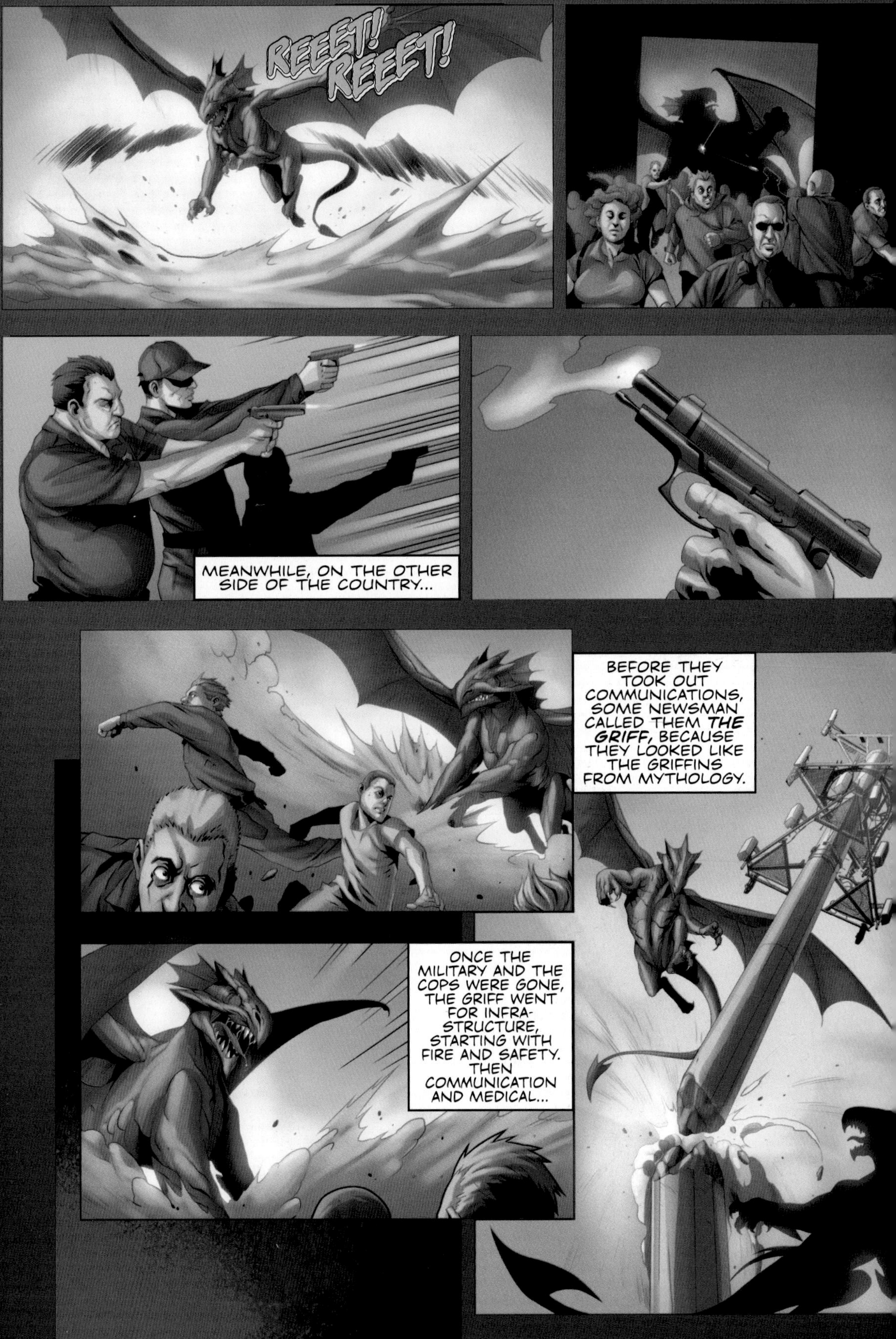
REEEET! REEEET!
MEANWHILE, ON THE OTHER SIDE OF THE COUNTRY...
BEFORE THEY TOOK OUT COMMUNICATIONS, SOME NEWSMAN CALLED THEM THE GRIFF, BECAUSE THEY LOOKED LIKE THE GRIFFINS FROM MYTHOLOGY.
ONCE THE MILITARY AND THE COPS WERE GONE, THE GRIFF WENT FOR INFRA-STRUCTURE, STARTING WITH FIRE AND SAFETY. THEN COMMUNICATION AND MEDICAL...

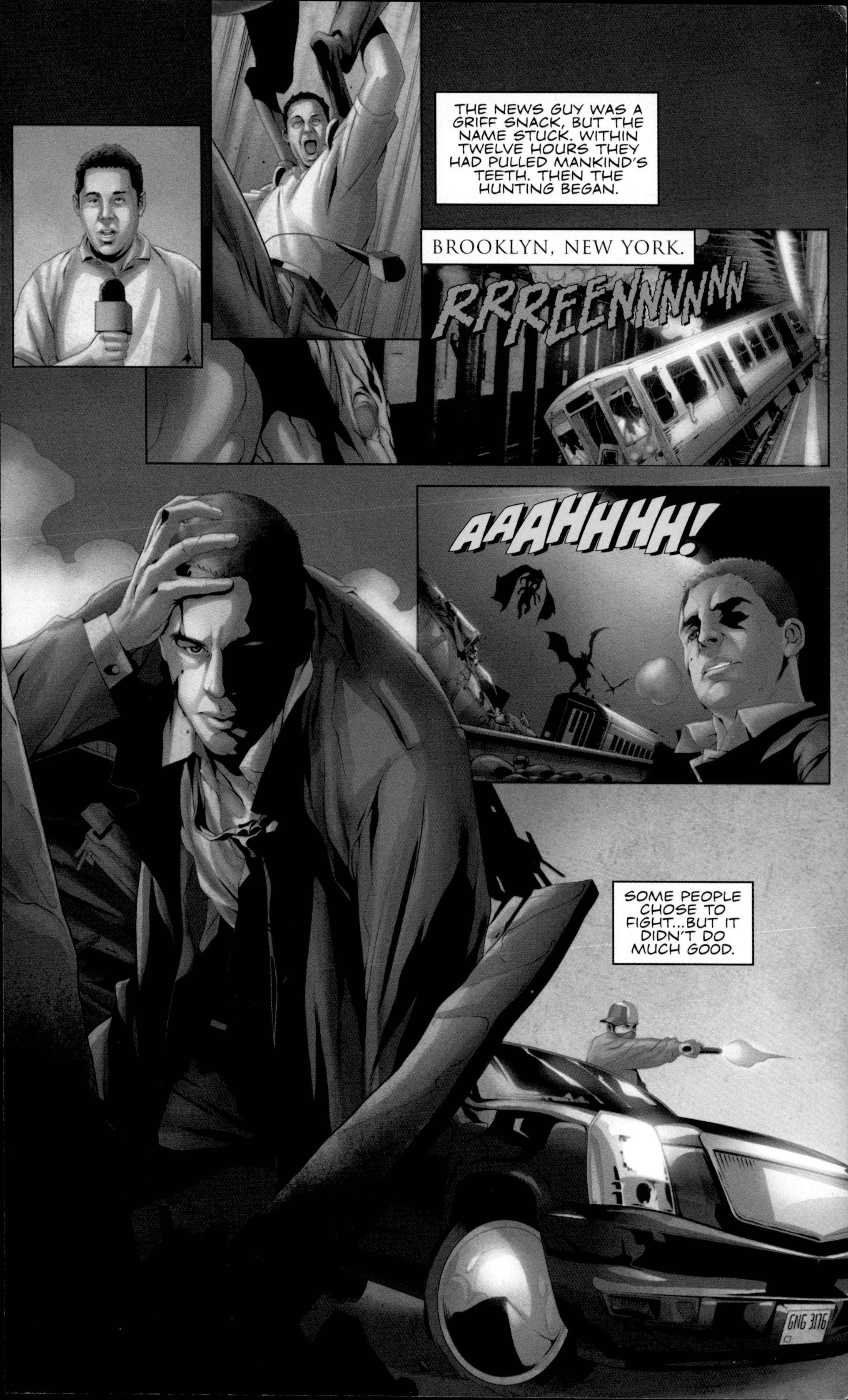
THE NEWS GUY WAS A GRIFF SNACK, BUT THE NAME STUCK. WITHIN TWELVE HOURS THEY HAD PULLED MANKIND'S TEETH. THEN THE HUNTING BEGAN.
BROOKLYN, NEW YORK.
RRREENNNNNN
AAAHHHH!
SOME PEOPLE CHOSE TO FIGHT...BUT IT DIDN'T DO MUCH GOOD.
GNG 3176

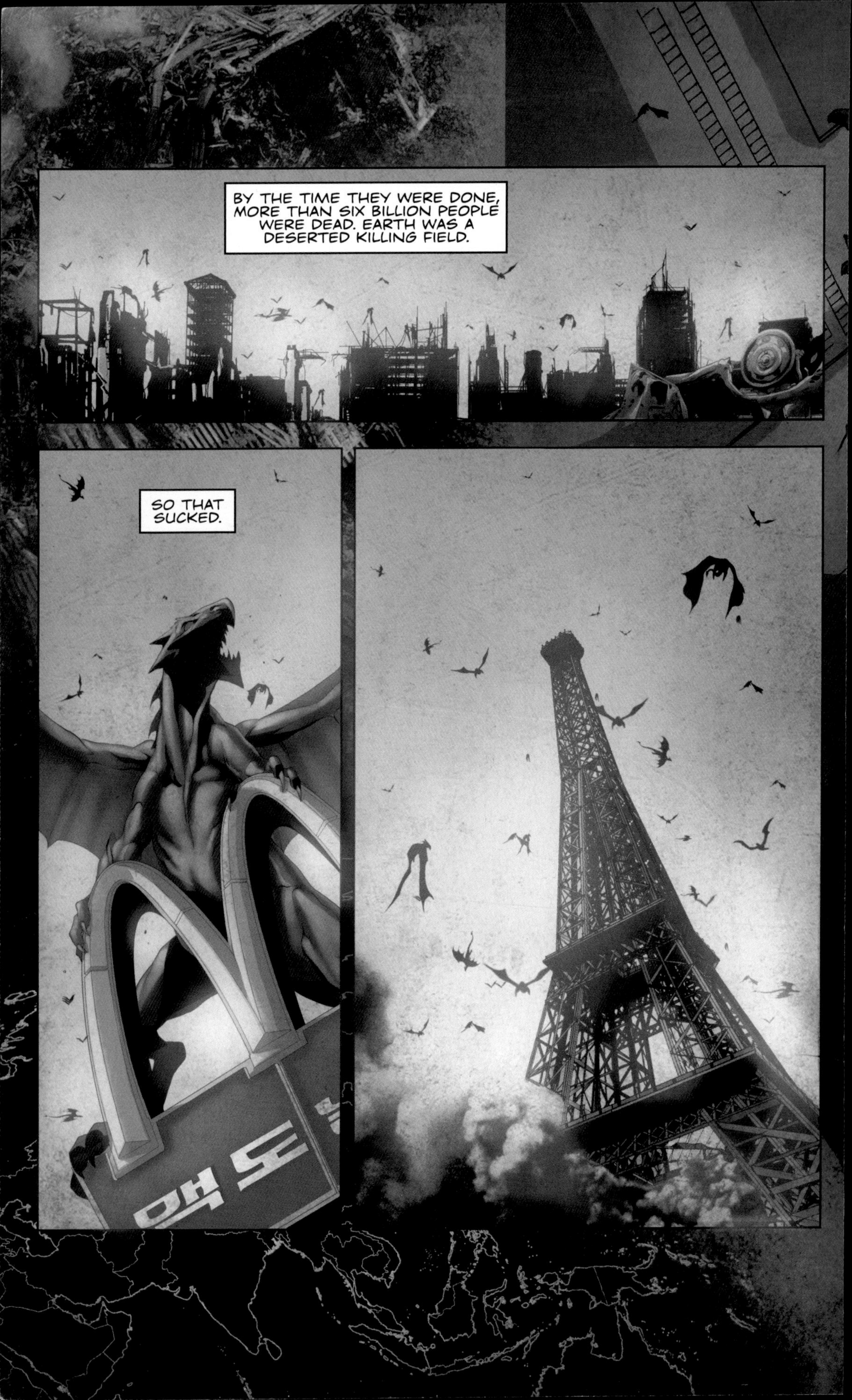
BY THE TIME THEY WERE DONE, MORE THAN SIX BILLION PEOPLE WERE DEAD. EARTH WAS A DESERTED KILLING FIELD.
SO THAT SUCKED.

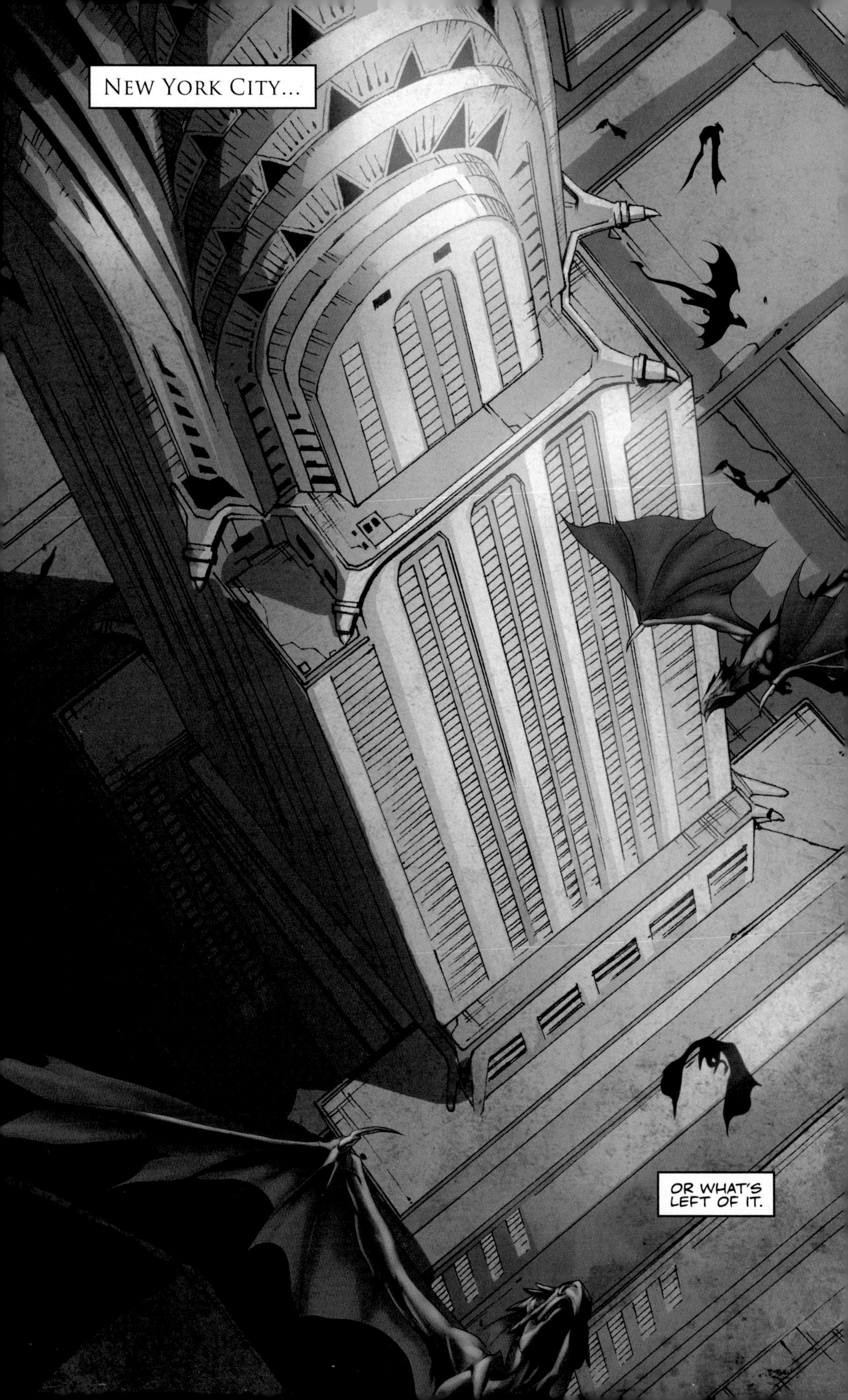
NEW YORK CITY...
OR WHAT'S LEFT OF IT.

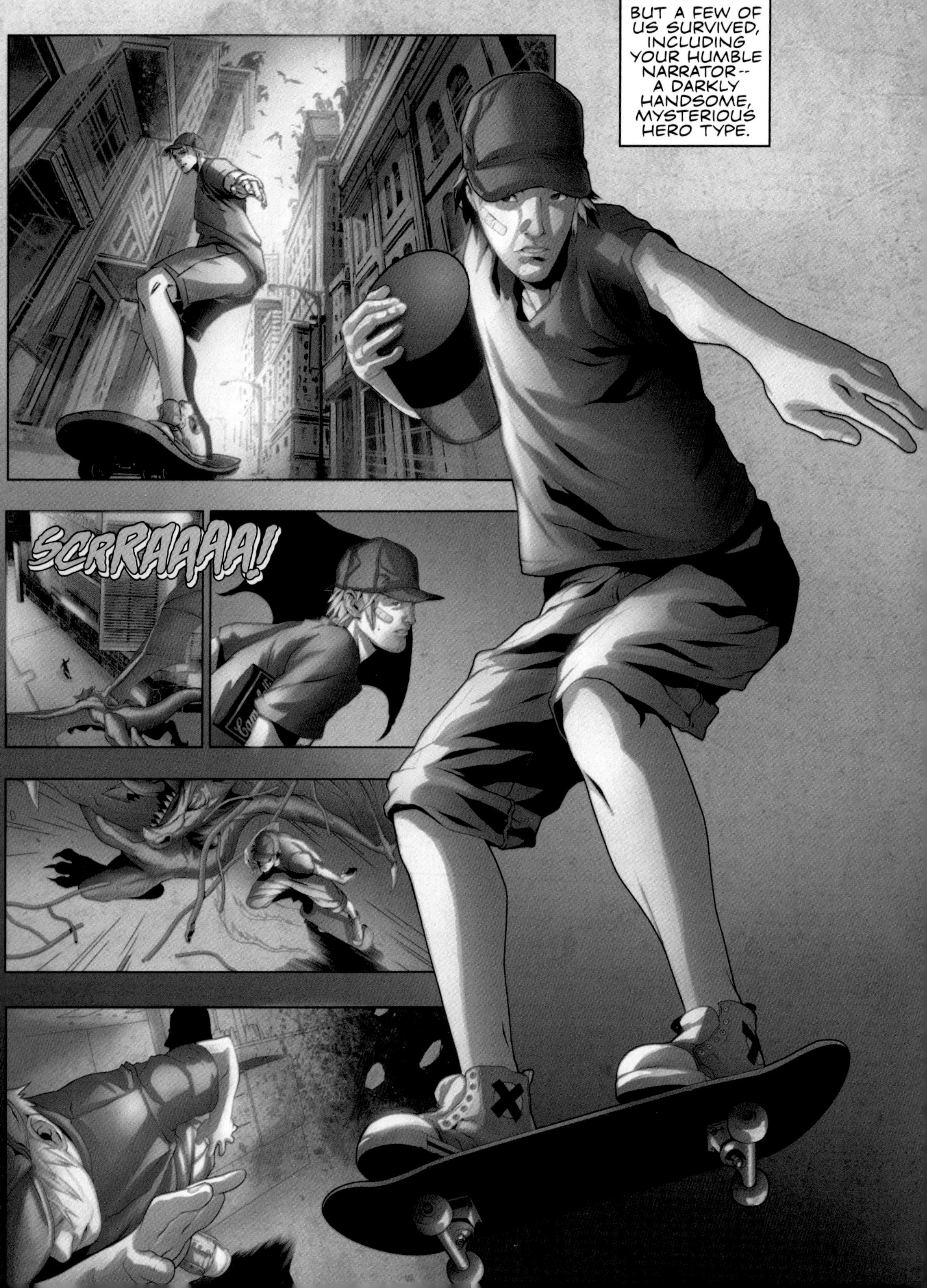
BUT A FEW OF US SURVIVED, INCLUDING YOUR HUMBLE NARRATOR-- A DARKLY HANDSOME, MYSTERIOUS HERO TYPE.
SCRRAAAA!

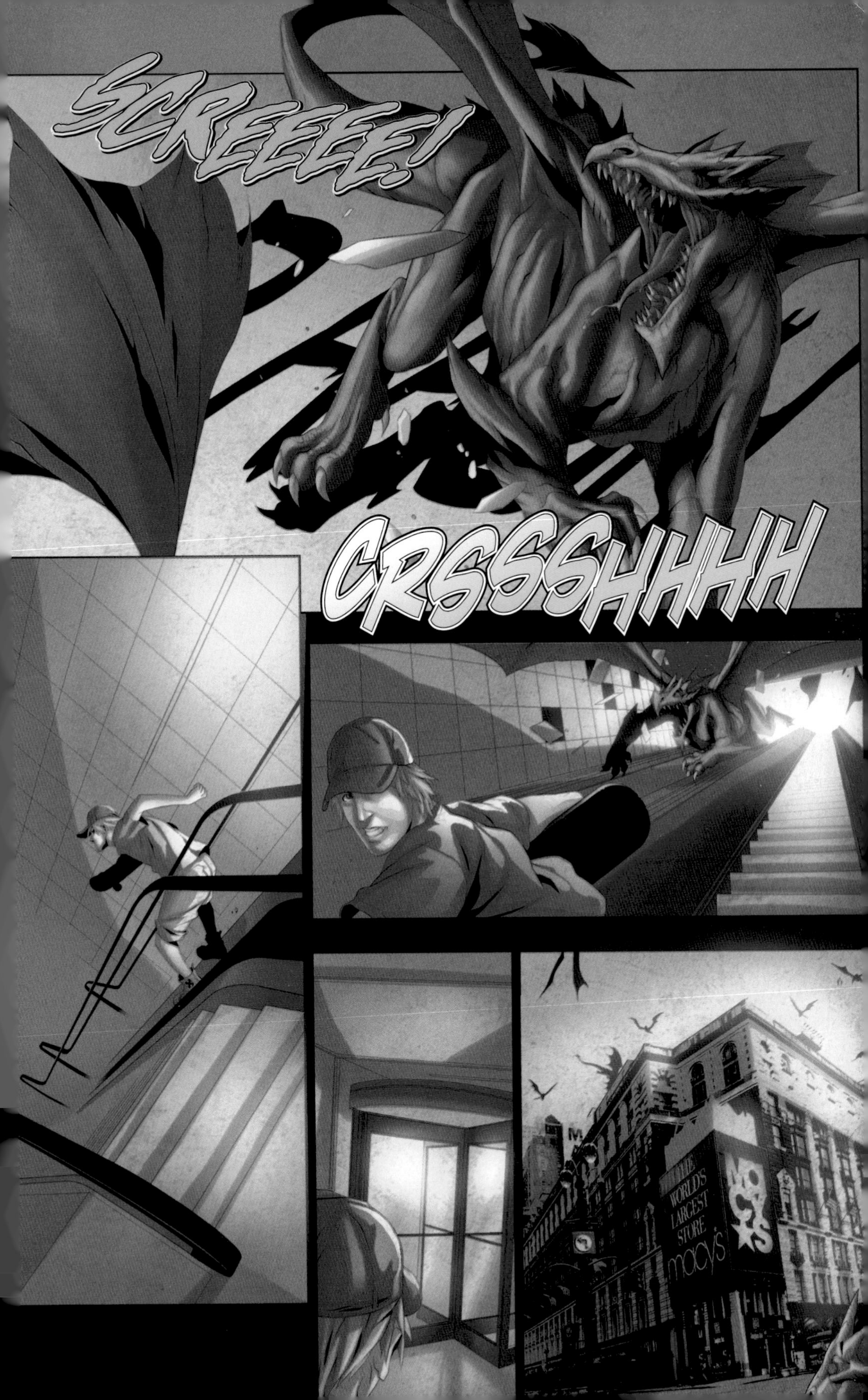
SCREEEEE!
CRSSSHHHH
THE WORLD'S LARGEST STORE
macy's
MACY'S

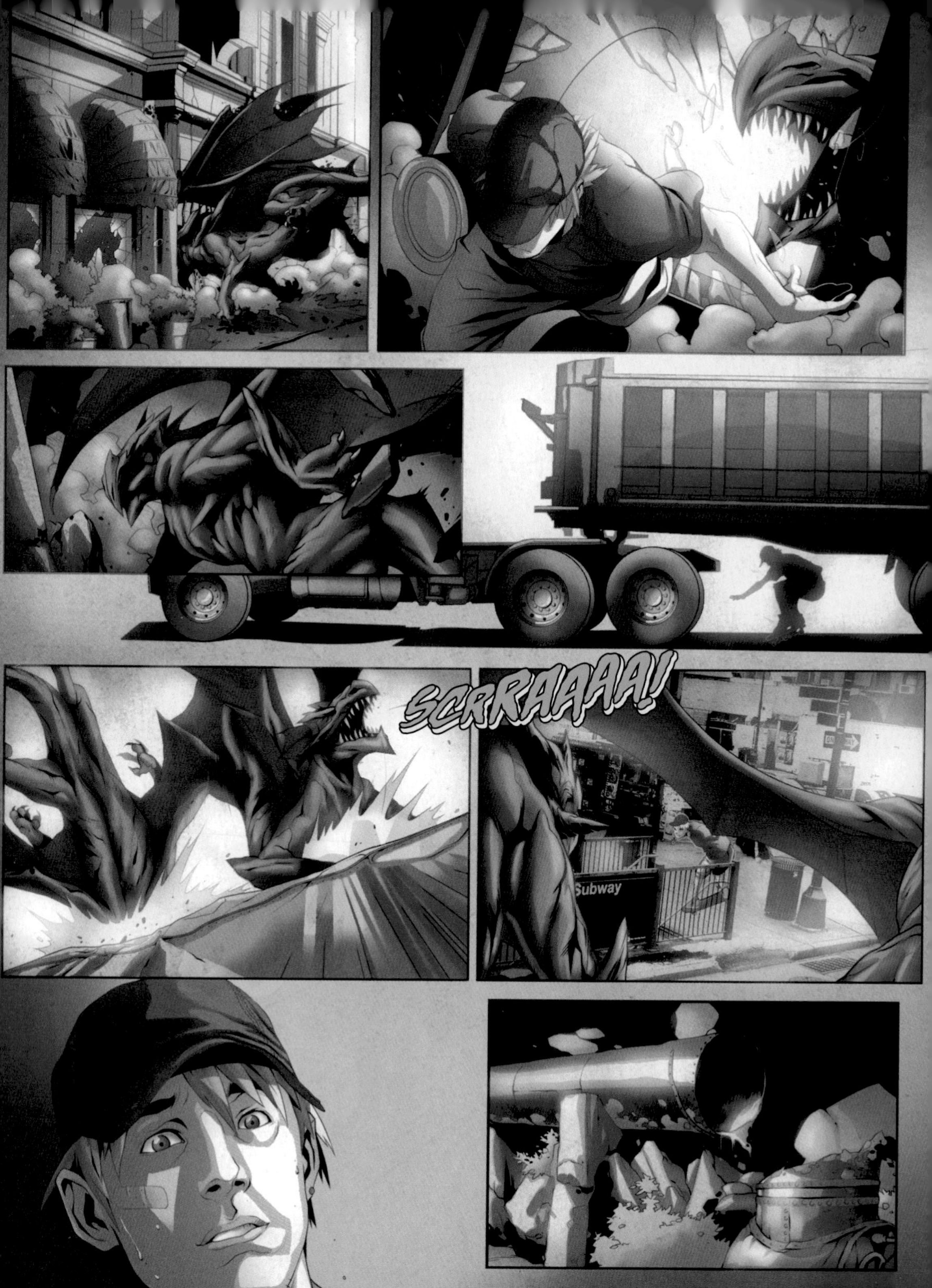
SCRRAAAAA!
Subway

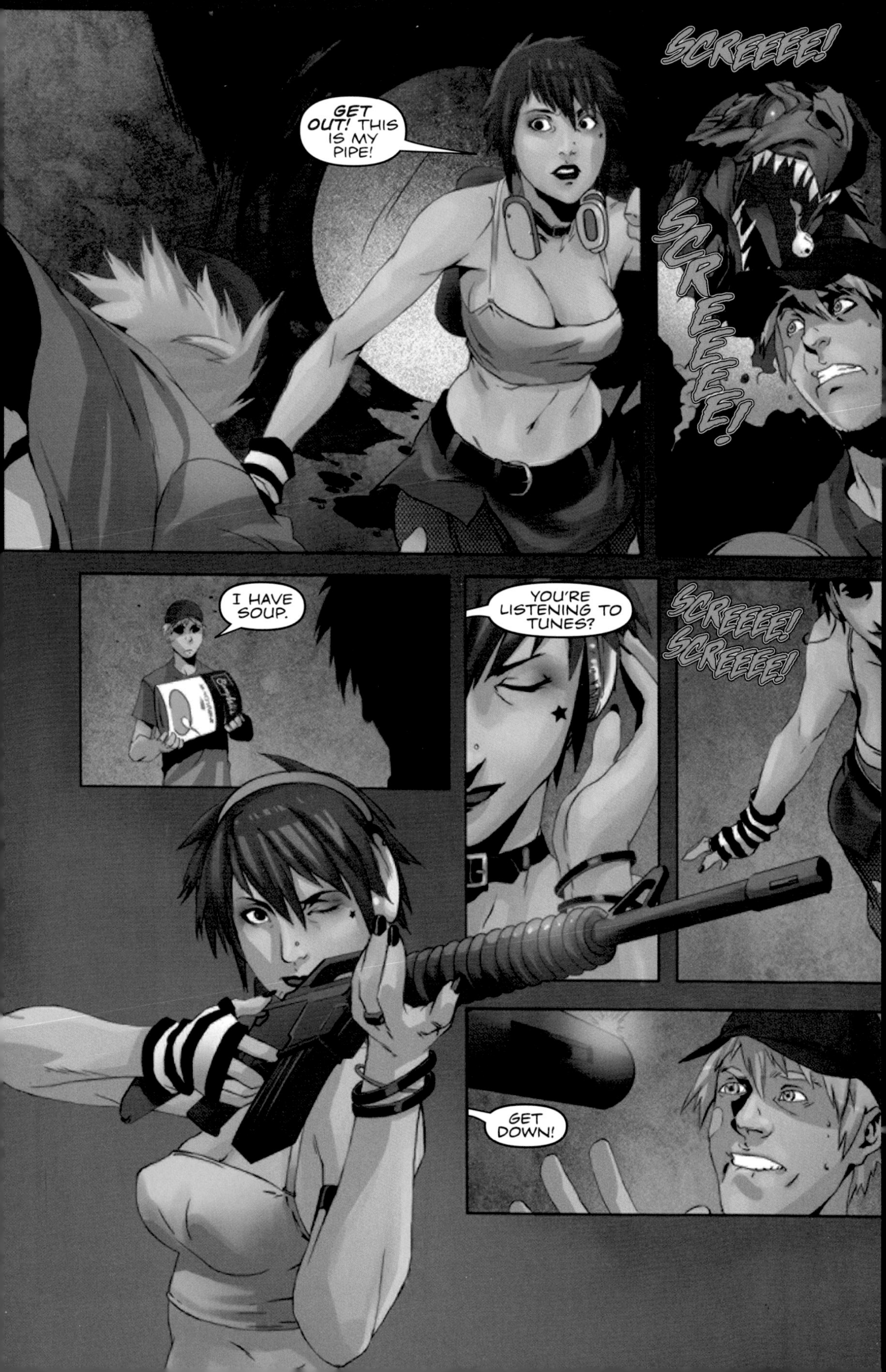
GET OUT! THIS IS MY PIPE!
SCREEEEE!
SCREEEEEE!
I HAVE SOUP.
YOU'RE LISTENING TO TUNES?
SCREEEEE! SCREEEEE!
GET DOWN!

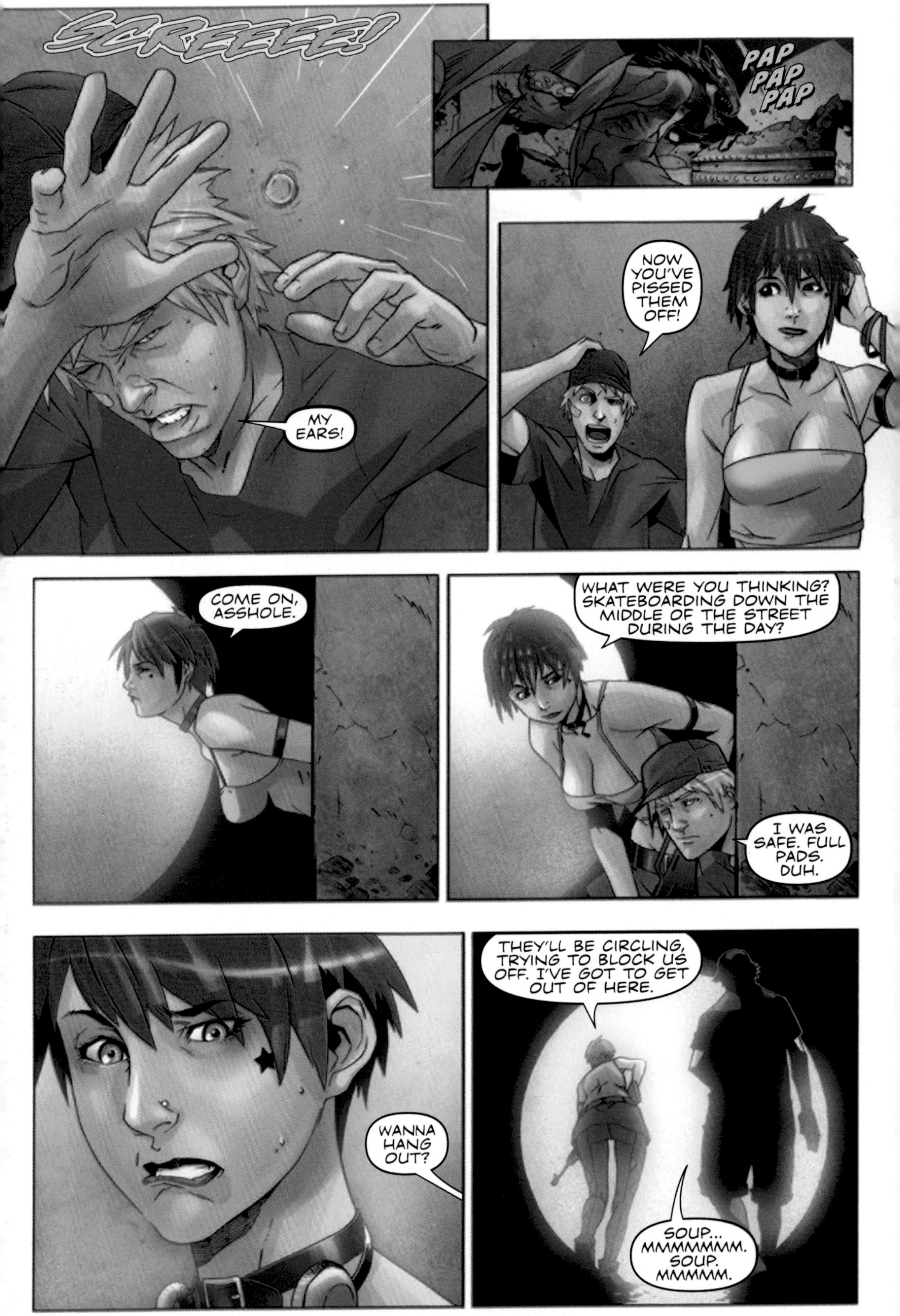
SCREEEEE!
MY EARS!
PAP PAP PAP
NOW YOU'VE PISSED THEM OFF!
COME ON, ASSHOLE.
WHAT WERE YOU THINKING? SKATEBOARDING DOWN THE MIDDLE OF THE STREET DURING THE DAY?
I WAS SAFE. FULL PADS. DUH.
WANNA HANG OUT?
THEY'LL BE CIRCLING, TRYING TO BLOCK US OFF. I'VE GOT TO GET OUT OF HERE.
SOUP... MMMMMMM. SOUP. MMMMM.

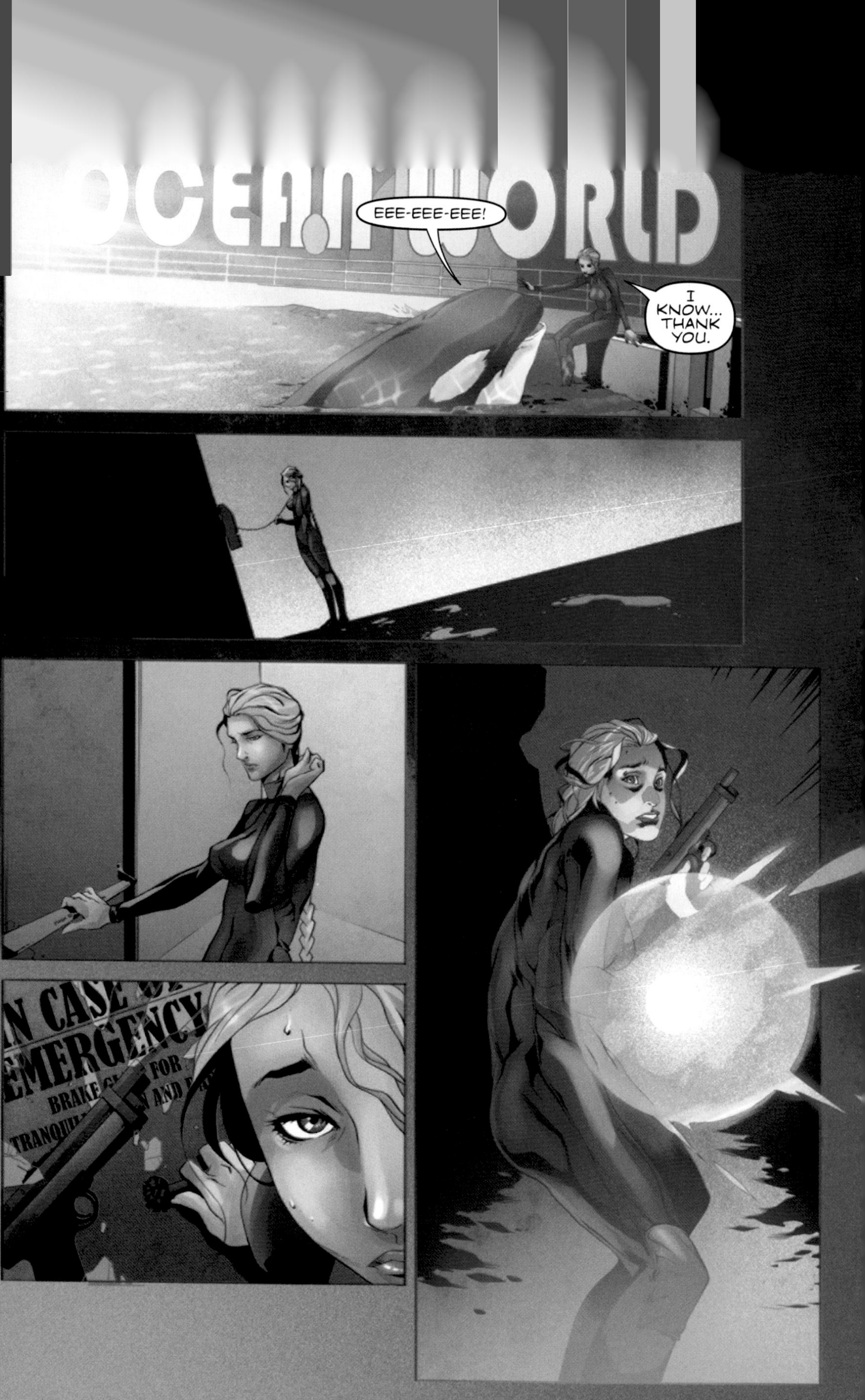
OCEAN WORLD
EEE-EEE-EEE!
I KNOW... THANK YOU.
N CASE
EMERGENCY
BRAKE
FOR

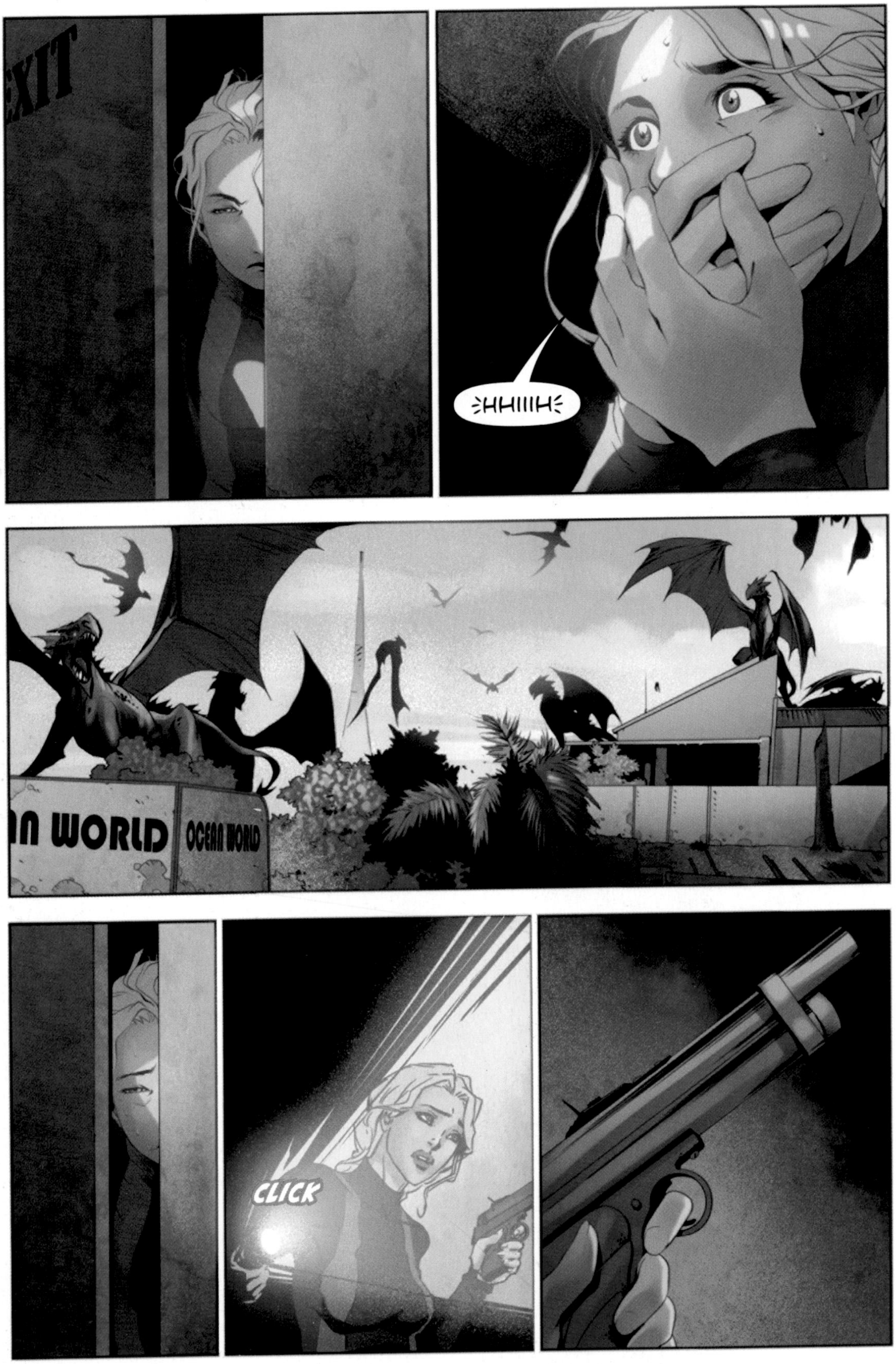
EXIT
HHIIIH
AN WORLD
OCEAN WORLD
CLICK

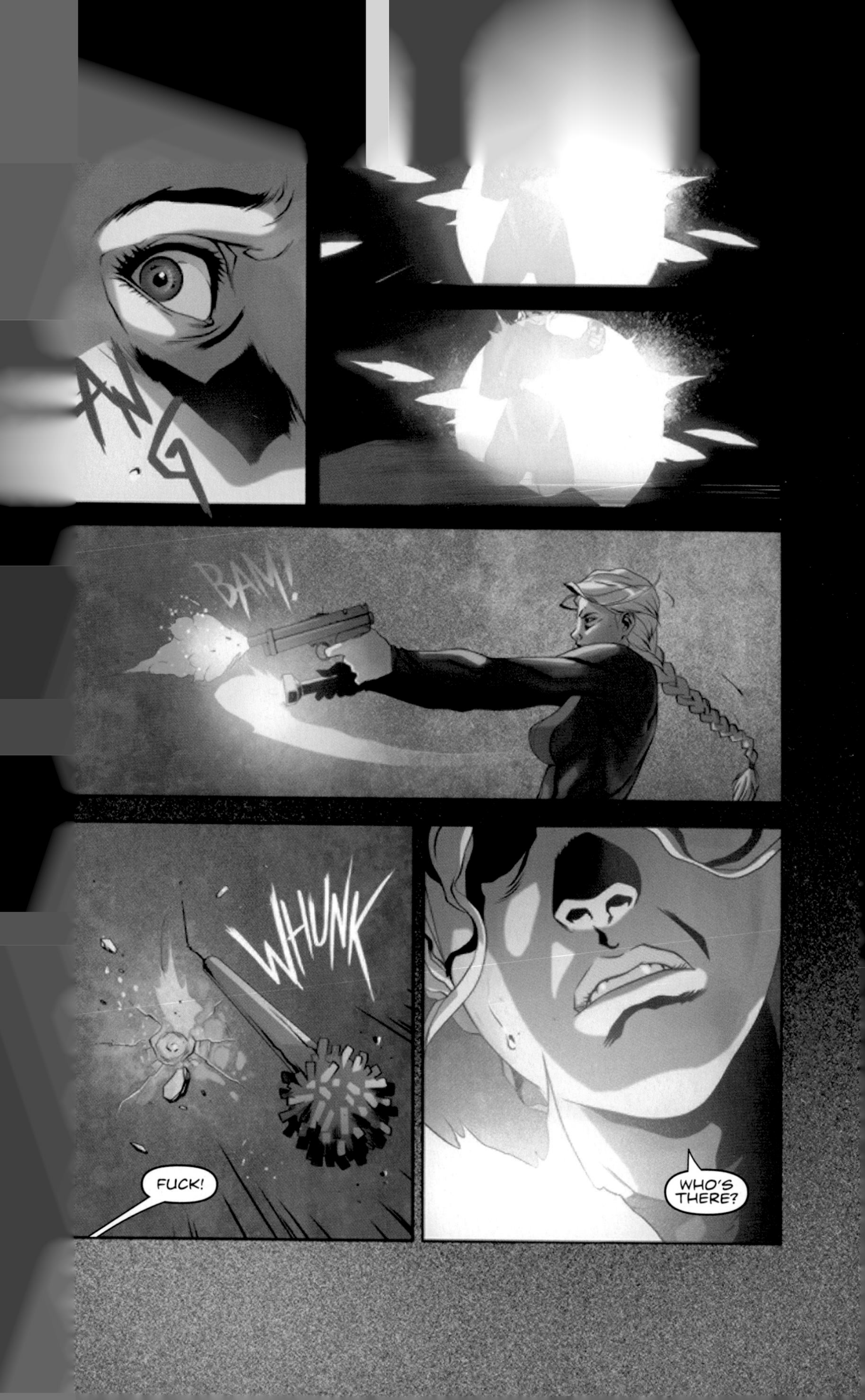
ANG
BAM!
WHUNK
FUCK!
WHO'S THERE?

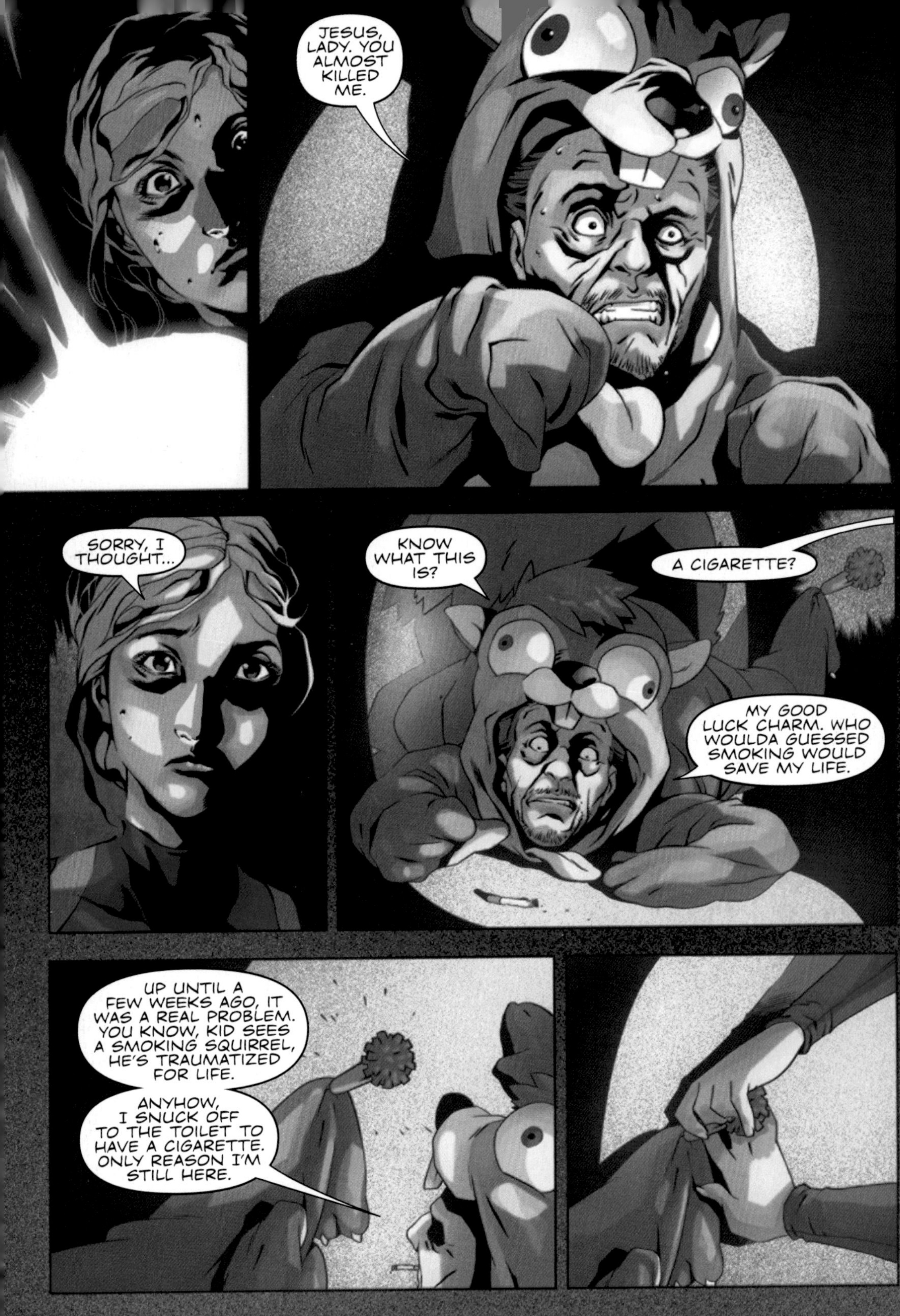

JESUS, LADY. YOU ALMOST KILLED ME.
SORRY, I THOUGHT...
KNOW WHAT THIS IS?
A CIGARETTE?
MY GOOD LUCK CHARM. WHO WOULDA GUESSED SMOKING WOULD SAVE MY LIFE.
UP UNTIL A FEW WEEKS AGO, IT WAS A REAL PROBLEM. YOU KNOW, KID SEES A SMOKING SQUIRREL, HE'S TRAUMATIZED FOR LIFE.
ANYHOW, I SNUCK OFF TO THE TOILET TO HAVE A CIGARETTE. ONLY REASON I'M STILL HERE.

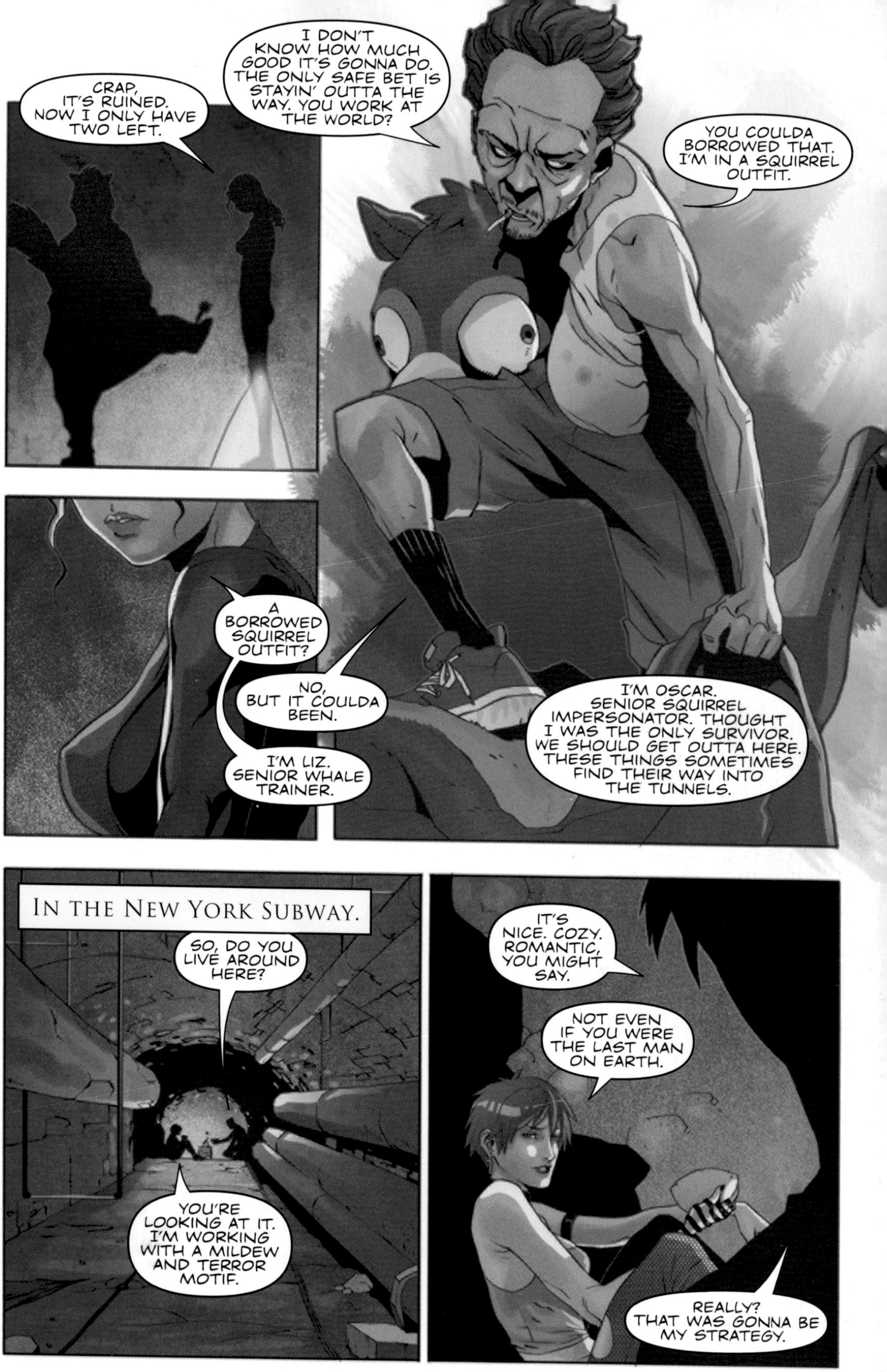
CRAP, IT'S RUINED. NOW I ONLY HAVE TWO LEFT.
I DON'T KNOW HOW MUCH GOOD IT'S GONNA DO. THE ONLY SAFE BET IS STAYIN' OUTTA THE WAY. YOU WORK AT THE WORLD?
YOU COULDA BORROWED THAT. I'M IN A SQUIRREL OUTFIT.
A BORROWED SQUIRREL OUTFIT?
NO, BUT IT COULDA BEEN.
I'M LIZ. SENIOR WHALE TRAINER.
I'M OSCAR. SENIOR SQUIRREL IMPERSONATOR. THOUGHT I WAS THE ONLY SURVIVOR. WE SHOULD GET OUTTA HERE. THESE THINGS SOMETIMES FIND THEIR WAY INTO THE TUNNELS.
IN THE NEW YORK SUBWAY.
SO, DO YOU LIVE AROUND HERE?
YOU'RE LOOKING AT IT. I'M WORKING WITH A MILDEW AND TERROR MOTIF.
IT'S NICE. COZY. ROMANTIC, YOU MIGHT SAY.
NOT EVEN IF YOU WERE THE LAST MAN ON EARTH.
REALLY? THAT WAS GONNA BE MY STRATEGY.

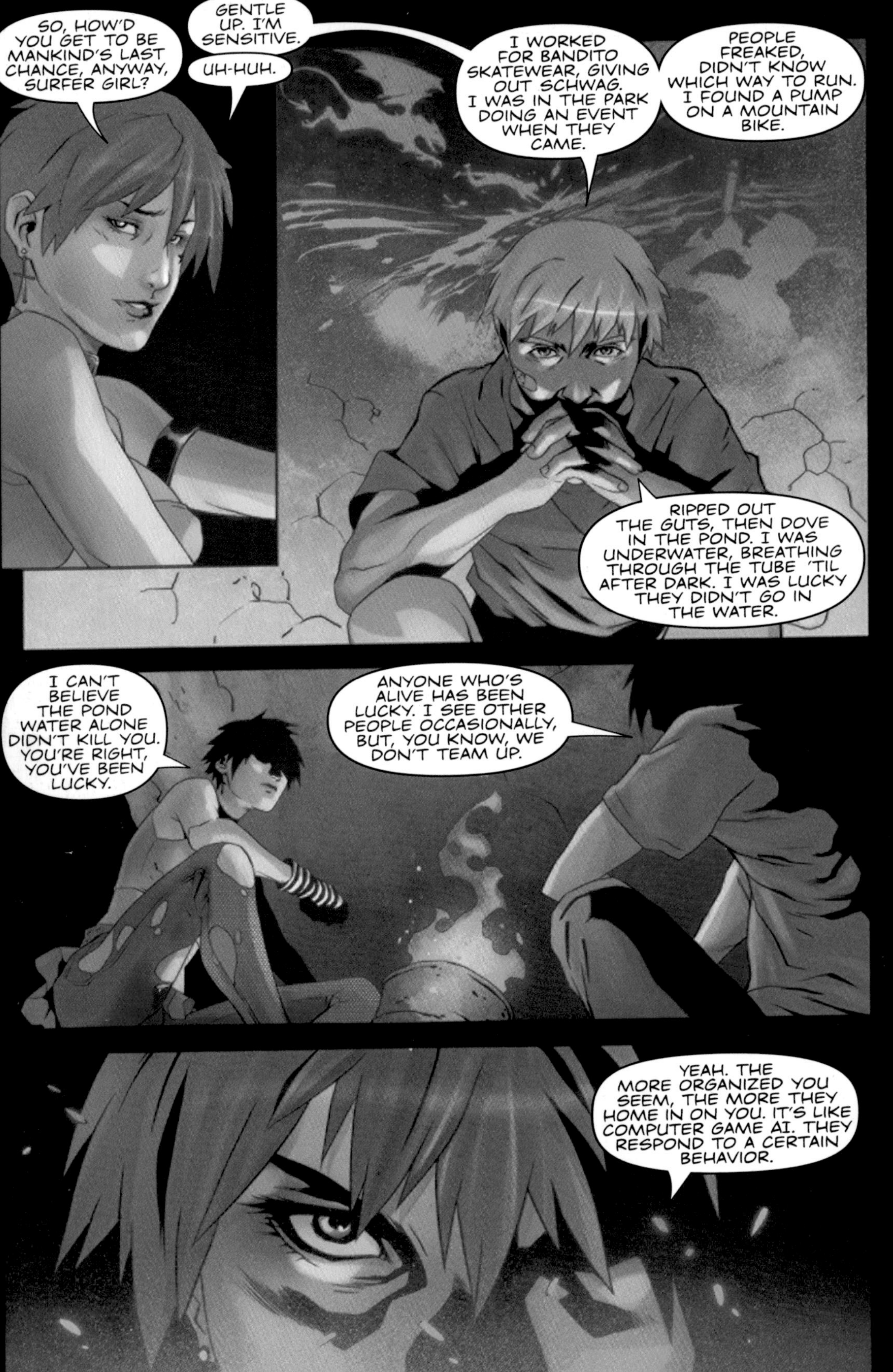
SO, HOW'D YOU GET TO BE MANKIND'S LAST CHANCE, ANYWAY, SURFER GIRL?
GENTLE UP. I'M SENSITIVE.
UH-HUH.
I WORKED FOR BANDITO SKATEWEAR, GIVING OUT SCHWAG. I WAS IN THE PARK DOING AN EVENT WHEN THEY CAME.
PEOPLE FREAKED, DIDN'T KNOW WHICH WAY TO RUN. I FOUND A PUMP ON A MOUNTAIN BIKE.
RIPPED OUT THE GUTS, THEN DOVE IN THE POND. I WAS UNDERWATER, BREATHING THROUGH THE TUBE 'TIL AFTER DARK. I WAS LUCKY THEY DIDN'T GO IN THE WATER.
I CAN'T BELIEVE THE POND WATER ALONE DIDN'T KILL YOU. YOU'RE RIGHT, YOU'VE BEEN LUCKY.
ANYONE WHO'S ALIVE HAS BEEN LUCKY. I SEE OTHER PEOPLE OCCASIONALLY, BUT, YOU KNOW, WE DON'T TEAM UP.
YEAH. THE MORE ORGANIZED YOU SEEM, THE MORE THEY HOME IN ON YOU. IT'S LIKE COMPUTER GAME AI. THEY RESPOND TO A CERTAIN BEHAVIOR.

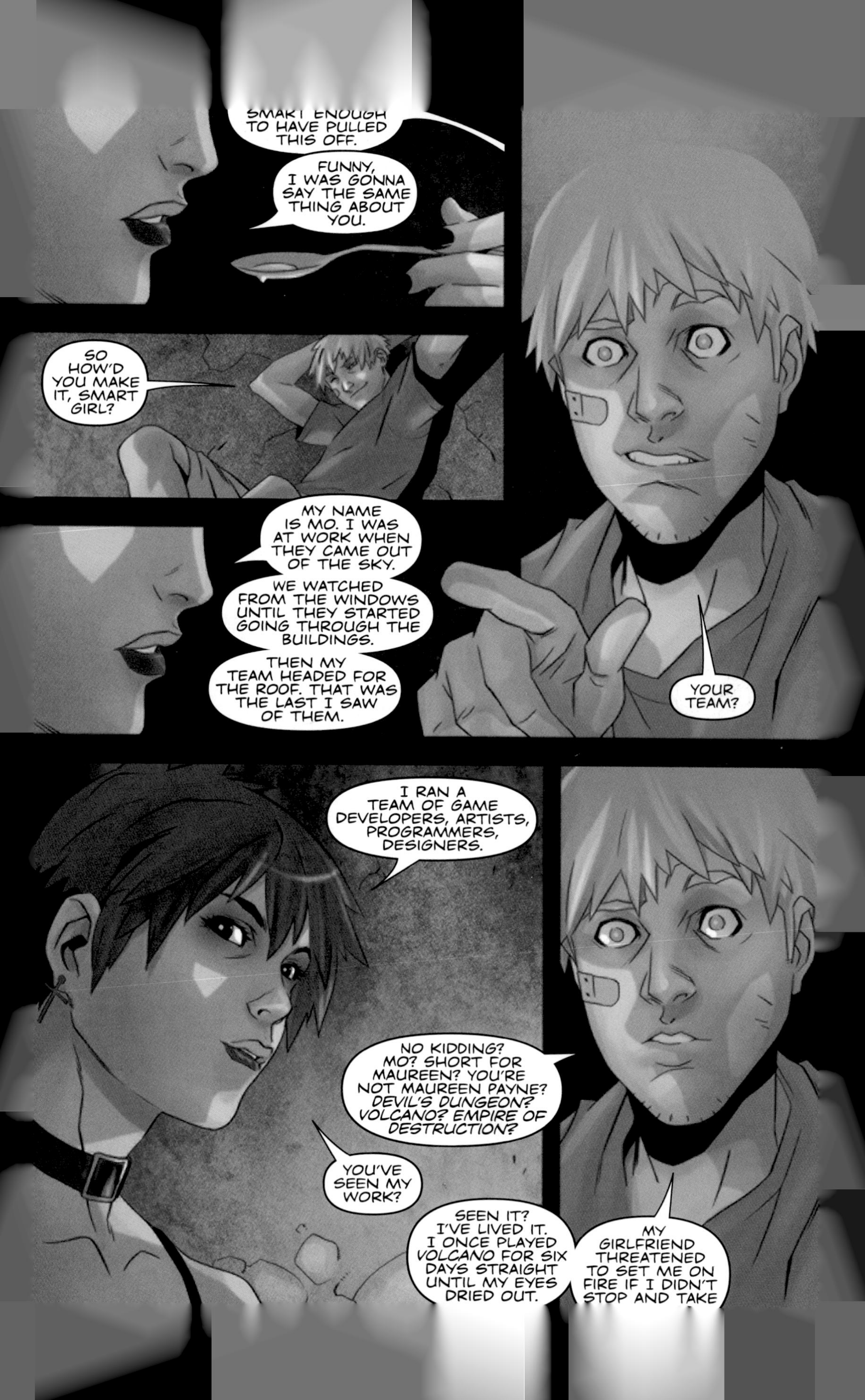
SMART ENOUGH TO HAVE PULLED THIS OFF.
FUNNY, I WAS GONNA SAY THE SAME THING ABOUT YOU.
SO HOW'D YOU MAKE IT, SMART GIRL?
MY NAME IS MO. I WAS AT WORK WHEN THEY CAME OUT OF THE SKY.
WE WATCHED FROM THE WINDOWS UNTIL THEY STARTED GOING THROUGH THE BUILDINGS.
THEN MY TEAM HEADED FOR THE ROOF. THAT WAS THE LAST I SAW OF THEM.
YOUR TEAM?
I RAN A TEAM OF GAME DEVELOPERS, ARTISTS, PROGRAMMERS, DESIGNERS.
NO KIDDING? MO? SHORT FOR MAUREEN? YOU'RE NOT MAUREEN PAYNE? *DEVIL'S DUNGEON? VOLCANO? EMPIRE OF DESTRUCTION?*
YOU'VE SEEN MY WORK?
SEEN IT? I'VE LIVED IT. I ONCE PLAYED *VOLCANO* FOR SIX DAYS STRAIGHT UNTIL MY EYES DRIED OUT.
MY GIRLFRIEND THREATENED TO SET ME ON FIRE IF I DIDN'T STOP AND TAKE

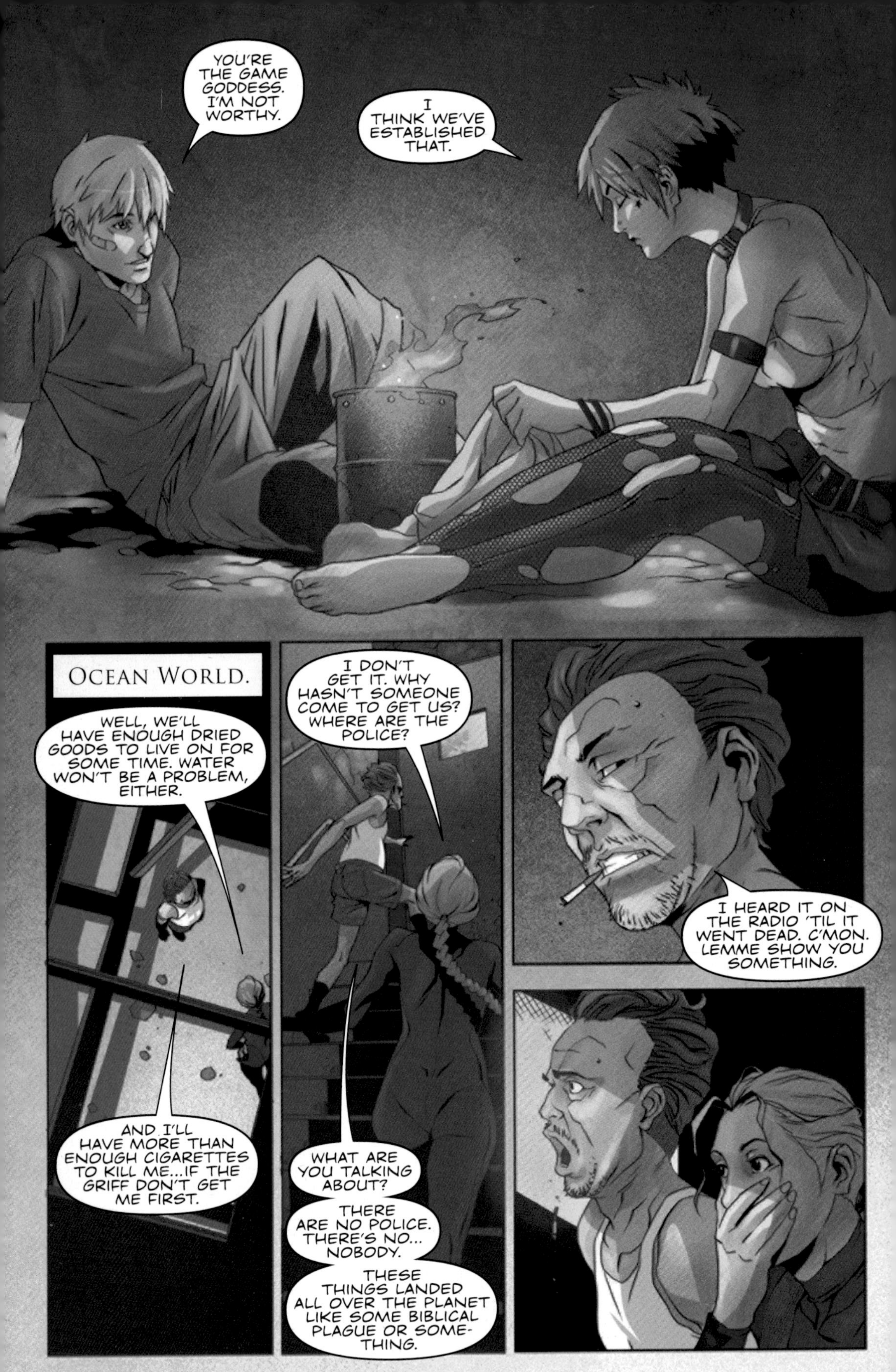
YOU'RE THE GAME GODDESS. I'M NOT WORTHY.
I THINK WE'VE ESTABLISHED THAT.
OCEAN WORLD.
WELL, WE'LL HAVE ENOUGH DRIED GOODS TO LIVE ON FOR SOME TIME. WATER WON'T BE A PROBLEM, EITHER.
AND I'LL HAVE MORE THAN ENOUGH CIGARETTES TO KILL ME...IF THE GRIFF DON'T GET ME FIRST.
I DON'T GET IT. WHY HASN'T SOMEONE COME TO GET US? WHERE ARE THE POLICE?
WHAT ARE YOU TALKING ABOUT?
THERE ARE NO POLICE. THERE'S NO... NOBODY.
THESE THINGS LANDED ALL OVER THE PLANET LIKE SOME BIBLICAL PLAGUE OR SOME-THING.
I HEARD IT ON THE RADIO 'TIL IT WENT DEAD. C'MON. LEMME SHOW YOU SOMETHING.

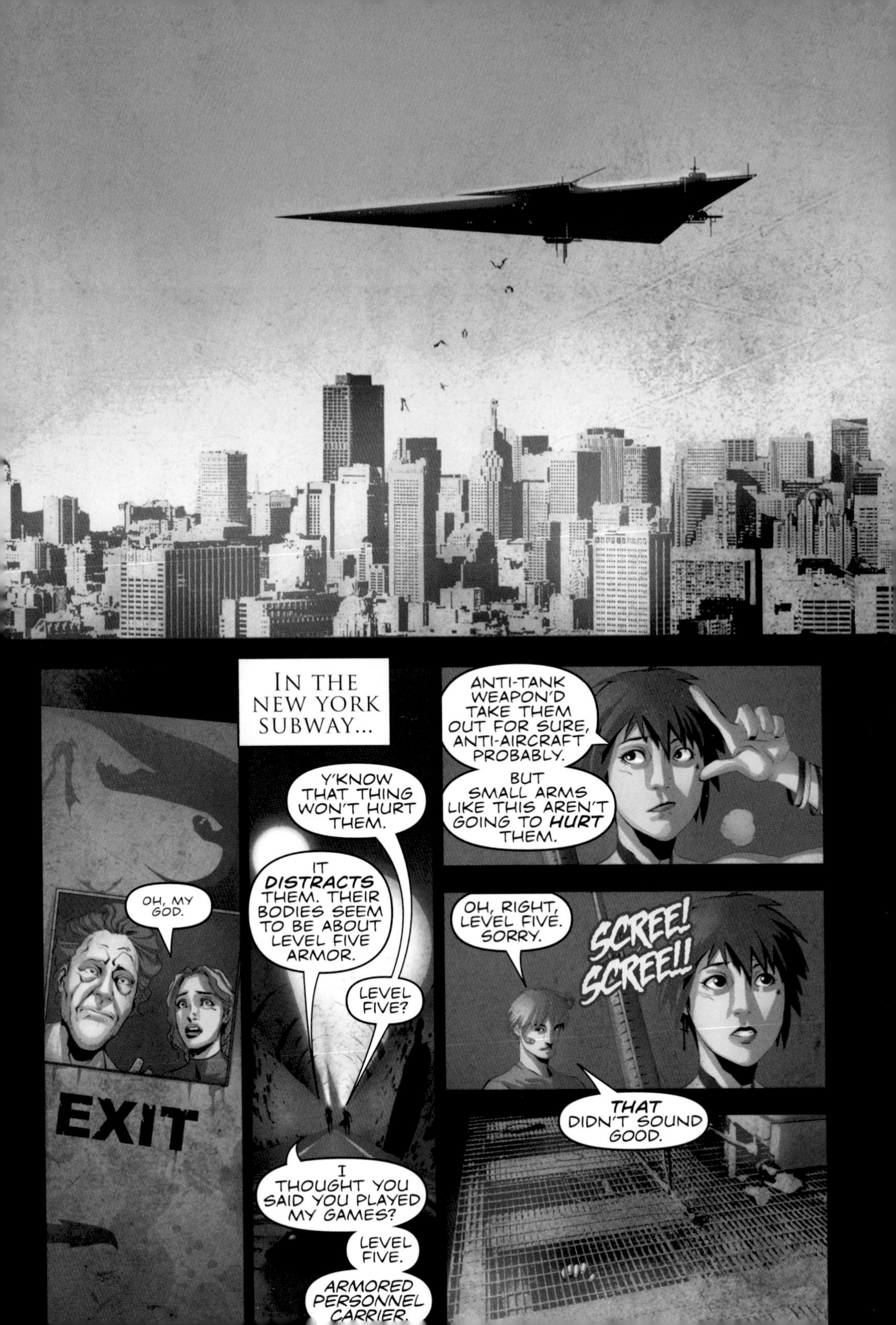
IN THE NEW YORK SUBWAY...
OH, MY GOD.
EXIT
Y'KNOW THAT THING WON'T HURT THEM.
IT DISTRACTS THEM. THEIR BODIES SEEM TO BE ABOUT LEVEL FIVE ARMOR.
LEVEL FIVE?
I THOUGHT YOU SAID YOU PLAYED MY GAMES?
LEVEL FIVE.
ARMORED PERSONNEL CARRIER.
ANTI-TANK WEAPON'D TAKE THEM OUT FOR SURE, ANTI-AIRCRAFT PROBABLY.
BUT SMALL ARMS LIKE THIS AREN'T GOING TO HURT THEM.
OH, RIGHT, LEVEL FIVE. SORRY.
SCREE! SCREE!!
THAT DIDN'T SOUND GOOD.

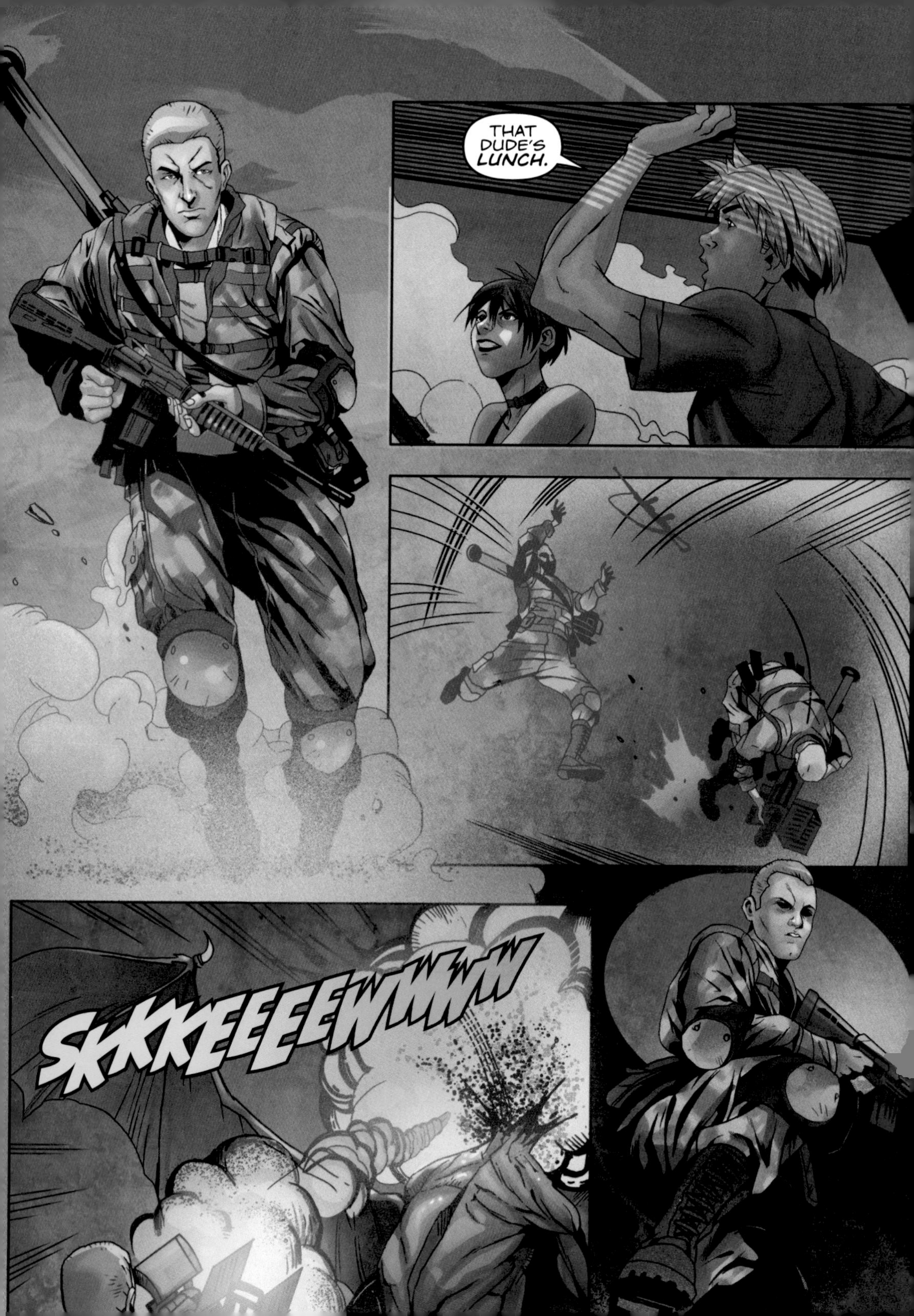
THAT DUDE'S LUNCH.
SKKREEEEEWWWN

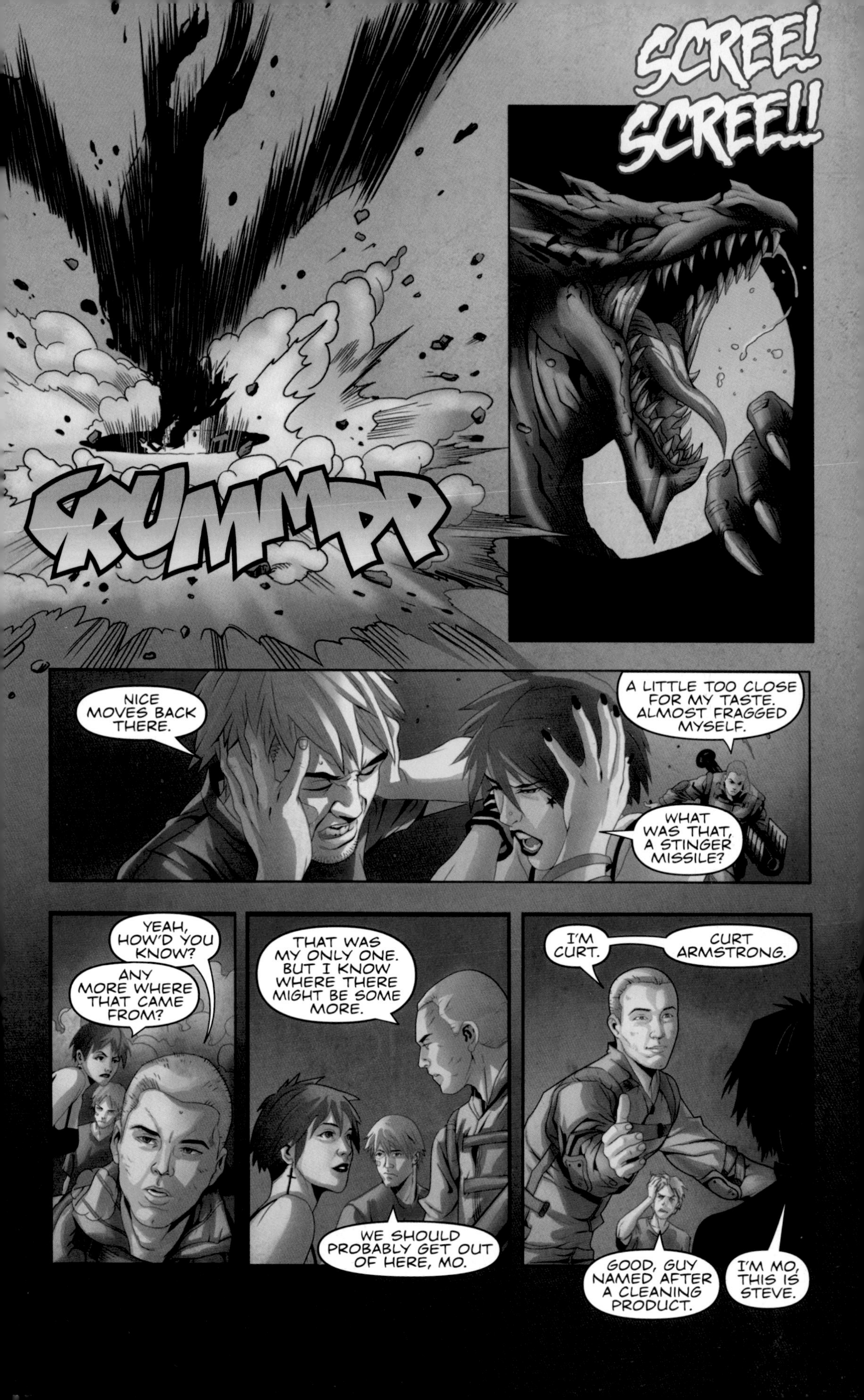
SCREE! SCREE!!
GRUMMPP
NICE MOVES BACK THERE.
A LITTLE TOO CLOSE FOR MY TASTE. ALMOST FRAGGED MYSELF.
WHAT WAS THAT, A STINGER MISSILE?
YEAH, HOW'D YOU KNOW?
ANY MORE WHERE THAT CAME FROM?
THAT WAS MY ONLY ONE. BUT I KNOW WHERE THERE MIGHT BE SOME MORE.
WE SHOULD PROBABLY GET OUT OF HERE, MO.
I'M CURT.
CURT ARMSTRONG.
GOOD, GUY NAMED AFTER A CLEANING PRODUCT.
I'M MO, THIS IS STEVE.

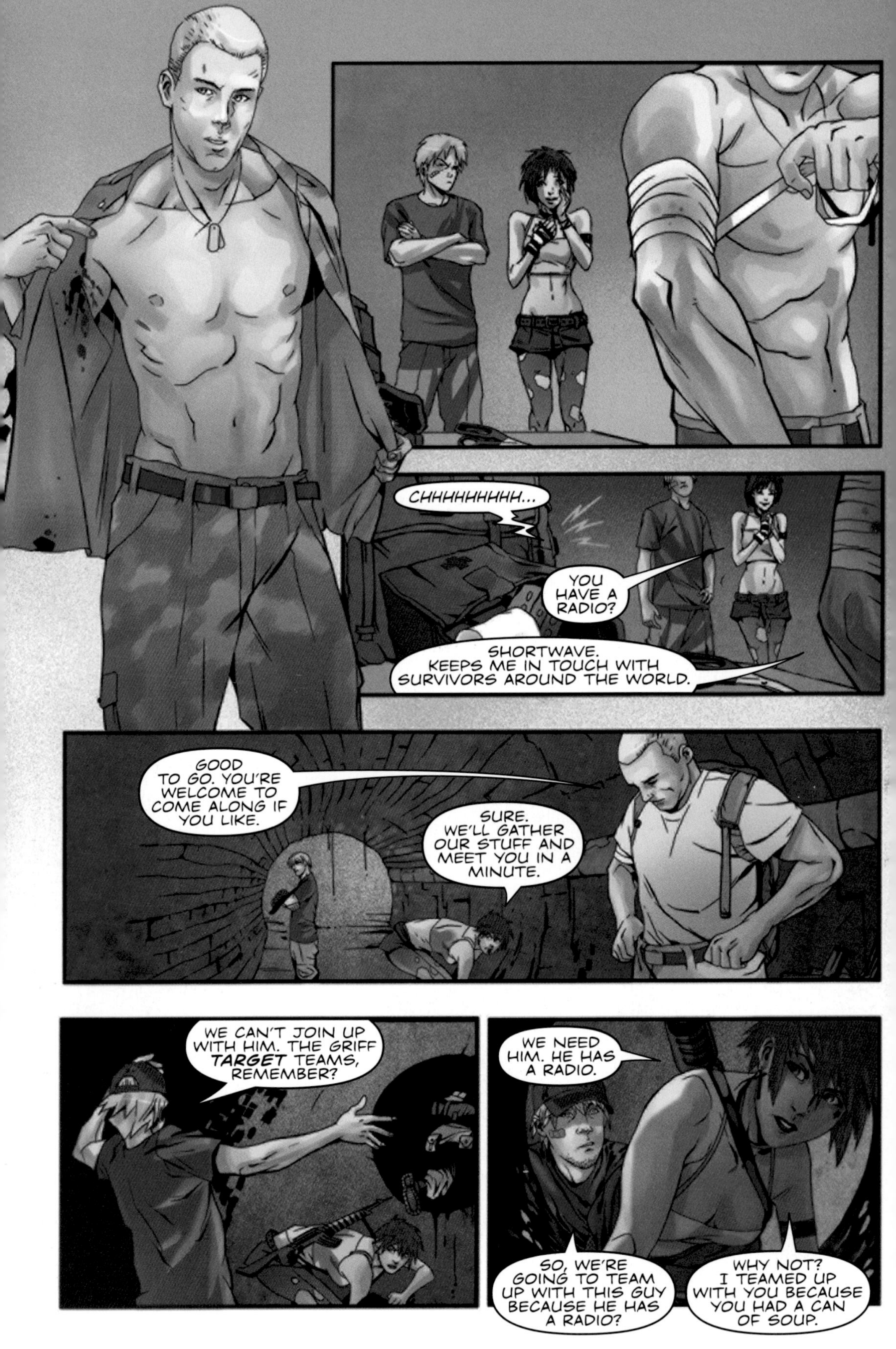
CHHHHHHHHH...
YOU HAVE A RADIO?
SHORTWAVE. KEEPS ME IN TOUCH WITH SURVIVORS AROUND THE WORLD.
GOOD TO GO. YOU'RE WELCOME TO COME ALONG IF YOU LIKE.
SURE. WE'LL GATHER OUR STUFF AND MEET YOU IN A MINUTE.
WE CAN'T JOIN UP WITH HIM. THE GRIFF TARGET TEAMS, REMEMBER?
WE NEED HIM. HE HAS A RADIO.
SO, WE'RE GOING TO TEAM UP WITH THIS GUY BECAUSE HE HAS A RADIO?
WHY NOT? I TEAMED UP WITH YOU BECAUSE YOU HAD A CAN OF SOUP.

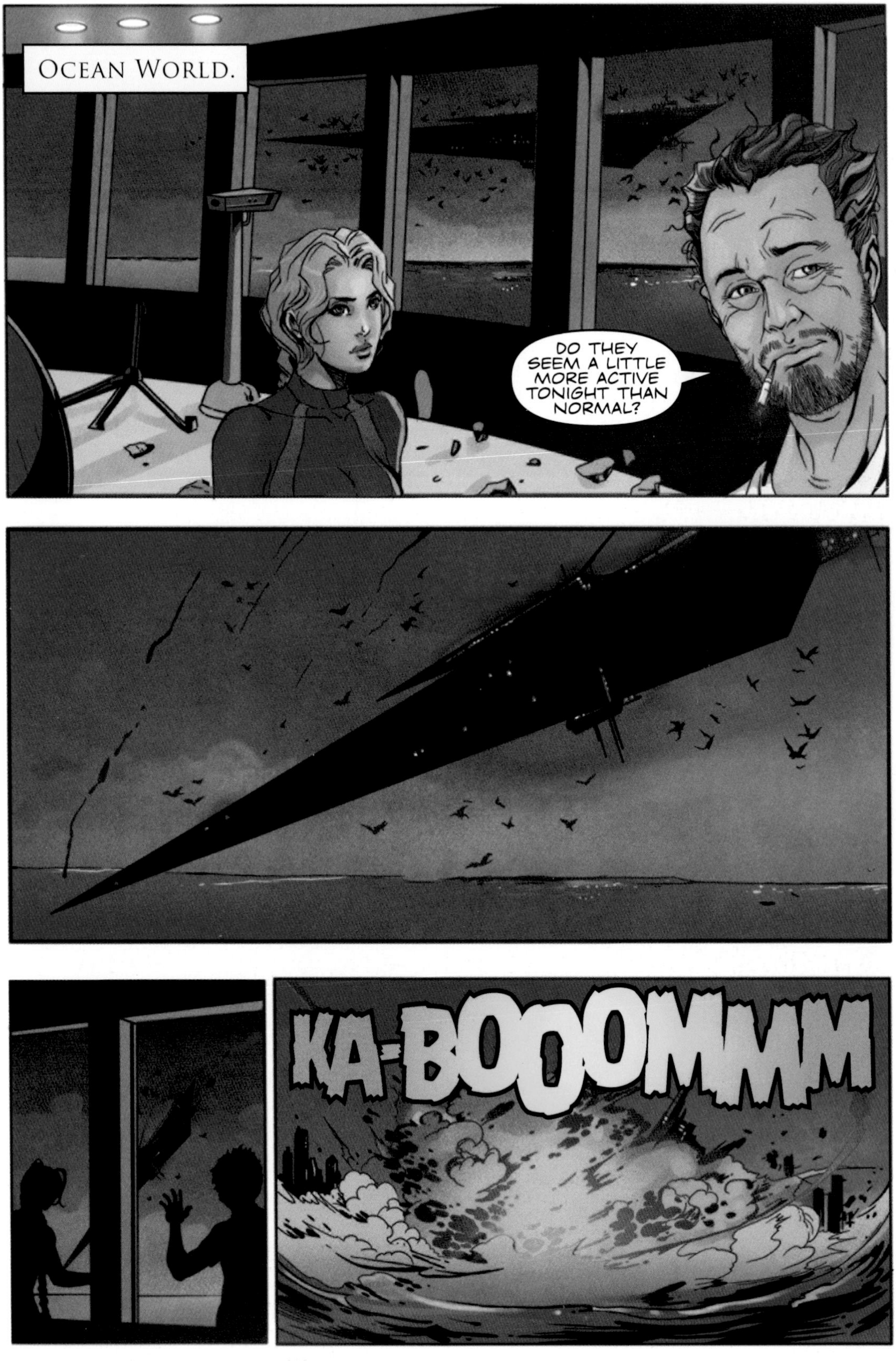
OCEAN WORLD.
DO THEY SEEM A LITTLE MORE ACTIVE TONIGHT THAN NORMAL?
KA-BOOOMMM

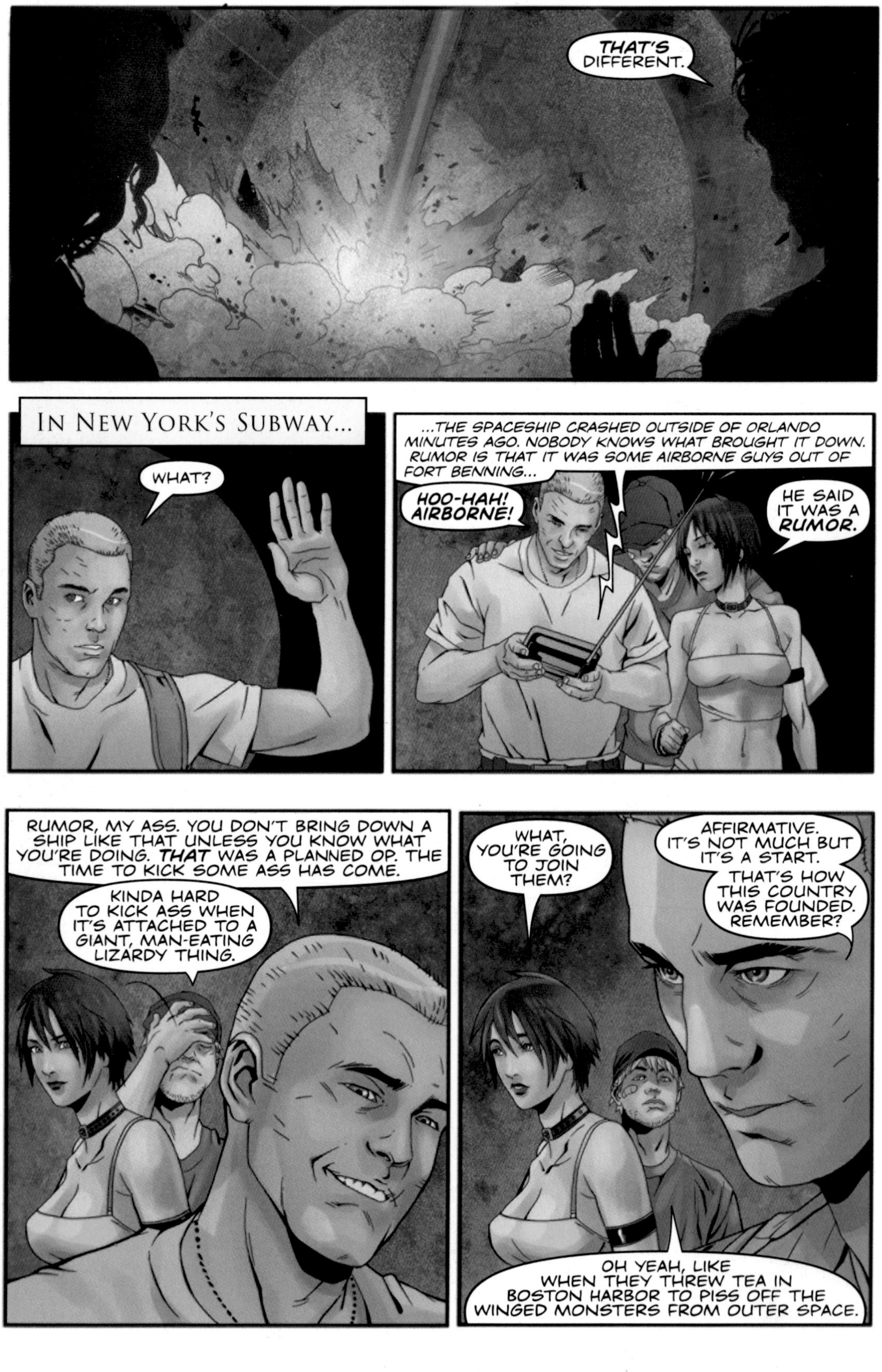
THAT'S DIFFERENT.
IN NEW YORK'S SUBWAY...
WHAT?
...THE SPACESHIP CRASHED OUTSIDE OF ORLANDO MINUTES AGO. NOBODY KNOWS WHAT BROUGHT IT DOWN. RUMOR IS THAT IT WAS SOME AIRBORNE GUYS OUT OF FORT BENNING...
HOO-HAH! AIRBORNE!
HE SAID IT WAS A RUMOR.
RUMOR, MY ASS. YOU DON'T BRING DOWN A SHIP LIKE THAT UNLESS YOU KNOW WHAT YOU'RE DOING. THAT WAS A PLANNED OP. THE TIME TO KICK SOME ASS HAS COME.
KINDA HARD TO KICK ASS WHEN IT'S ATTACHED TO A GIANT, MAN-EATING LIZARDY THING.
WHAT, YOU'RE GOING TO JOIN THEM?
AFFIRMATIVE. IT'S NOT MUCH BUT IT'S A START.
THAT'S HOW THIS COUNTRY WAS FOUNDED. REMEMBER?
OH YEAH, LIKE WHEN THEY THREW TEA IN BOSTON HARBOR TO PISS OFF THE WINGED MONSTERS FROM OUTER SPACE.

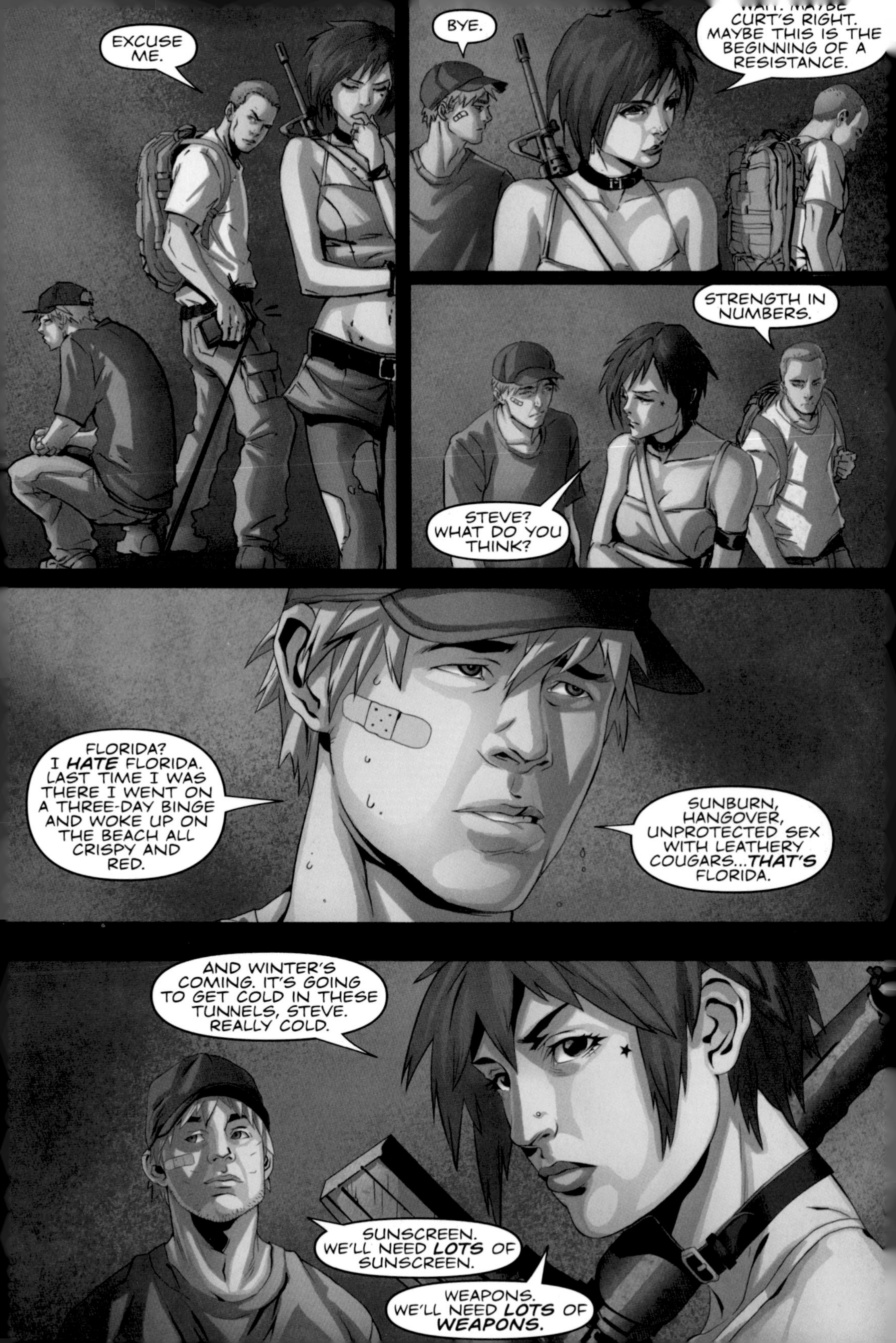
EXCUSE ME.
BYE.
CURT'S RIGHT. MAYBE THIS IS THE BEGINNING OF A RESISTANCE.
STRENGTH IN NUMBERS.
STEVE? WHAT DO YOU THINK?
FLORIDA? I **HATE** FLORIDA. LAST TIME I WAS THERE I WENT ON A THREE-DAY BINGE AND WOKE UP ON THE BEACH ALL CRISPY AND RED.
SUNBURN, HANGOVER, UNPROTECTED SEX WITH LEATHERY COUGARS...**THAT'S** FLORIDA.
AND WINTER'S COMING. IT'S GOING TO GET COLD IN THESE TUNNELS, STEVE. REALLY COLD.
SUNSCREEN. WE'LL NEED **LOTS** OF SUNSCREEN.
WEAPONS. WE'LL NEED **LOTS** OF **WEAPONS.**

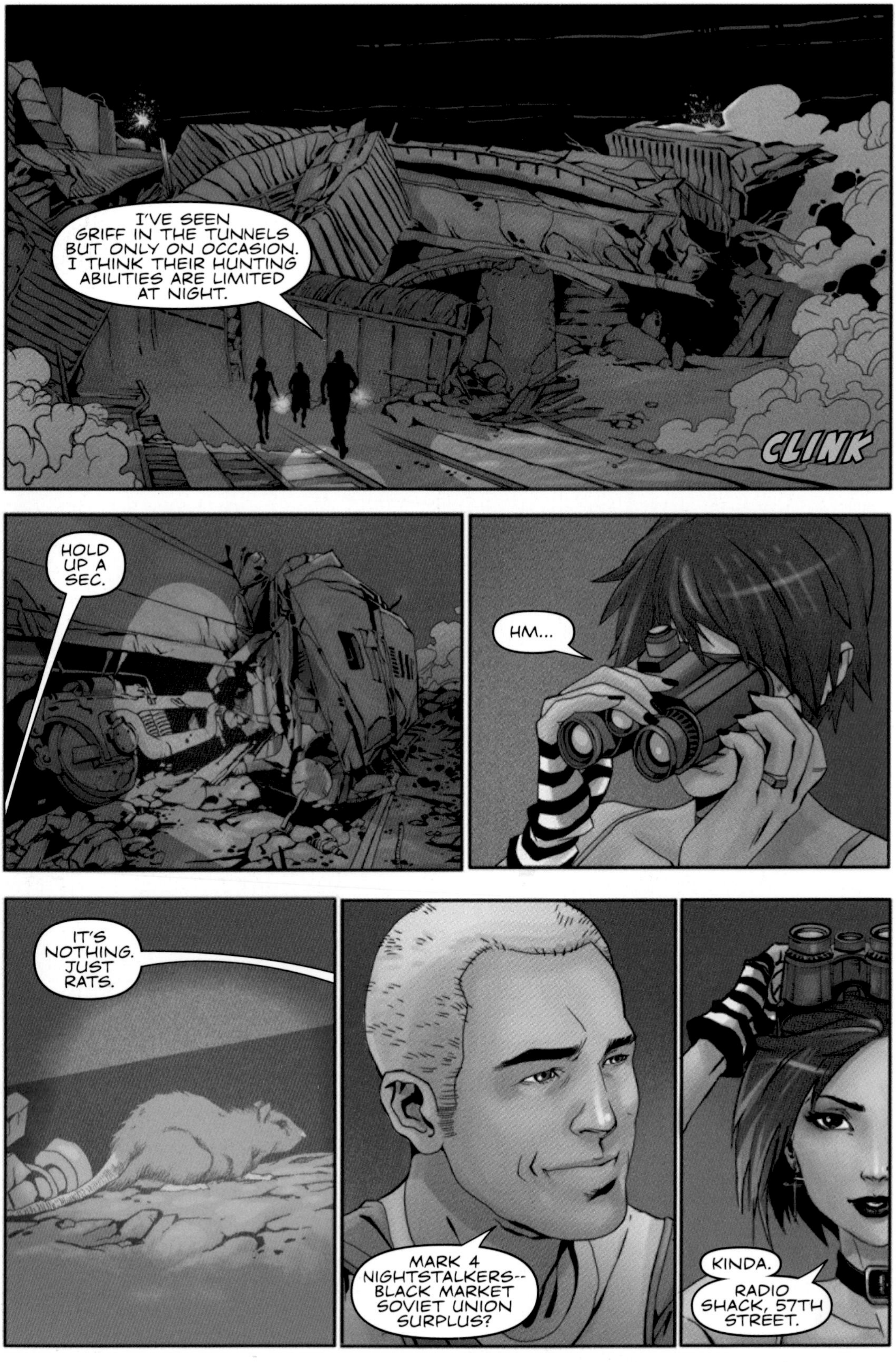
I'VE SEEN GRIFF IN THE TUNNELS BUT ONLY ON OCCASION. I THINK THEIR HUNTING ABILITIES ARE LIMITED AT NIGHT.
CLINK
HOLD UP A SEC.
HM...
IT'S NOTHING. JUST RATS.
MARK 4 NIGHTSTALKERS-- BLACK MARKET SOVIET UNION SURPLUS?
KINDA.
RADIO SHACK, 57TH STREET.

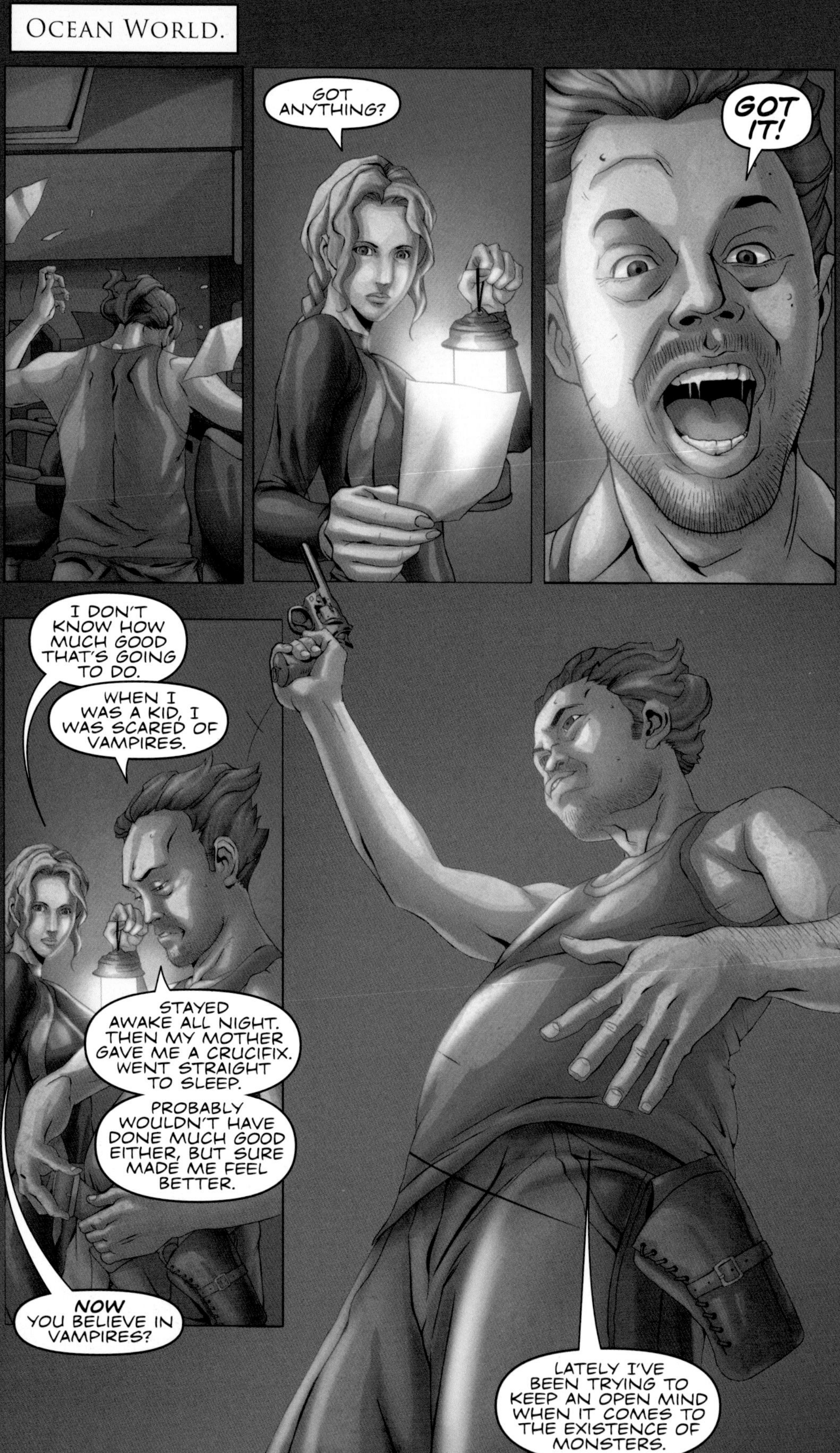
OCEAN WORLD.
GOT ANYTHING?
GOT IT!
I DON'T KNOW HOW MUCH GOOD THAT'S GOING TO DO.
WHEN I WAS A KID, I WAS SCARED OF VAMPIRES.
STAYED AWAKE ALL NIGHT. THEN MY MOTHER GAVE ME A CRUCIFIX. WENT STRAIGHT TO SLEEP.
PROBABLY WOULDN'T HAVE DONE MUCH GOOD EITHER, BUT SURE MADE ME FEEL BETTER.
NOW YOU BELIEVE IN VAMPIRES?
LATELY I'VE BEEN TRYING TO KEEP AN OPEN MIND WHEN IT COMES TO THE EXISTENCE OF MONSTERS.

NEW YORK CITY.

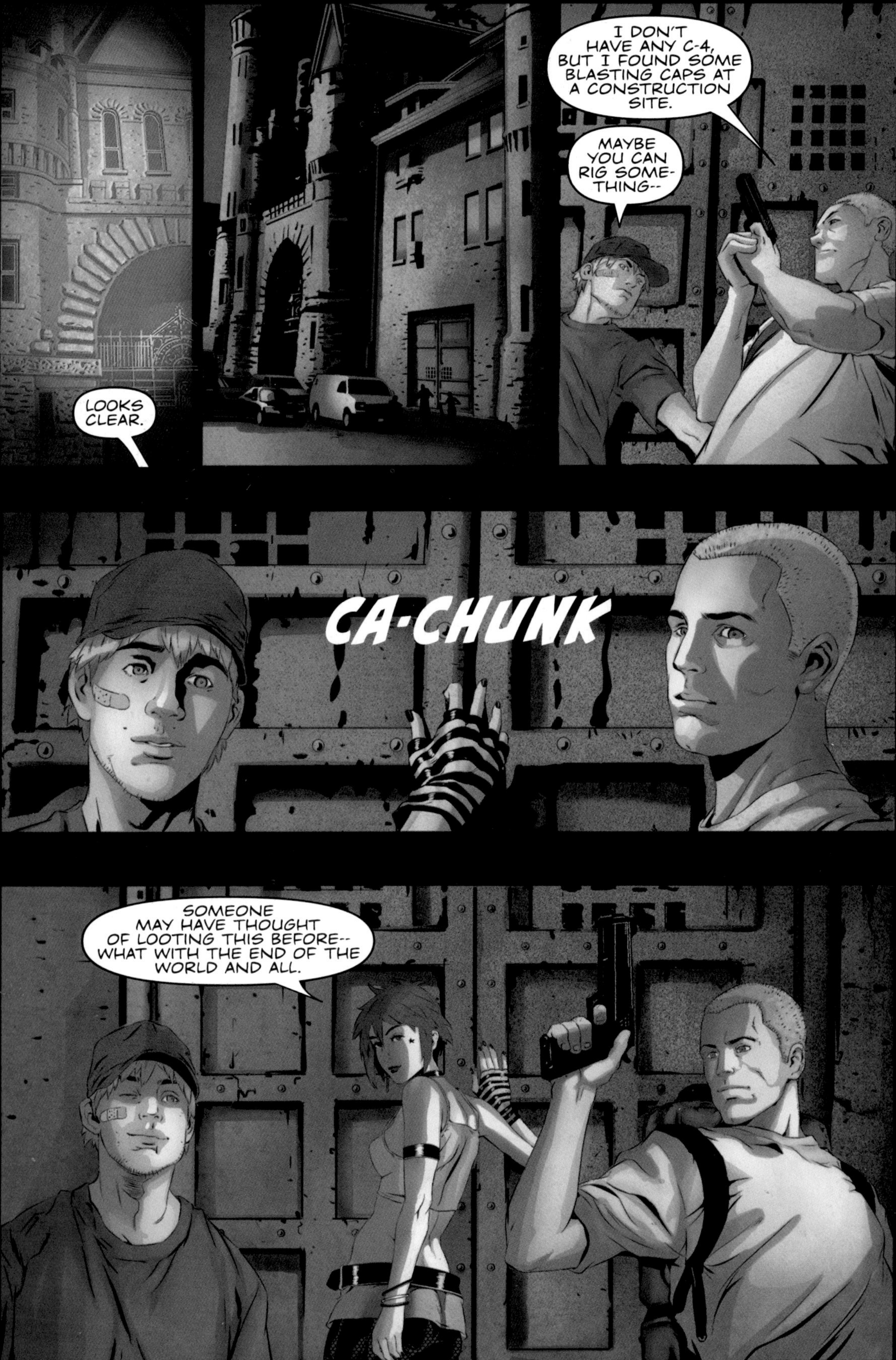
LOOKS CLEAR.
I DON'T HAVE ANY C-4, BUT I FOUND SOME BLASTING CAPS AT A CONSTRUCTION SITE.
MAYBE YOU CAN RIG SOME-THING--
CA-CHUNK
SOMEONE MAY HAVE THOUGHT OF LOOTING THIS BEFORE-- WHAT WITH THE END OF THE WORLD AND ALL.

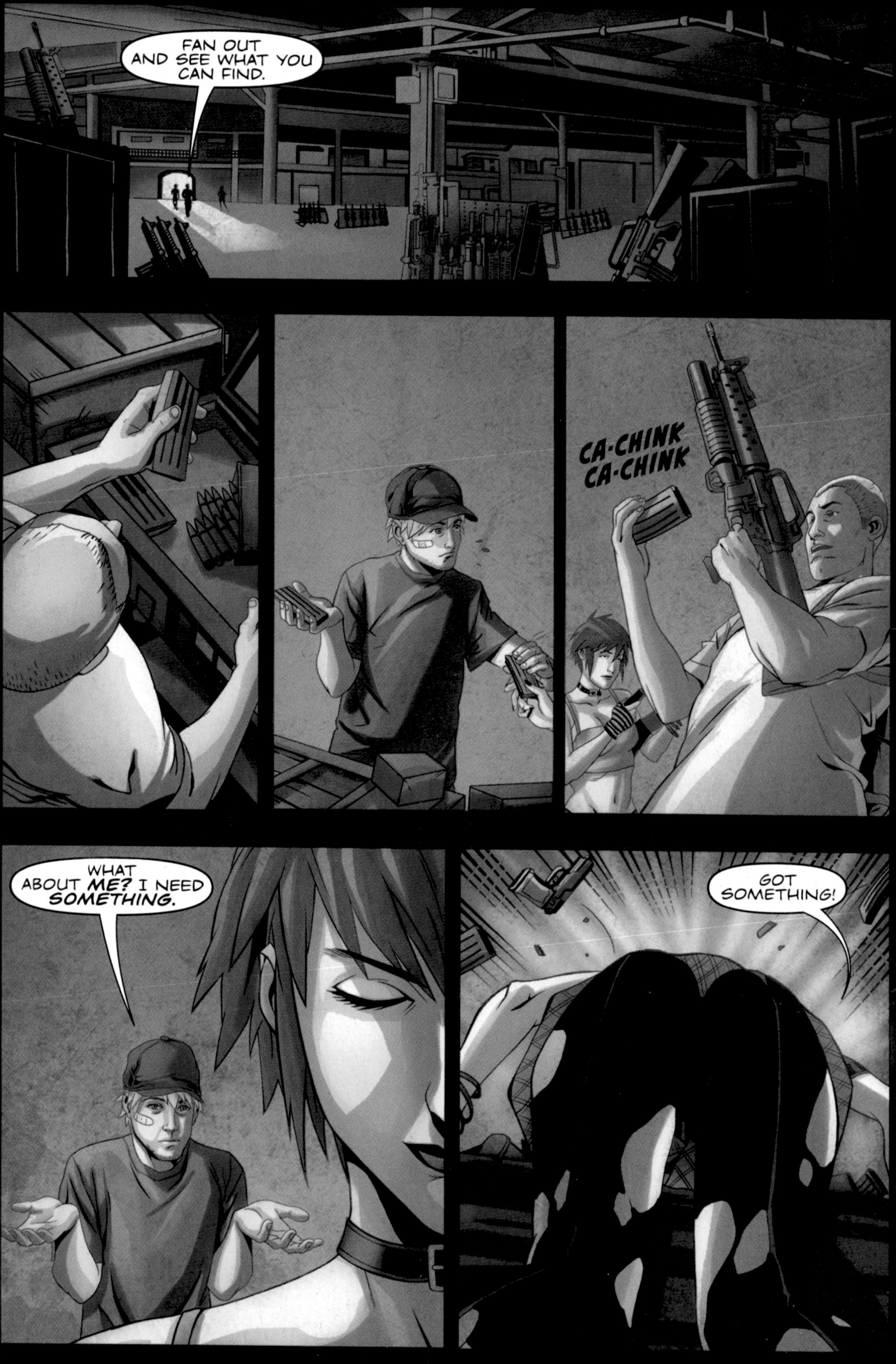
FAN OUT AND SEE WHAT YOU CAN FIND.
CA-CHINK CA-CHINK
WHAT ABOUT ME? I NEED SOMETHING.
GOT SOMETHING!

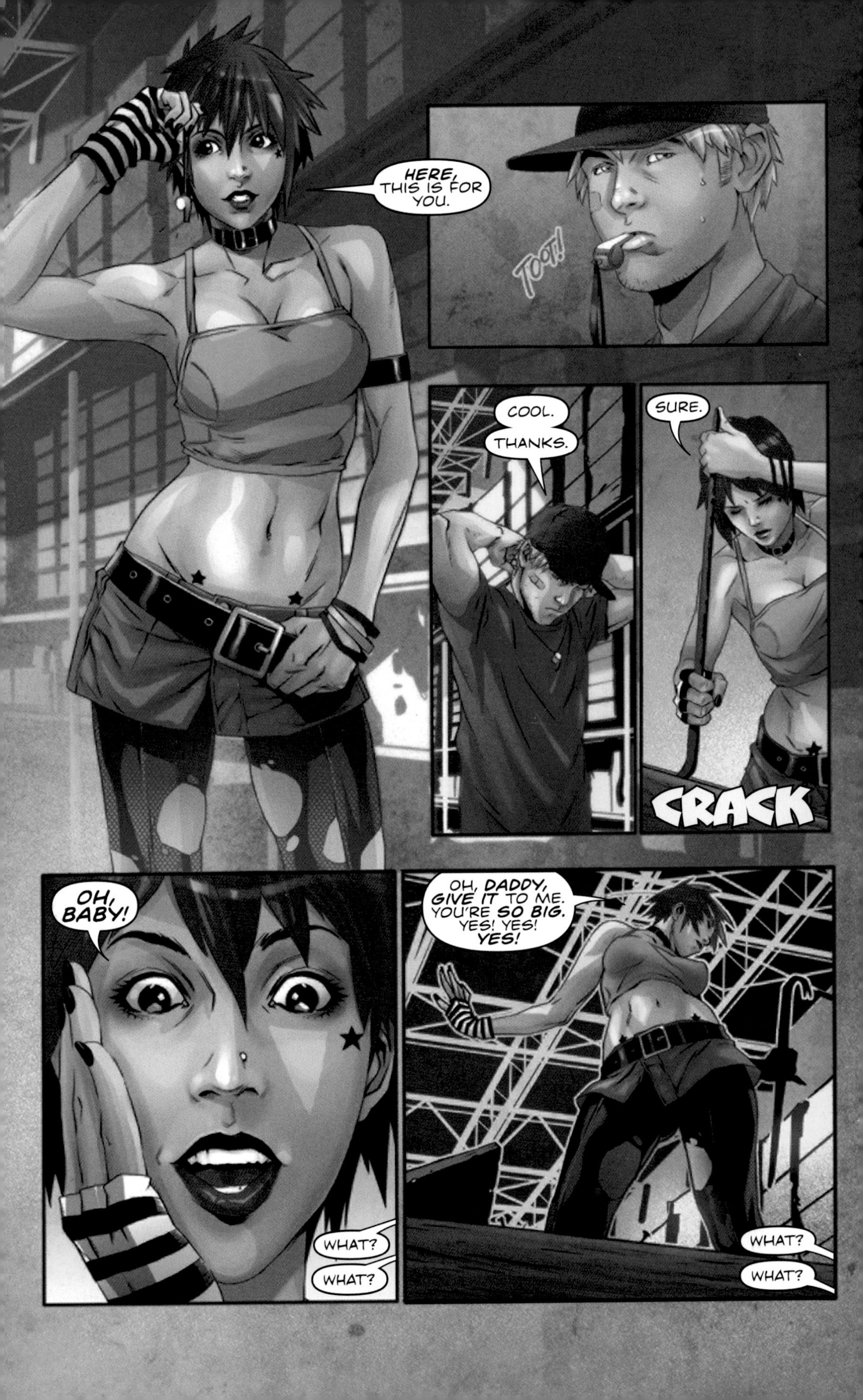
HERE, THIS IS FOR YOU.
TOOT!
COOL.
THANKS.
SURE.
CRACK
OH, BABY!
WHAT?
WHAT?
OH, DADDY, GIVE IT TO ME. YOU'RE SO BIG. YES! YES! YES!
WHAT?
WHAT?

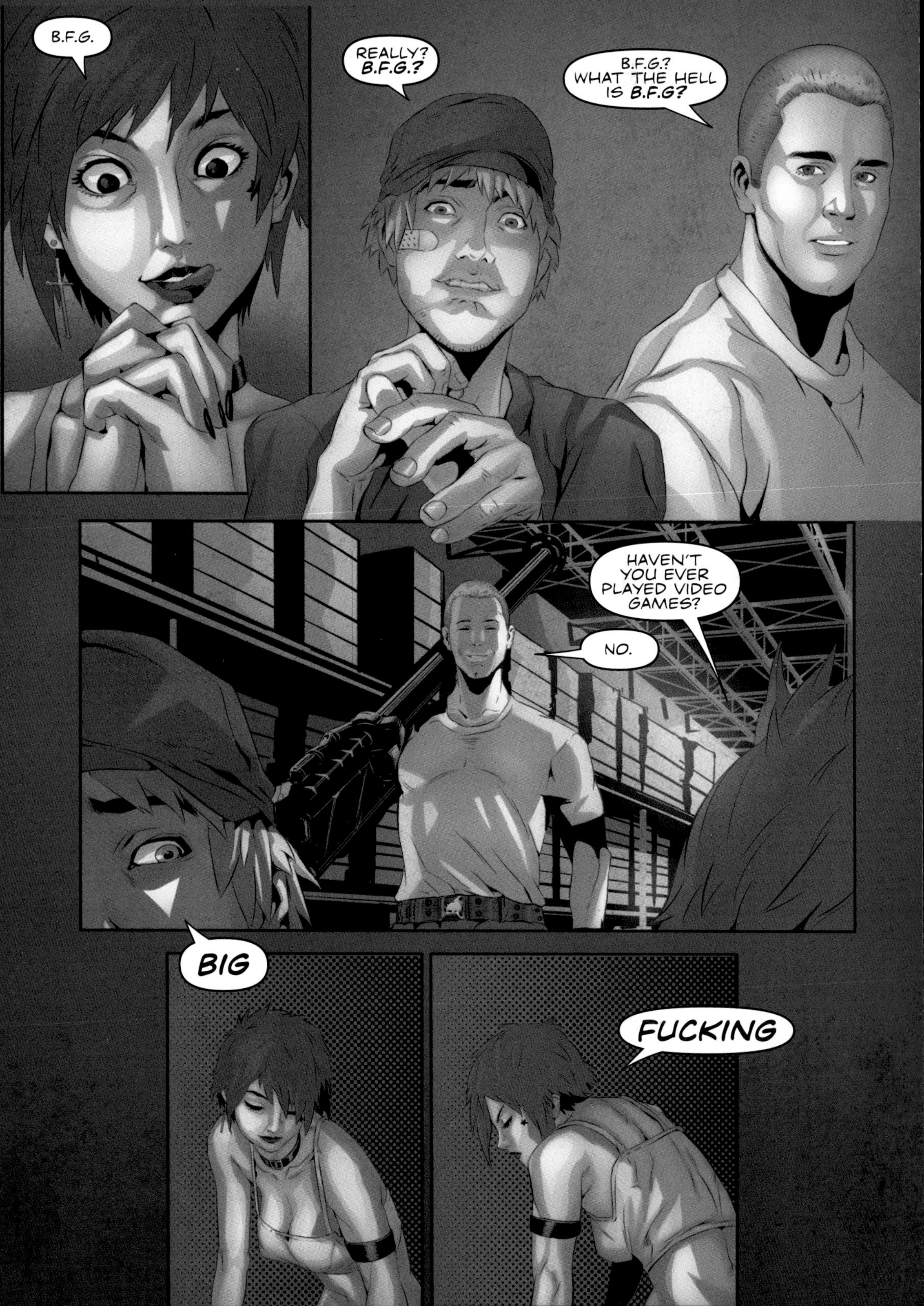
B.F.G.
REALLY? B.F.G.?
B.F.G.? WHAT THE HELL IS B.F.G?
HAVEN'T YOU EVER PLAYED VIDEO GAMES?
NO.
BIG
FUCKING

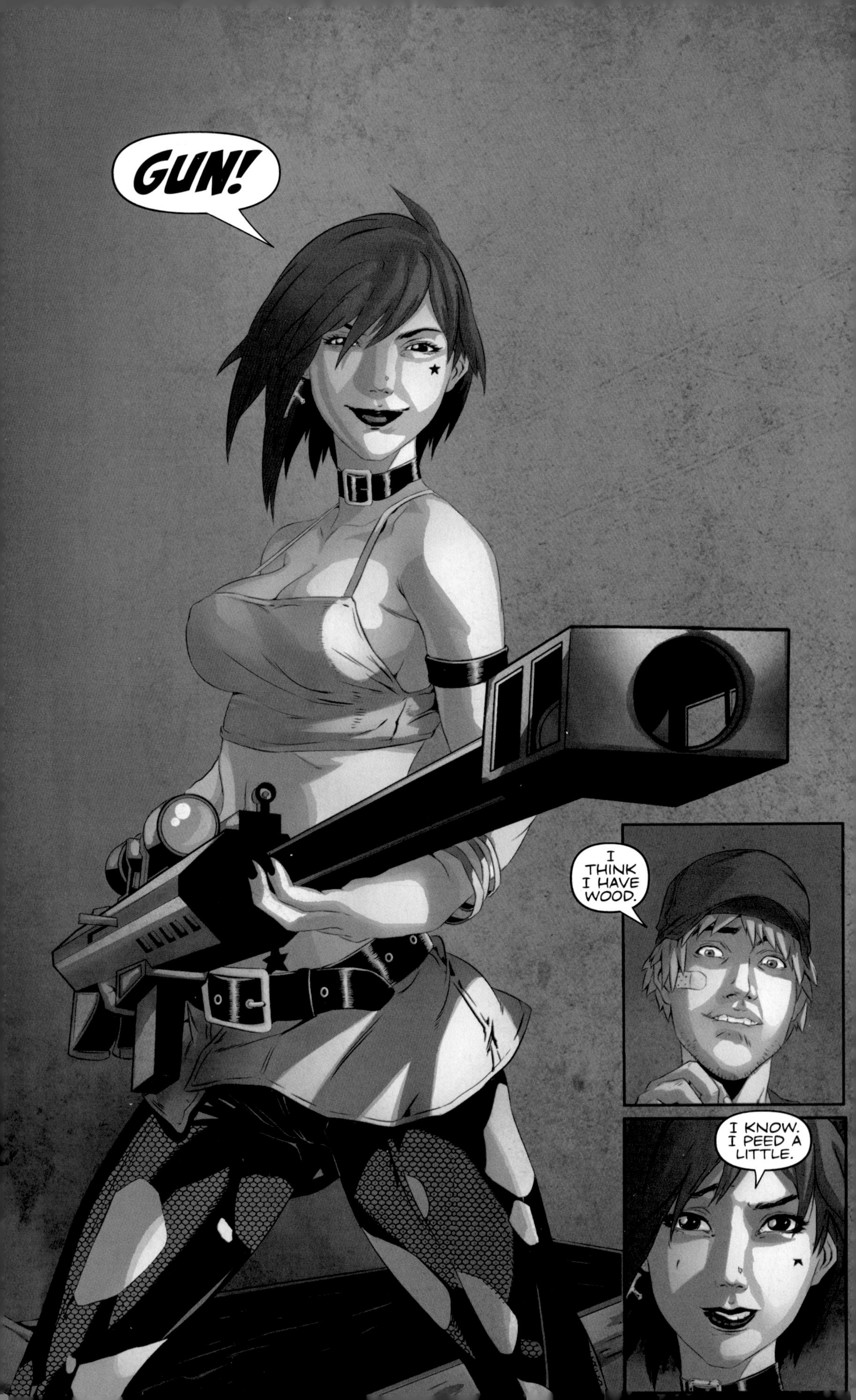
GUN!
I THINK I HAVE WOOD.
I KNOW. I PEED A LITTLE.

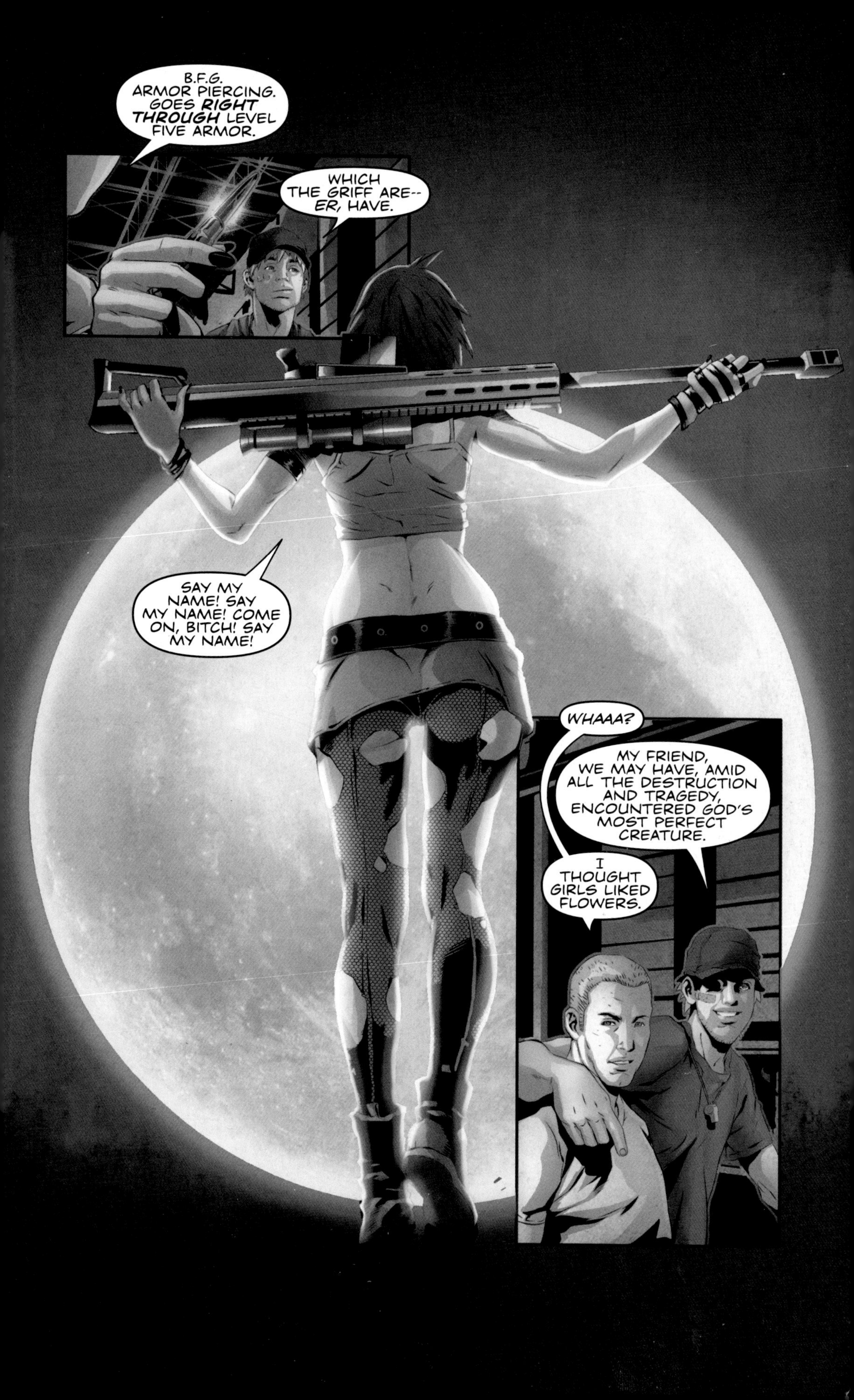
B.F.G. ARMOR PIERCING. GOES **RIGHT THROUGH** LEVEL FIVE ARMOR.
WHICH THE GRIFF ARE-- ER, HAVE.
SAY MY NAME! SAY MY NAME! COME ON, BITCH! SAY MY NAME!
WHAAA?
MY FRIEND, WE MAY HAVE, AMID ALL THE DESTRUCTION AND TRAGEDY, ENCOUNTERED GOD'S MOST PERFECT CREATURE.
I THOUGHT GIRLS LIKED FLOWERS.

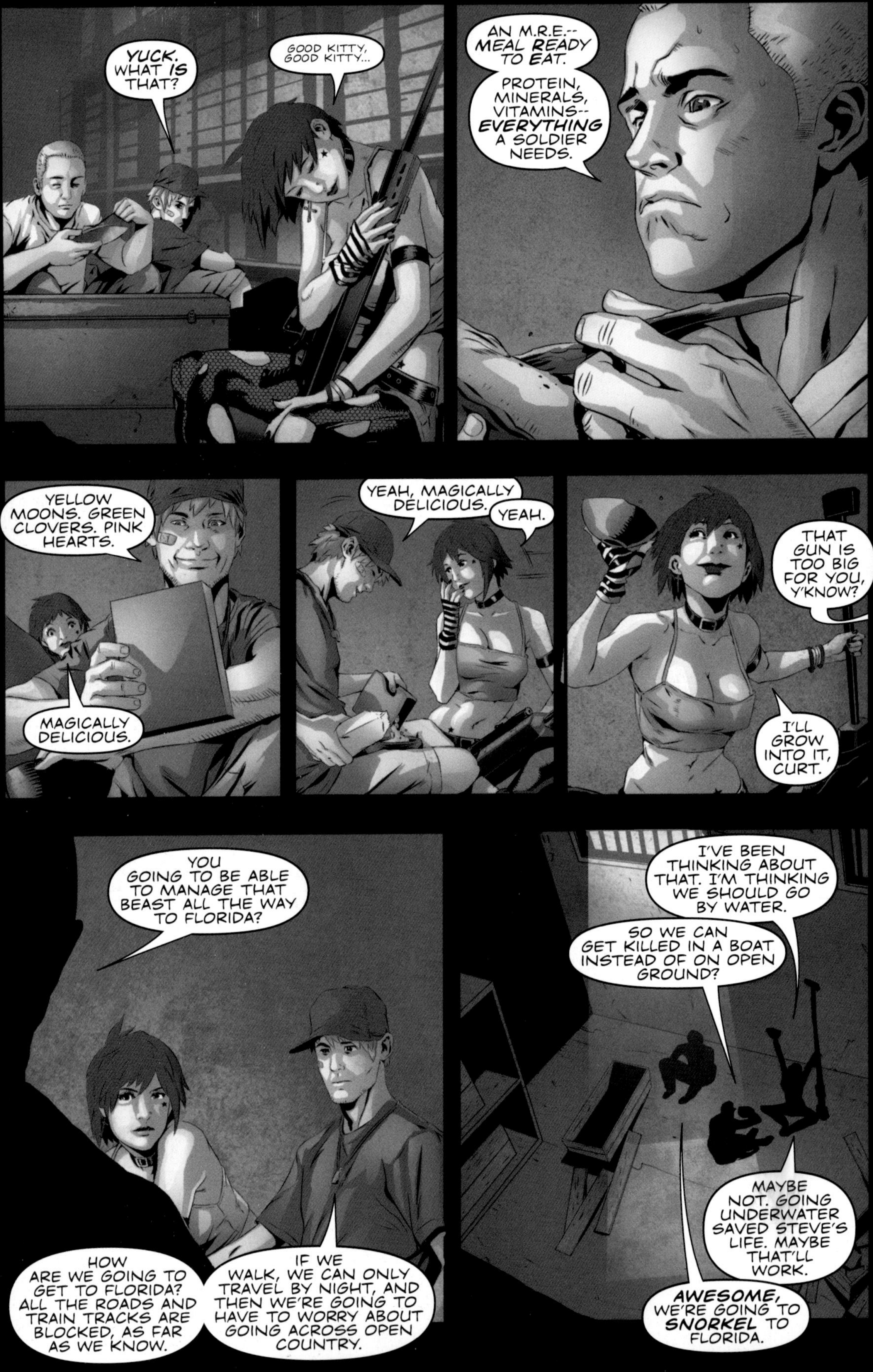
YUCK. WHAT IS THAT?
GOOD KITTY, GOOD KITTY...
AN M.R.E.-- MEAL READY TO EAT.
PROTEIN, MINERALS, VITAMINS-- EVERYTHING A SOLDIER NEEDS.
YELLOW MOONS. GREEN CLOVERS. PINK HEARTS.
MAGICALLY DELICIOUS.
YEAH, MAGICALLY DELICIOUS.
YEAH.
THAT GUN IS TOO BIG FOR YOU, Y'KNOW?
I'LL GROW INTO IT, CURT.
YOU GOING TO BE ABLE TO MANAGE THAT BEAST ALL THE WAY TO FLORIDA?
HOW ARE WE GOING TO GET TO FLORIDA? ALL THE ROADS AND TRAIN TRACKS ARE BLOCKED, AS FAR AS WE KNOW.
IF WE WALK, WE CAN ONLY TRAVEL BY NIGHT, AND THEN WE'RE GOING TO HAVE TO WORRY ABOUT GOING ACROSS OPEN COUNTRY.
I'VE BEEN THINKING ABOUT THAT. I'M THINKING WE SHOULD GO BY WATER.
SO WE CAN GET KILLED IN A BOAT INSTEAD OF ON OPEN GROUND?
MAYBE NOT. GOING UNDERWATER SAVED STEVE'S LIFE. MAYBE THAT'LL WORK.
AWESOME, WE'RE GOING TO SNORKEL TO FLORIDA.

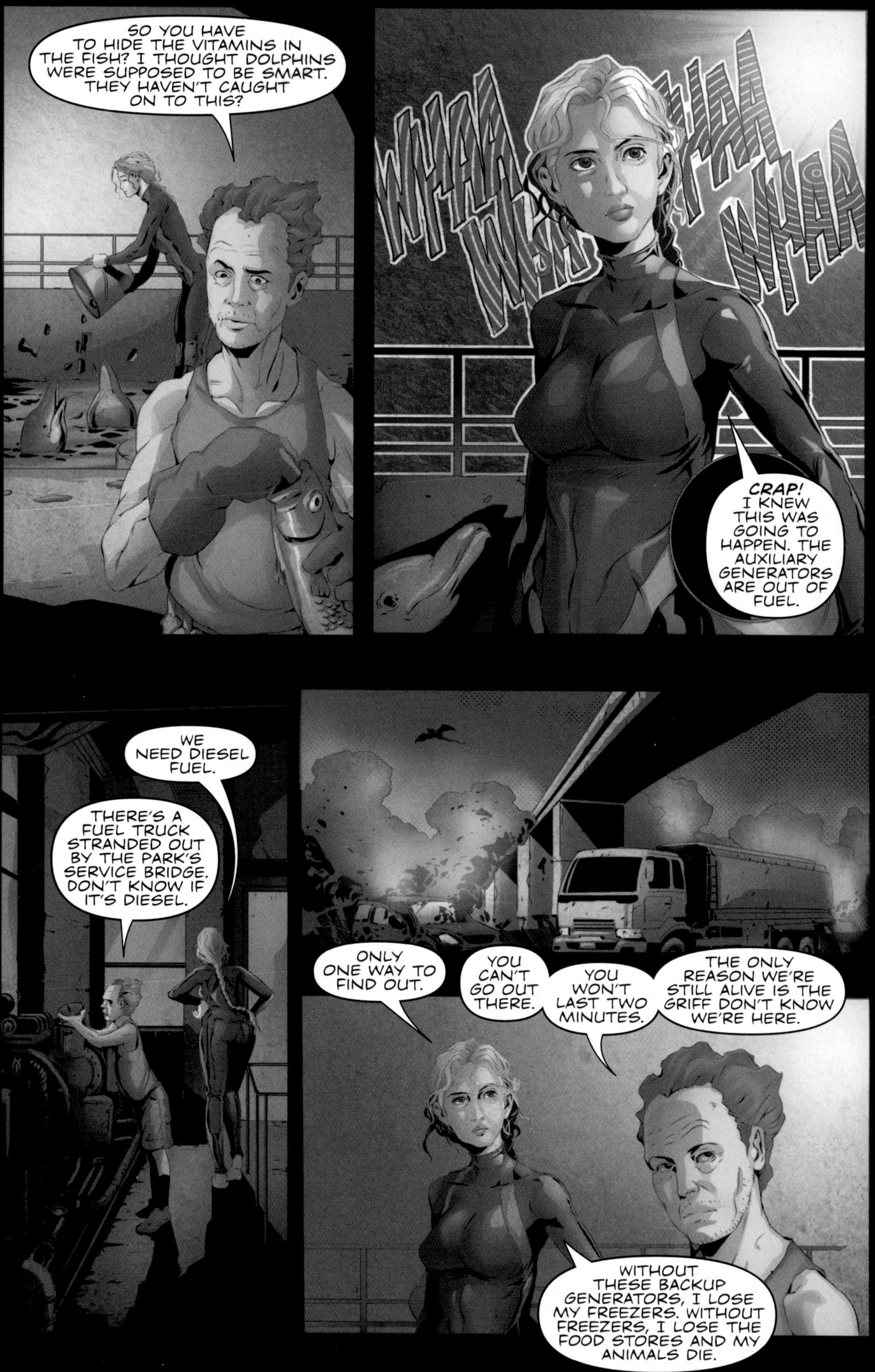
SO YOU HAVE TO HIDE THE VITAMINS IN THE FISH? I THOUGHT DOLPHINS WERE SUPPOSED TO BE SMART. THEY HAVEN'T CAUGHT ON TO THIS?
WHAA WHAA WHAA WHAA
CRAP! I KNEW THIS WAS GOING TO HAPPEN. THE AUXILIARY GENERATORS ARE OUT OF FUEL.
WE NEED DIESEL FUEL.
THERE'S A FUEL TRUCK STRANDED OUT BY THE PARK'S SERVICE BRIDGE. DON'T KNOW IF IT'S DIESEL.
ONLY ONE WAY TO FIND OUT.
YOU CAN'T GO OUT THERE.
YOU WON'T LAST TWO MINUTES.
THE ONLY REASON WE'RE STILL ALIVE IS THE GRIFF DON'T KNOW WE'RE HERE.
WITHOUT THESE BACKUP GENERATORS, I LOSE MY FREEZERS. WITHOUT FREEZERS, I LOSE THE FOOD STORES AND MY ANIMALS DIE.

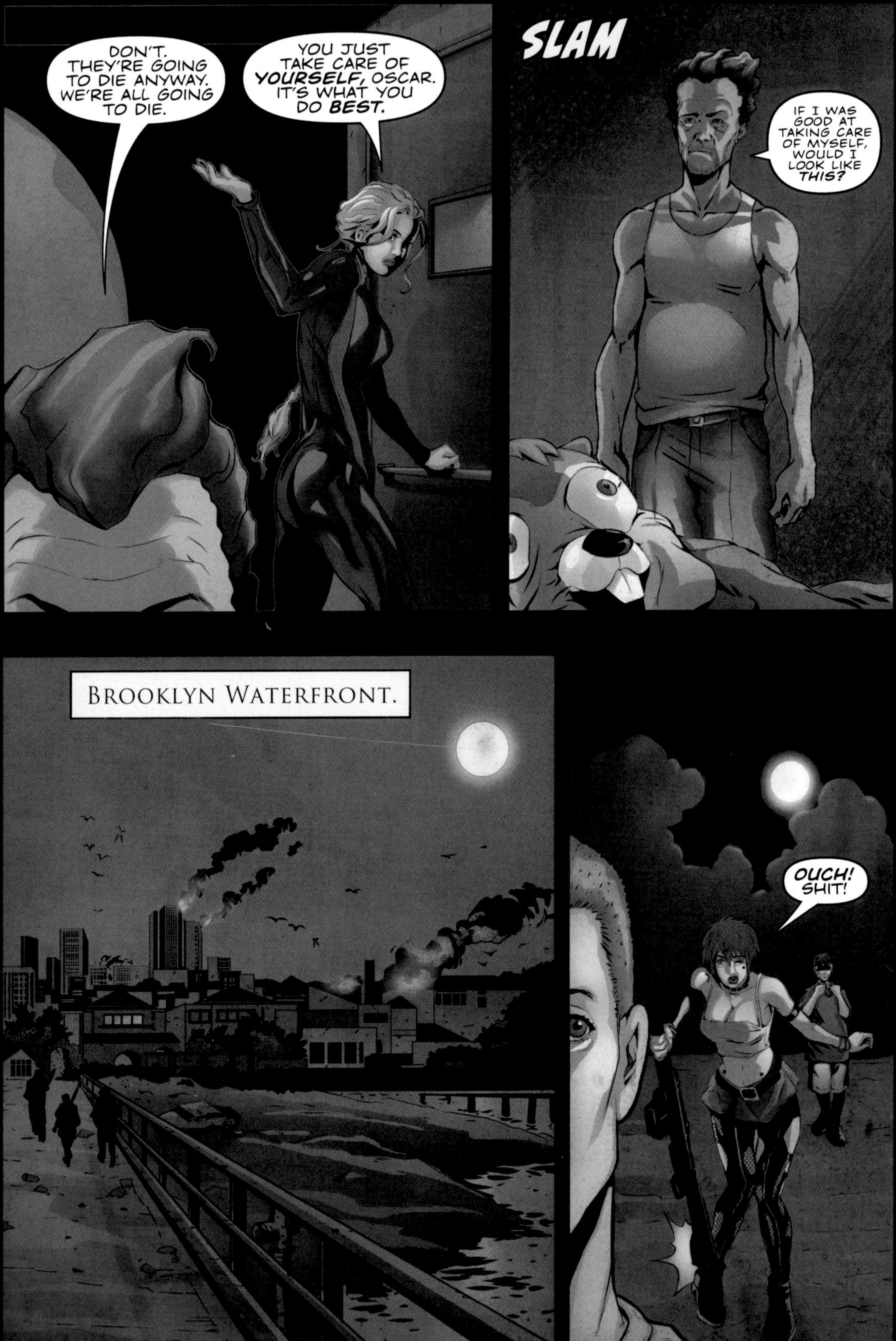
DON'T. THEY'RE GOING TO DIE ANYWAY. WE'RE ALL GOING TO DIE.
YOU JUST TAKE CARE OF **YOURSELF**, OSCAR. IT'S WHAT YOU DO **BEST**.
SLAM
IF I WAS GOOD AT TAKING CARE OF MYSELF, WOULD I LOOK LIKE **THIS?**
BROOKLYN WATERFRONT.
OUCH! SHIT!

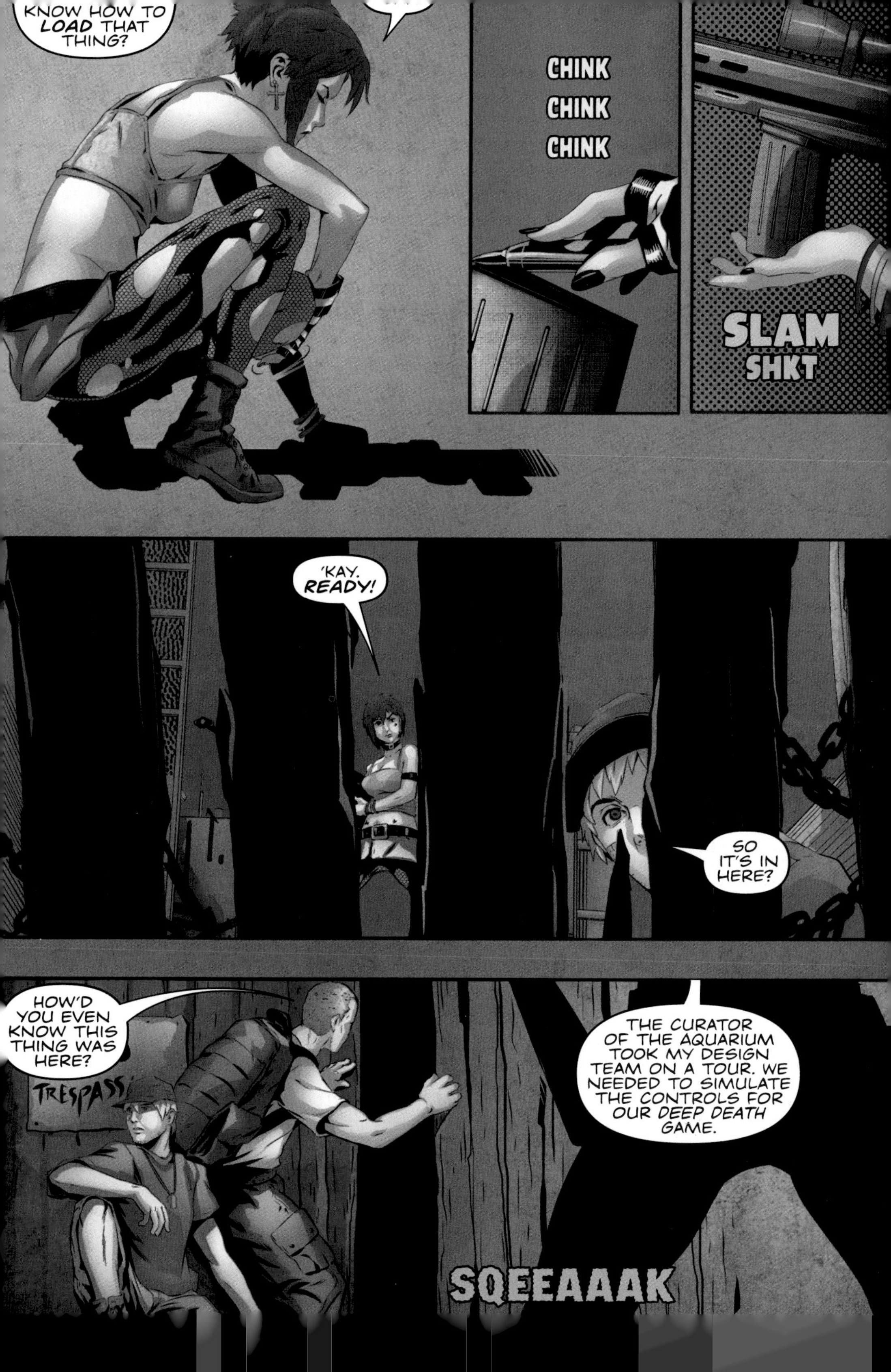
KNOW HOW TO LOAD THAT THING?
CHINK
CHINK
CHINK
SLAM
SHKT
'KAY. READY!
SO IT'S IN HERE?
HOW'D YOU EVEN KNOW THIS THING WAS HERE?
TRESPASS
THE CURATOR OF THE AQUARIUM TOOK MY DESIGN TEAM ON A TOUR. WE NEEDED TO SIMULATE THE CONTROLS FOR OUR DEEP DEATH GAME.
SQEEAAAK

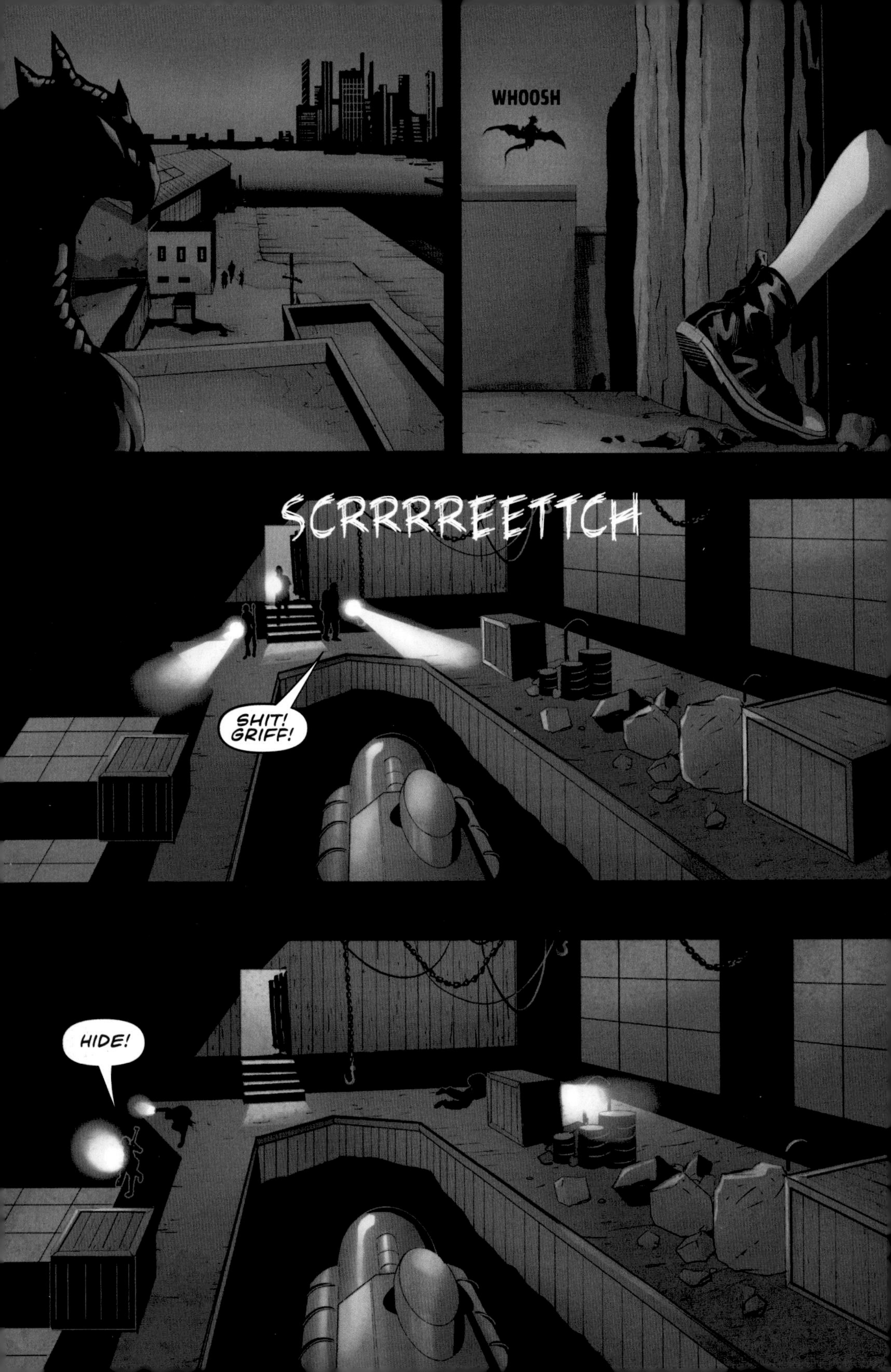
WHOOSH
SCRRRREETTCH
SHIT! GRIFF!
HIDE!

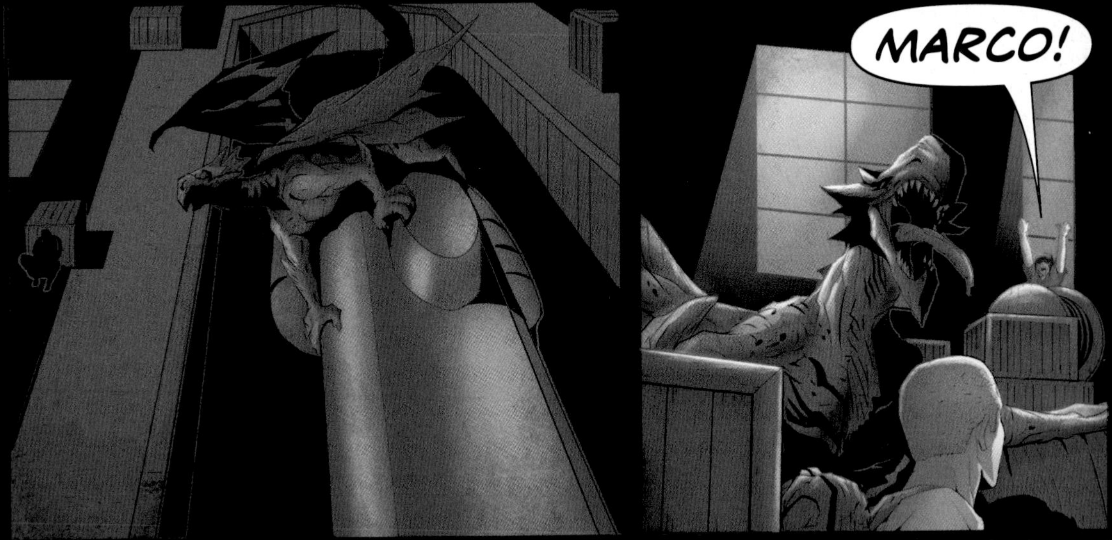
MARCO!

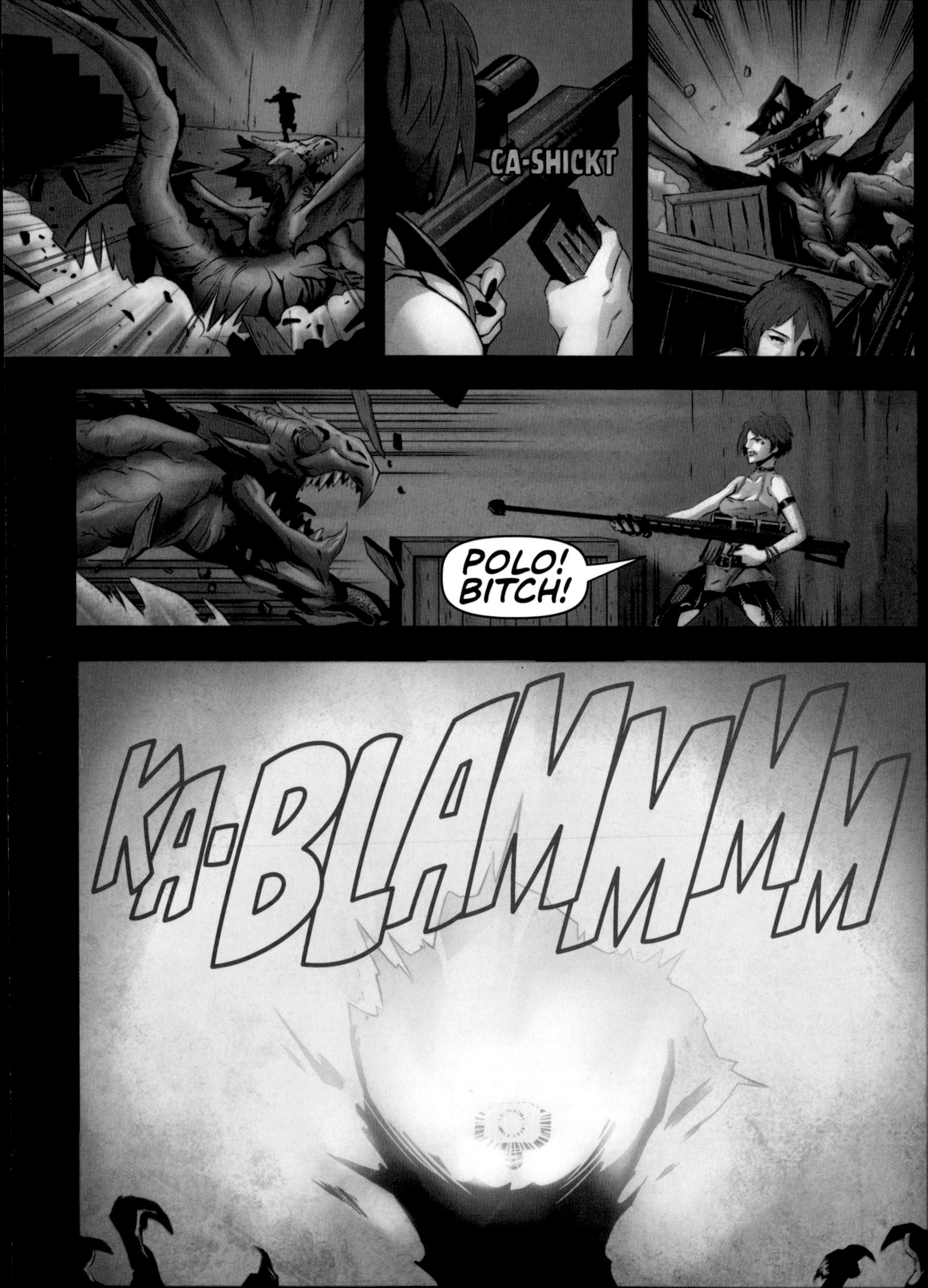
CA-SHICKT
POLO! BITCH!
KA-BLAMMMM

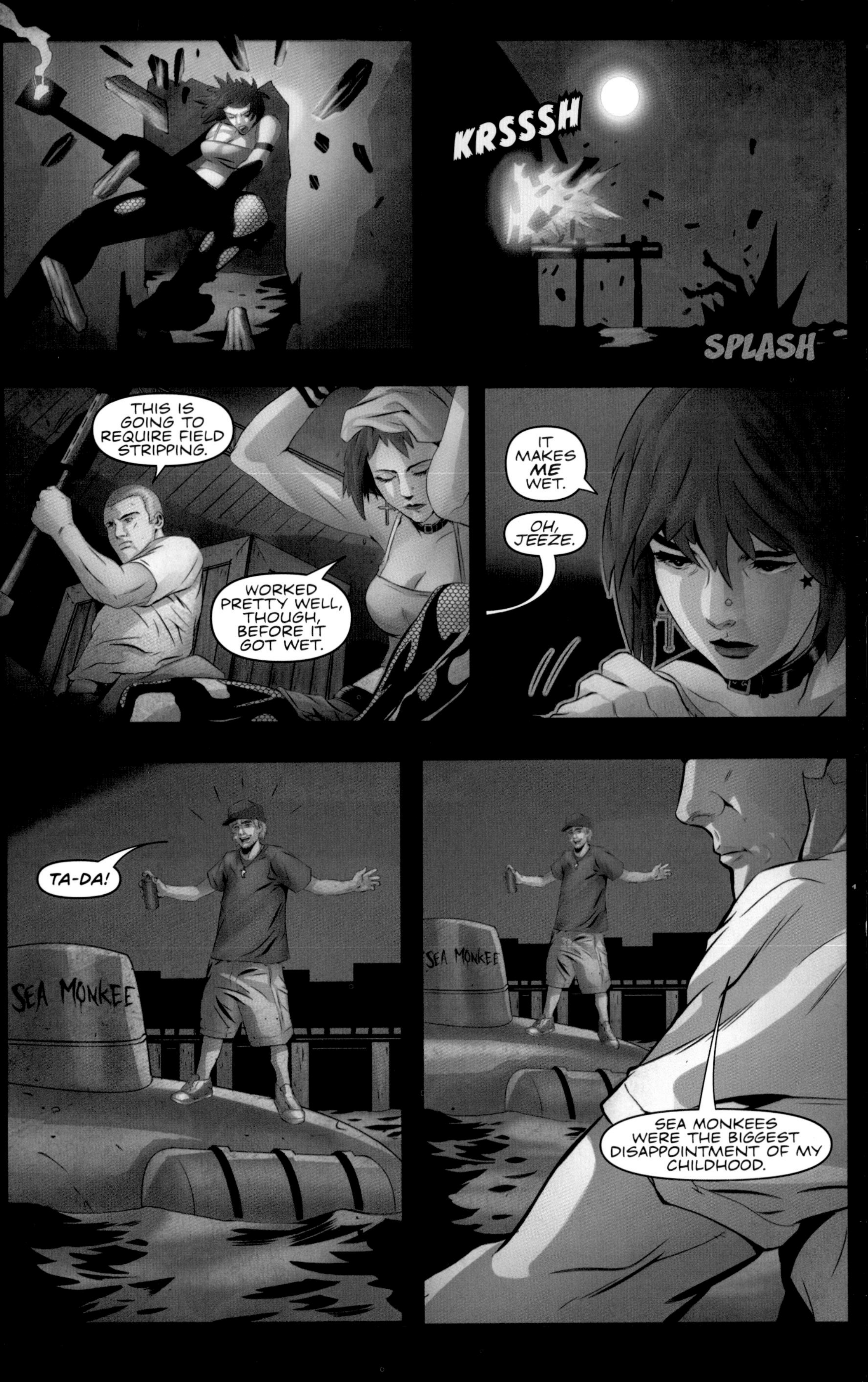
KRSSSH
SPLASH
THIS IS GOING TO REQUIRE FIELD STRIPPING.
WORKED PRETTY WELL, THOUGH, BEFORE IT GOT WET.
IT MAKES ME WET.
OH, JEEZE.
TA-DA!
SEA MONKEE
SEA MONKEE
SEA MONKEES WERE THE BIGGEST DISAPPOINTMENT OF MY CHILDHOOD.

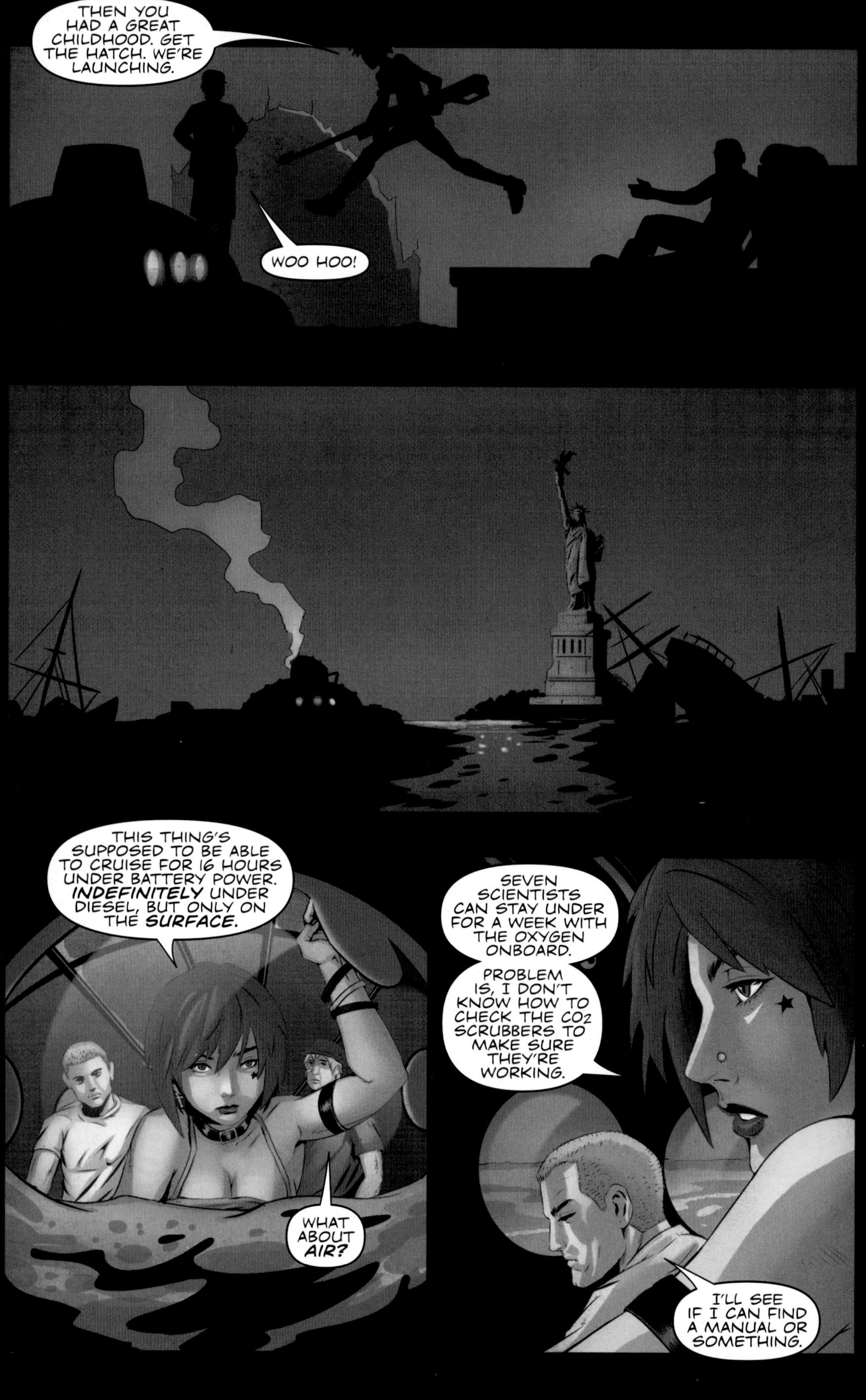
THEN YOU HAD A GREAT CHILDHOOD. GET THE HATCH. WE'RE LAUNCHING.
WOO HOO!
THIS THING'S SUPPOSED TO BE ABLE TO CRUISE FOR 16 HOURS UNDER BATTERY POWER. INDEFINITELY UNDER DIESEL, BUT ONLY ON THE SURFACE.
WHAT ABOUT AIR?
SEVEN SCIENTISTS CAN STAY UNDER FOR A WEEK WITH THE OXYGEN ONBOARD.
PROBLEM IS, I DON'T KNOW HOW TO CHECK THE CO2 SCRUBBERS TO MAKE SURE THEY'RE WORKING.
I'LL SEE IF I CAN FIND A MANUAL OR SOMETHING.

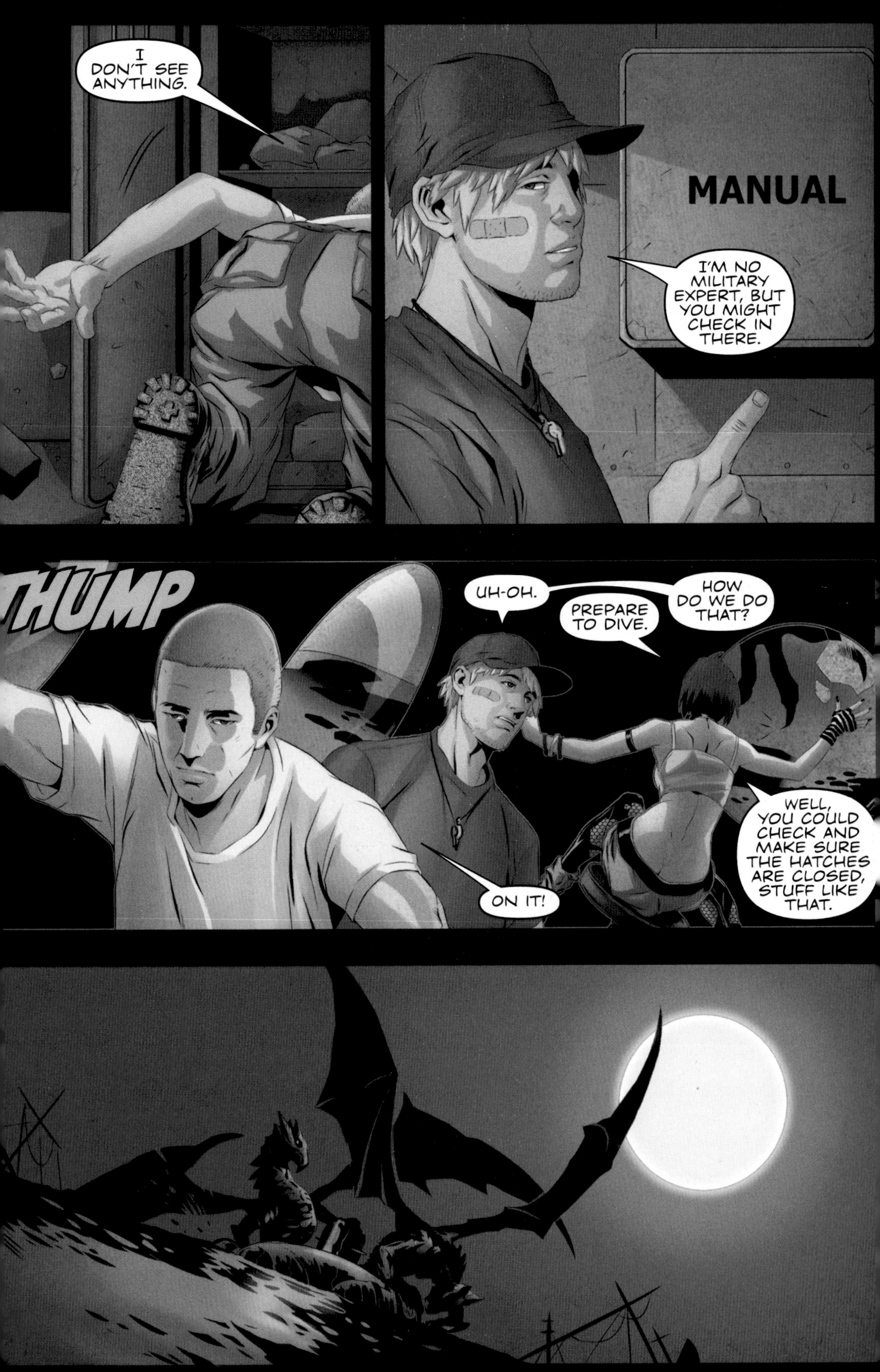
I DON'T SEE ANYTHING.
MANUAL
I'M NO MILITARY EXPERT, BUT YOU MIGHT CHECK IN THERE.
THUMP
UH-OH.
PREPARE TO DIVE.
HOW DO WE DO THAT?
WELL, YOU COULD CHECK AND MAKE SURE THE HATCHES ARE CLOSED, STUFF LIKE THAT.
ON IT!

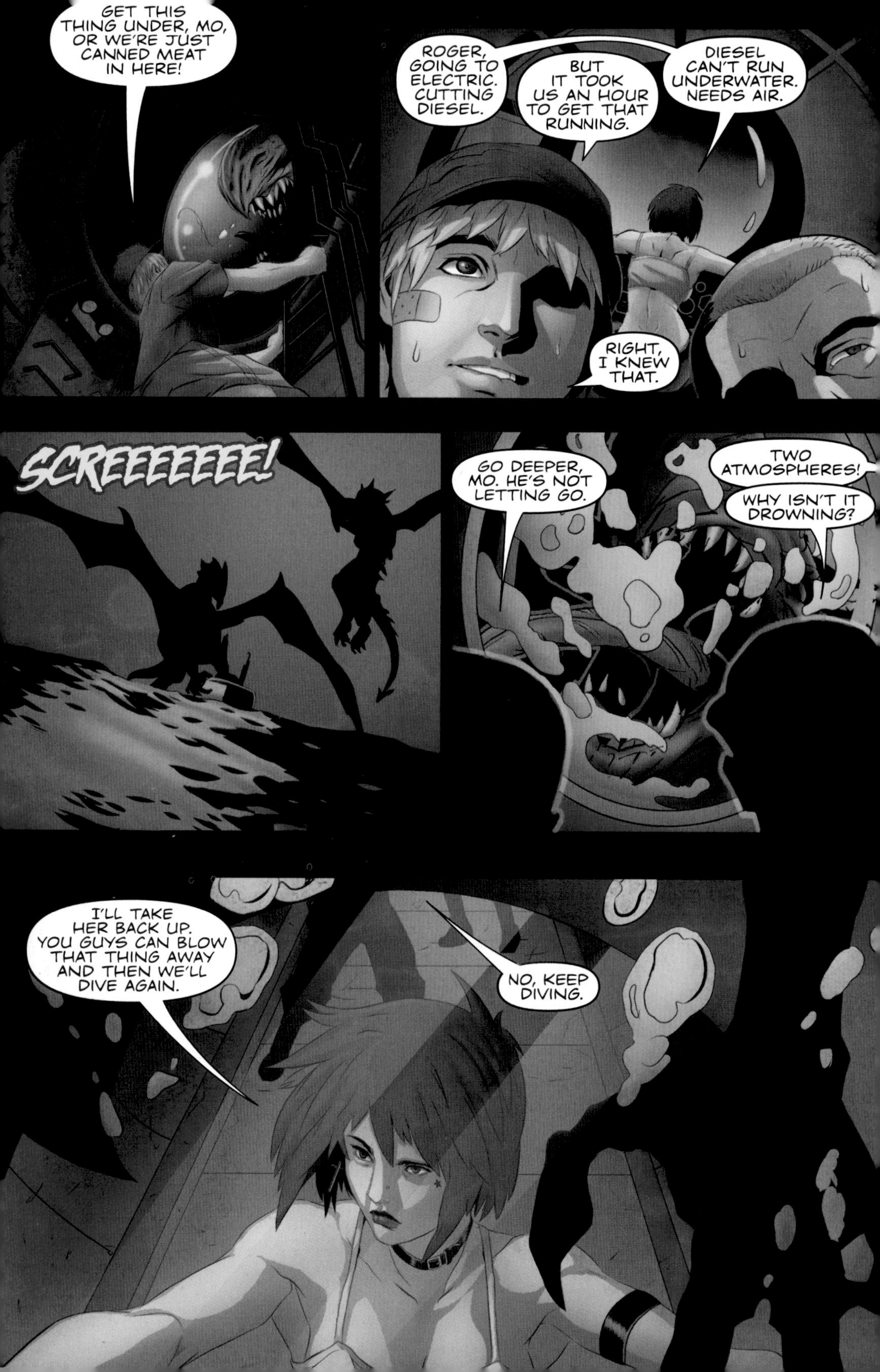
GET THIS THING UNDER, MO, OR WE'RE JUST CANNED MEAT IN HERE!
ROGER, GOING TO ELECTRIC. CUTTING DIESEL.
BUT IT TOOK US AN HOUR TO GET THAT RUNNING.
DIESEL CAN'T RUN UNDERWATER. NEEDS AIR.
RIGHT, I KNEW THAT.
SCREEEEEEEE!
GO DEEPER, MO. HE'S NOT LETTING GO.
TWO ATMOSPHERES!
WHY ISN'T IT DROWNING?
I'LL TAKE HER BACK UP. YOU GUYS CAN BLOW THAT THING AWAY AND THEN WE'LL DIVE AGAIN.
NO, KEEP DIVING.

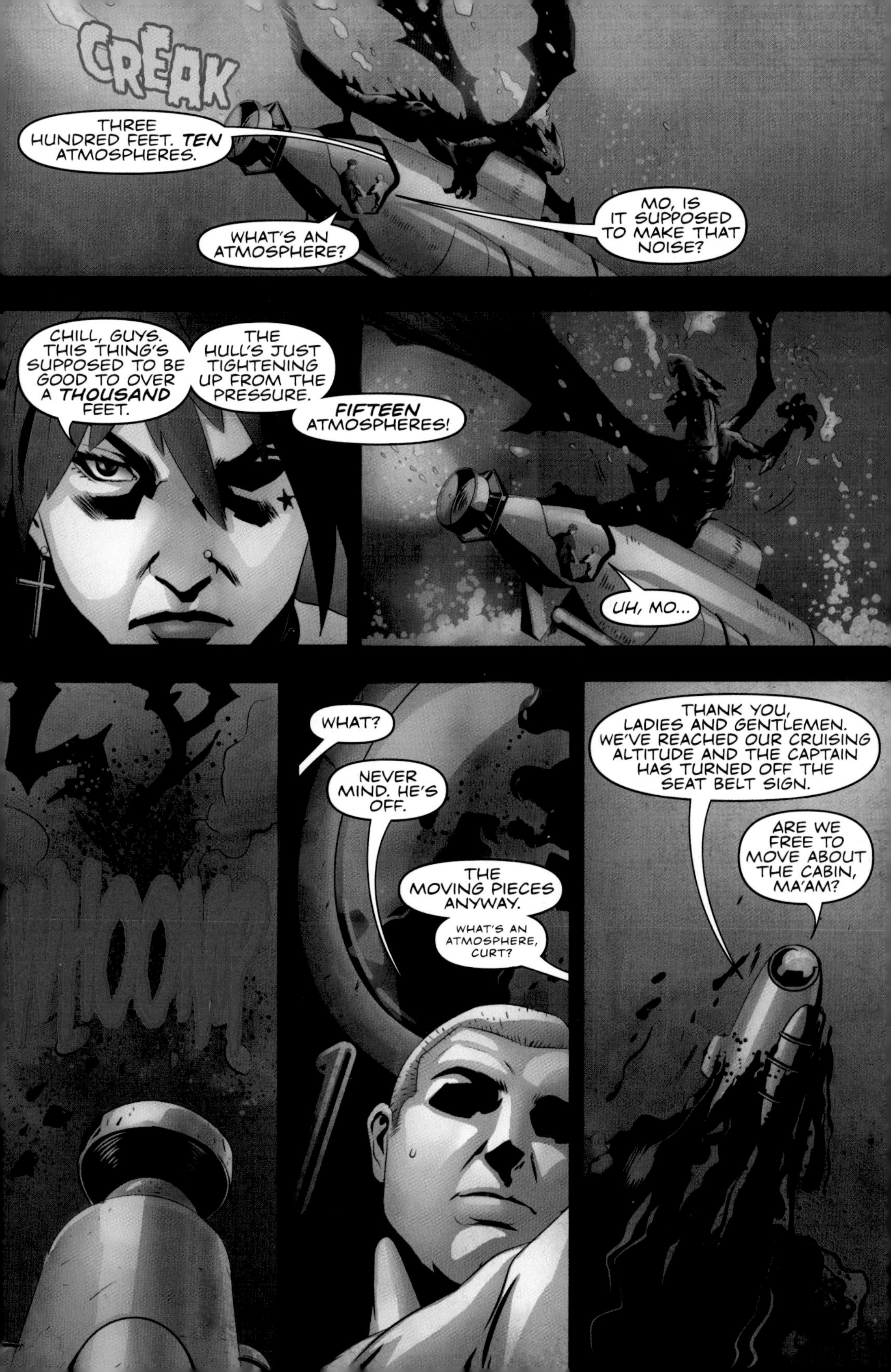
CREAK
THREE HUNDRED FEET. TEN ATMOSPHERES.
WHAT'S AN ATMOSPHERE?
MO, IS IT SUPPOSED TO MAKE THAT NOISE?
CHILL, GUYS. THIS THING'S SUPPOSED TO BE GOOD TO OVER A THOUSAND FEET.
THE HULL'S JUST TIGHTENING UP FROM THE PRESSURE.
FIFTEEN ATMOSPHERES!
UH, MO...
WHAT?
NEVER MIND. HE'S OFF.
THE MOVING PIECES ANYWAY.
WHAT'S AN ATMOSPHERE, CURT?
THANK YOU, LADIES AND GENTLEMEN. WE'VE REACHED OUR CRUISING ALTITUDE AND THE CAPTAIN HAS TURNED OFF THE SEAT BELT SIGN.
ARE WE FREE TO MOVE ABOUT THE CABIN, MA'AM?

SEE, I TOLD YOU. WE'LL NEVER GET IT OUT OF THAT JAM.

WE'RE NOT GOING TO HAVE TO.

OH, NO.

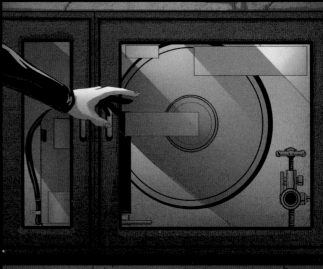

THIS WILL NEVER WORK.

I HATE THIS. HATE THIS. HATE THIS.

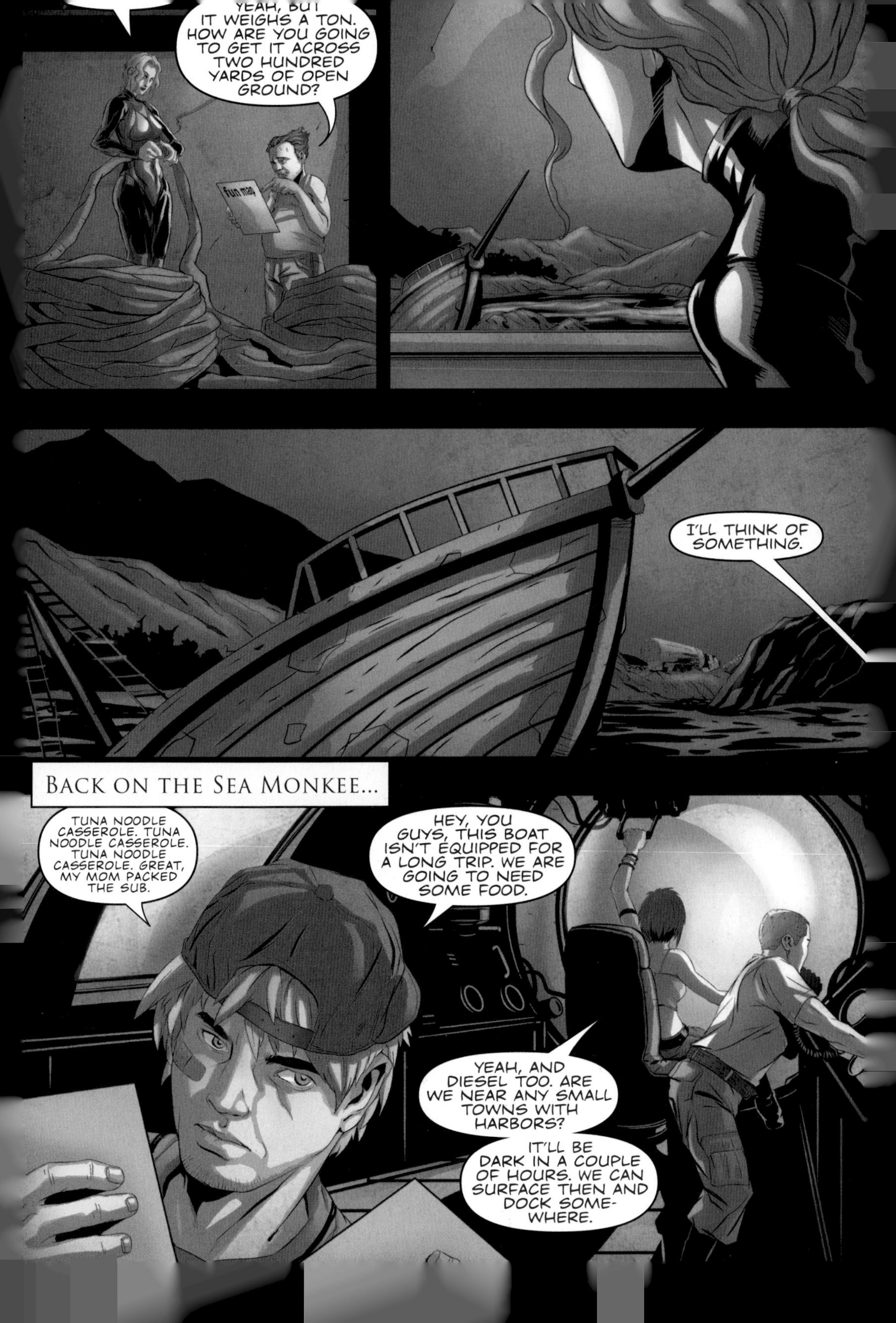
YEAH, BUT IT WEIGHS A TON. HOW ARE YOU GOING TO GET IT ACROSS TWO HUNDRED YARDS OF OPEN GROUND?
fun map
I'LL THINK OF SOMETHING.
BACK ON THE SEA MONKEE...
TUNA NOODLE CASSEROLE. TUNA NOODLE CASSEROLE. TUNA NOODLE CASSEROLE. GREAT, MY MOM PACKED THE SUB.
HEY, YOU GUYS, THIS BOAT ISN'T EQUIPPED FOR A LONG TRIP. WE ARE GOING TO NEED SOME FOOD.
YEAH, AND DIESEL TOO. ARE WE NEAR ANY SMALL TOWNS WITH HARBORS?
IT'LL BE DARK IN A COUPLE OF HOURS. WE CAN SURFACE THEN AND DOCK SOME-WHERE.

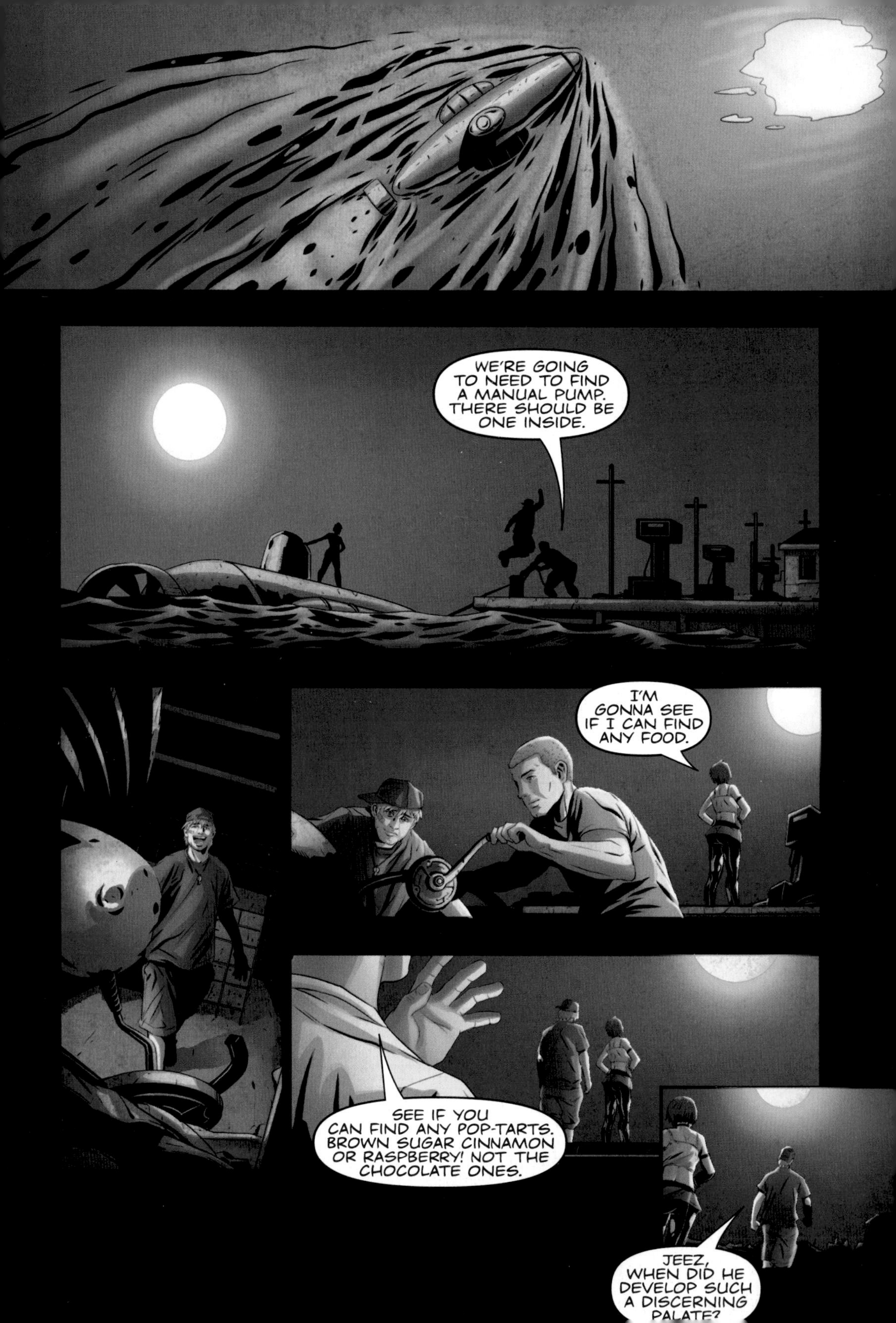
WE'RE GOING TO NEED TO FIND A MANUAL PUMP. THERE SHOULD BE ONE INSIDE.
I'M GONNA SEE IF I CAN FIND ANY FOOD.
SEE IF YOU CAN FIND ANY POP-TARTS. BROWN SUGAR CINNAMON OR RASPBERRY! NOT THE CHOCOLATE ONES.
JEEZ, WHEN DID HE DEVELOP SUCH A DISCERNING PALATE?

OCEAN WORLD.

SCRRRRR
WHAT WAS THAT?

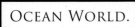

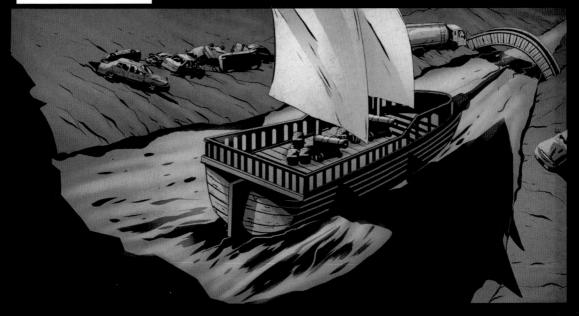

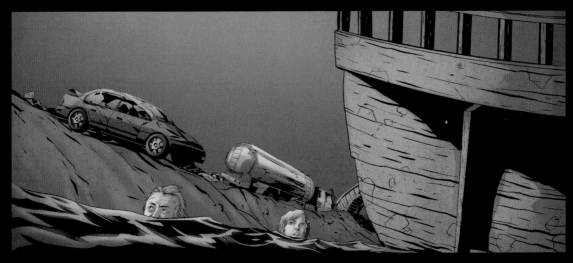

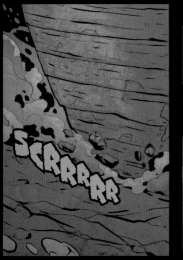

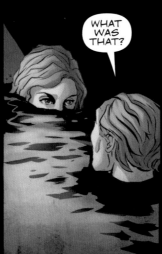

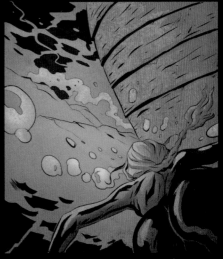

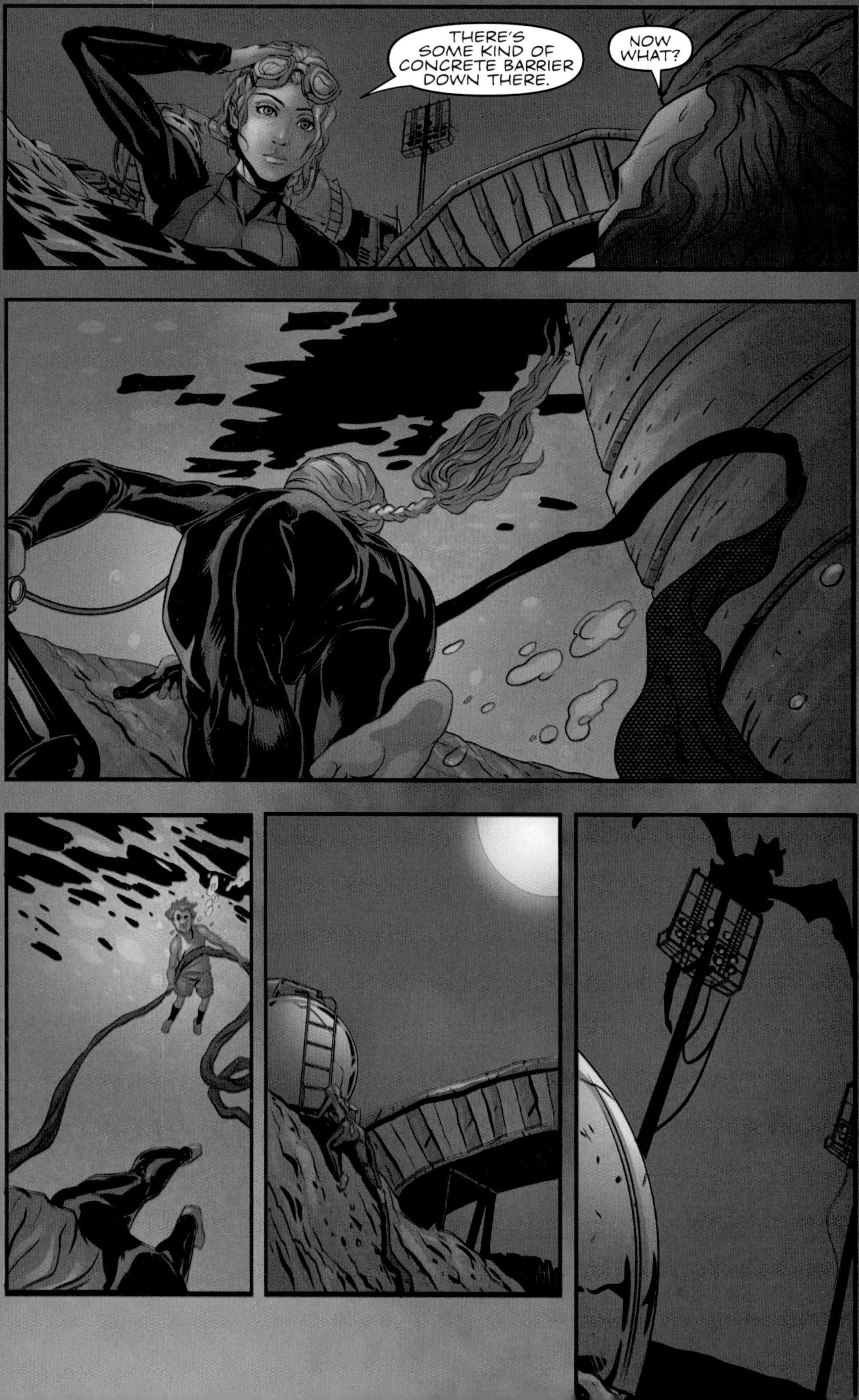
THERE'S SOME KIND OF CONCRETE BARRIER DOWN THERE.
NOW WHAT?

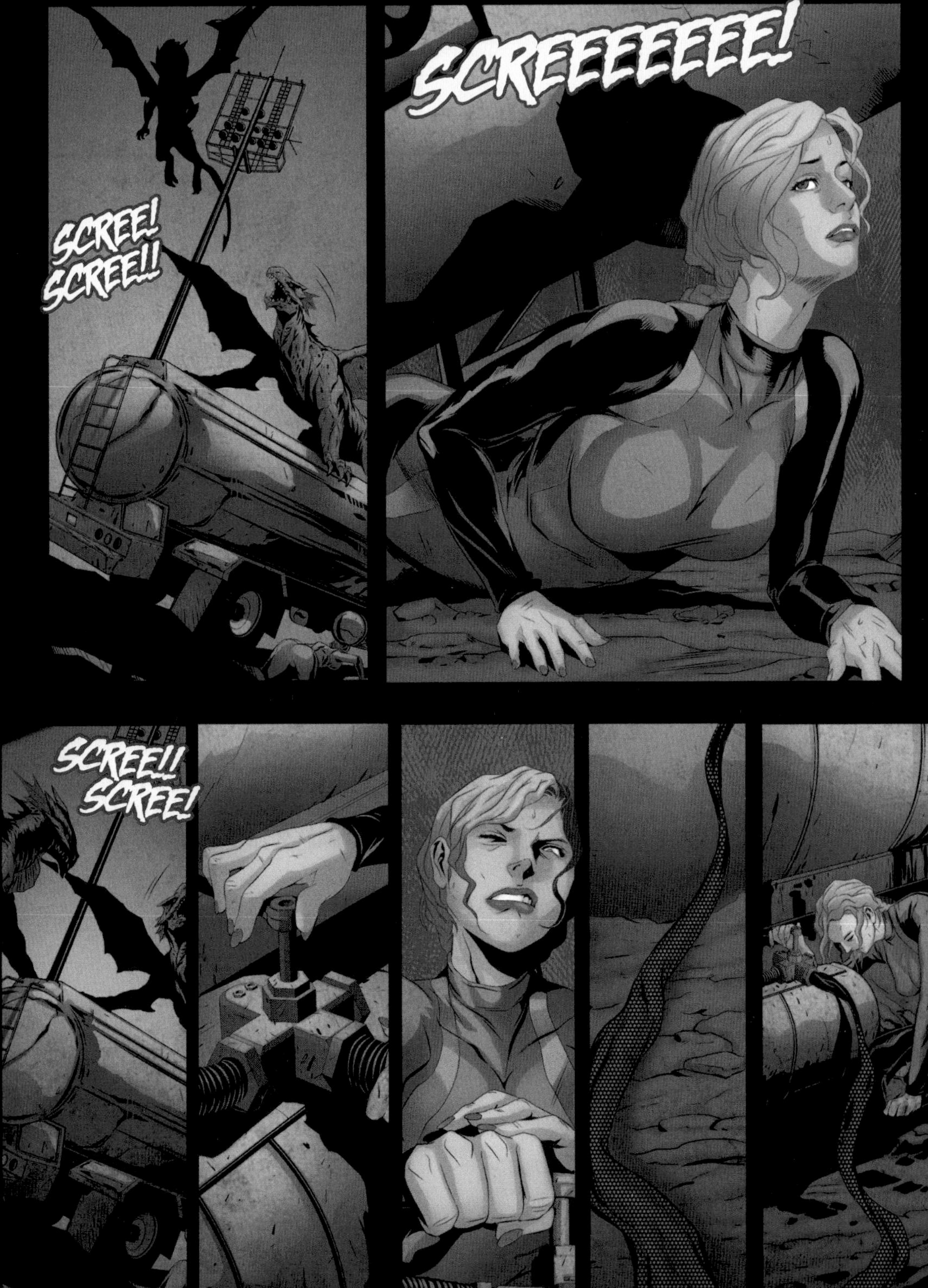
SCREE!
SCREE!!
SCREEEEEEEE!
SCREE!!
SCREE!

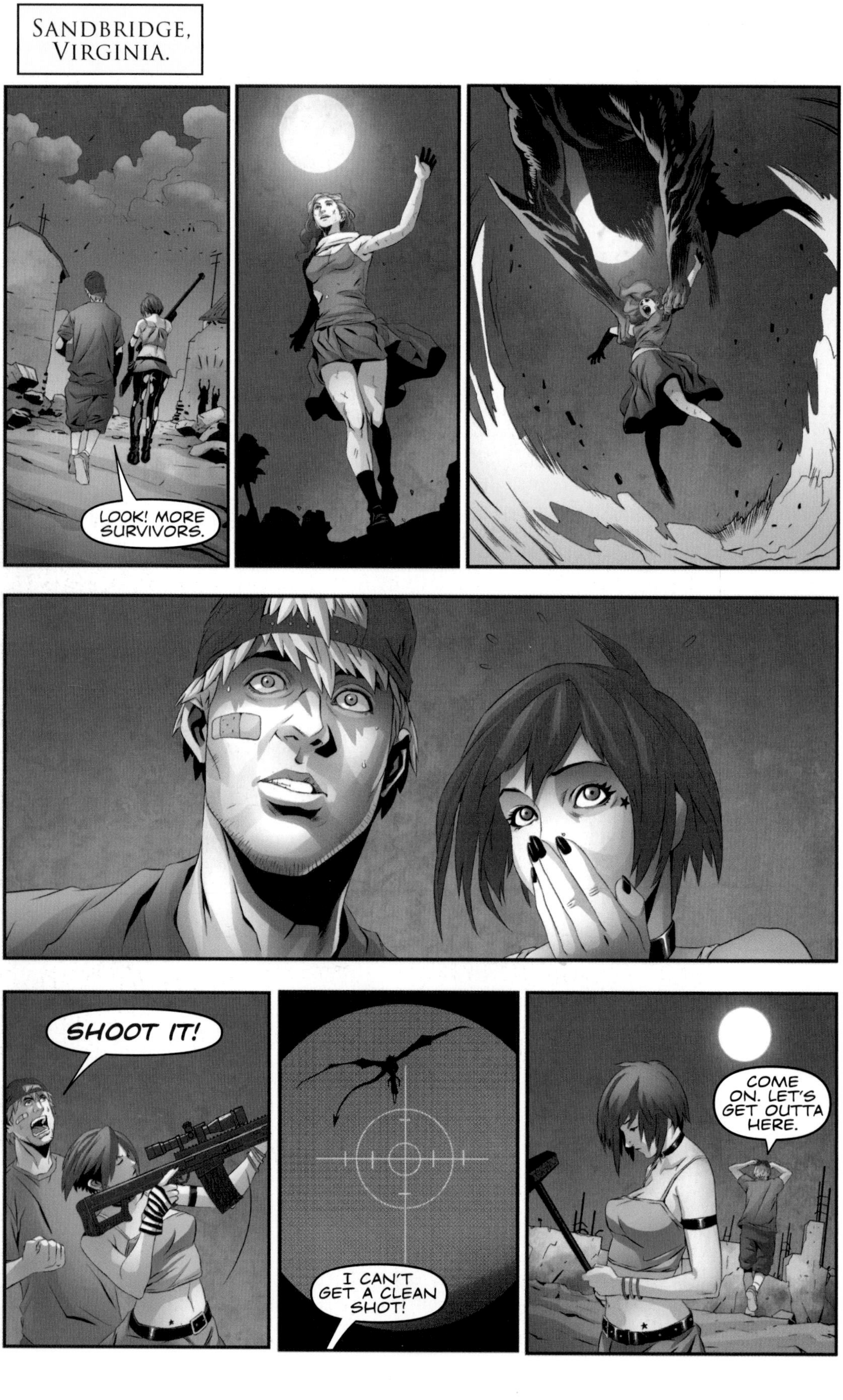
SANDBRIDGE, VIRGINIA.
LOOK! MORE SURVIVORS.
SHOOT IT!
I CAN'T GET A CLEAN SHOT!
COME ON. LET'S GET OUTTA HERE.

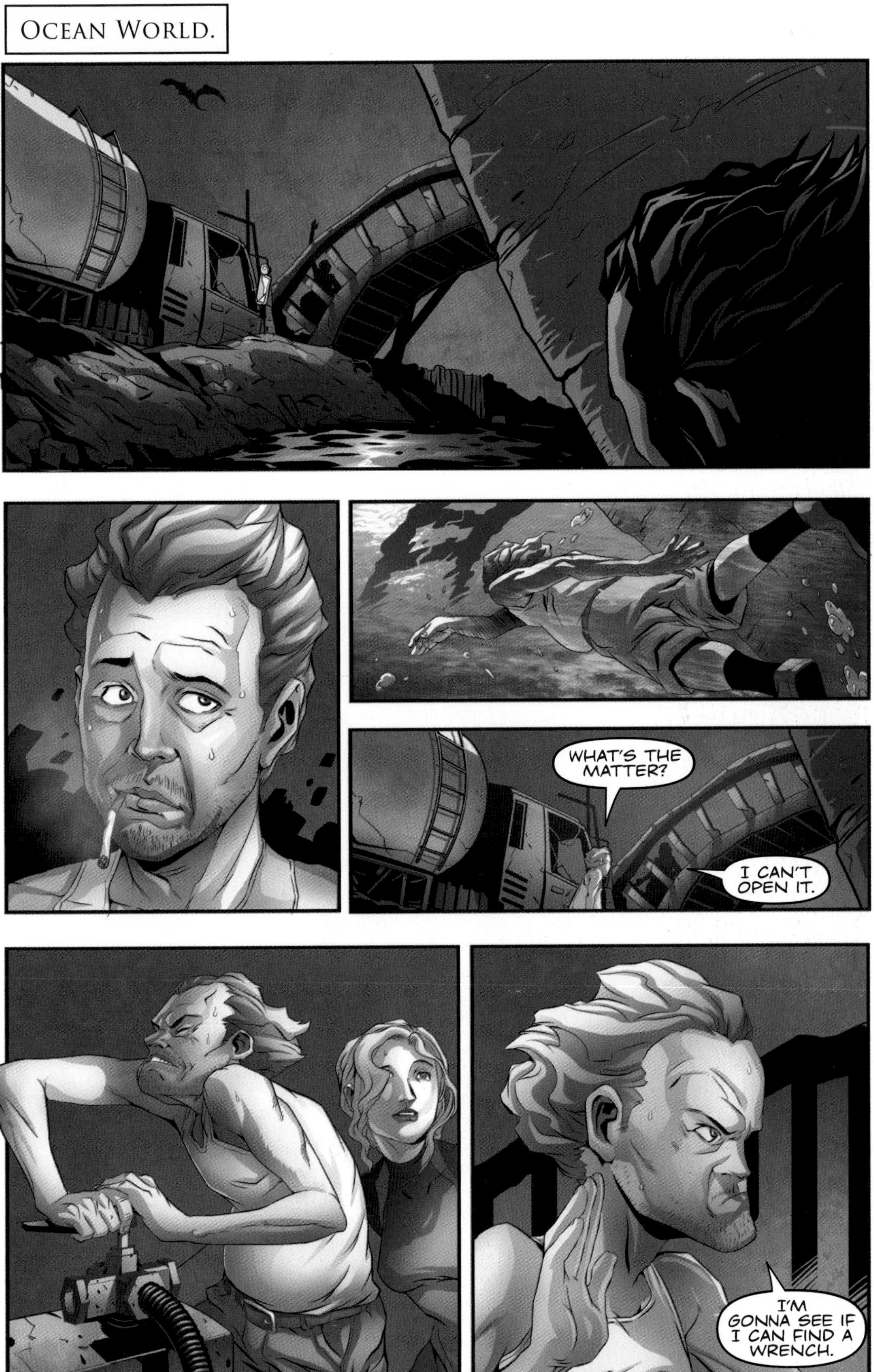
OCEAN WORLD.
WHAT'S THE MATTER?
I CAN'T OPEN IT.
I'M GONNA SEE IF I CAN FIND A WRENCH.

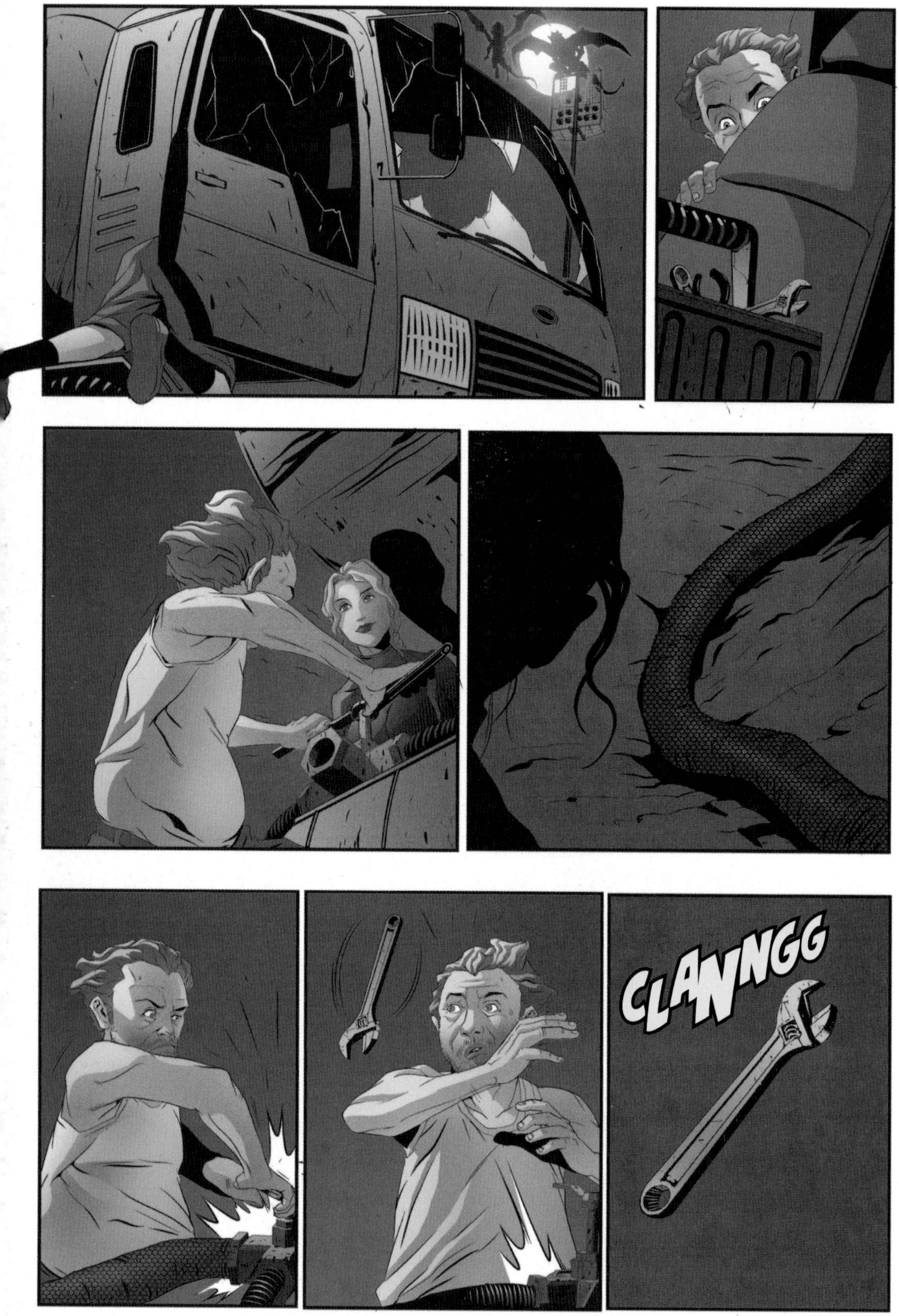
CLANNGG

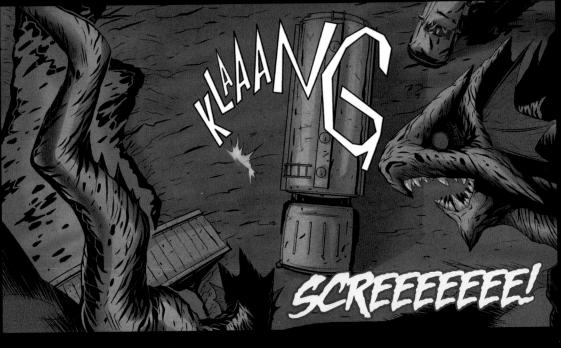

KLAAANG

SCREEEEEEE!

THUMP

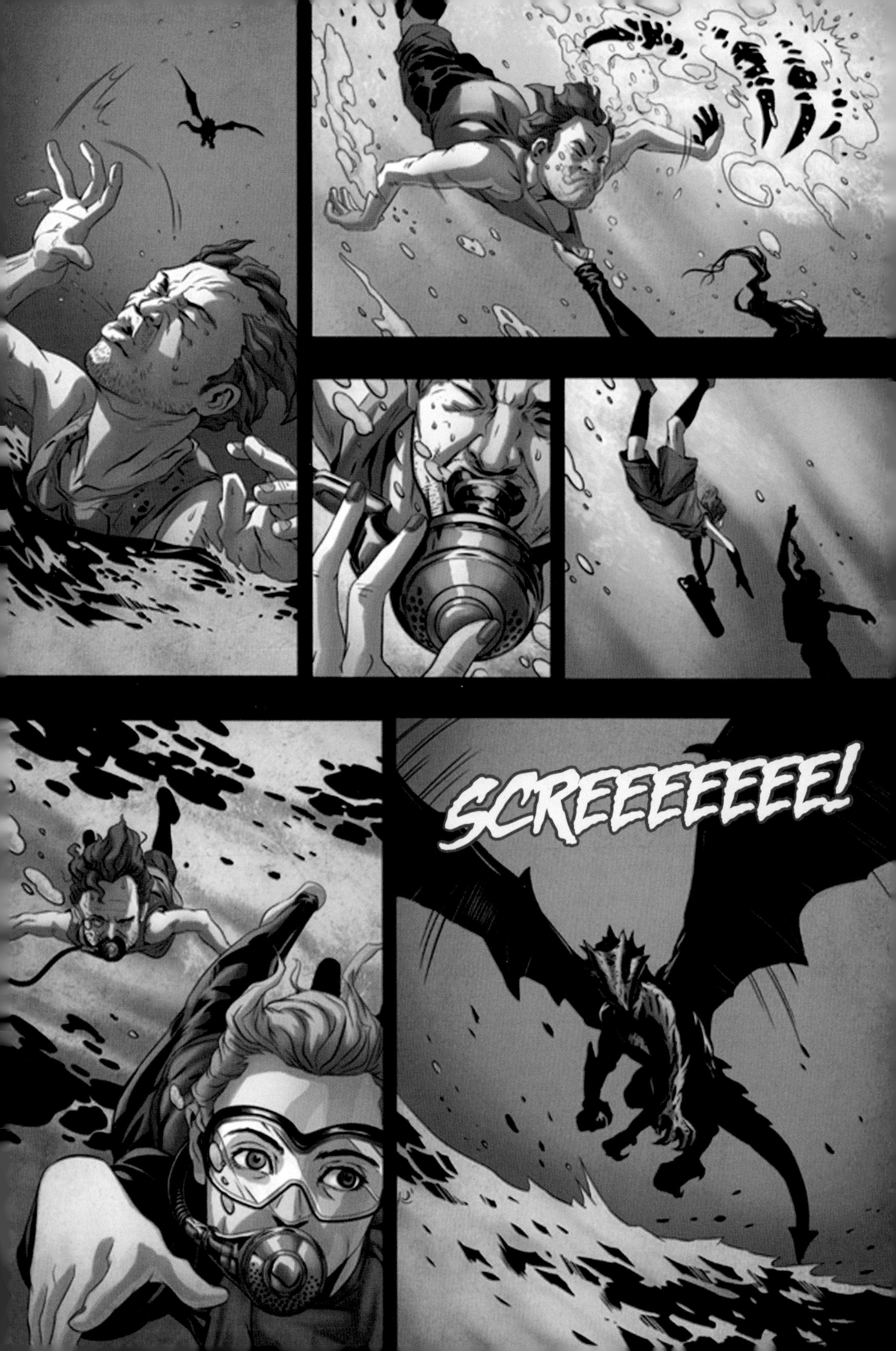
SCREEEEEEEE!

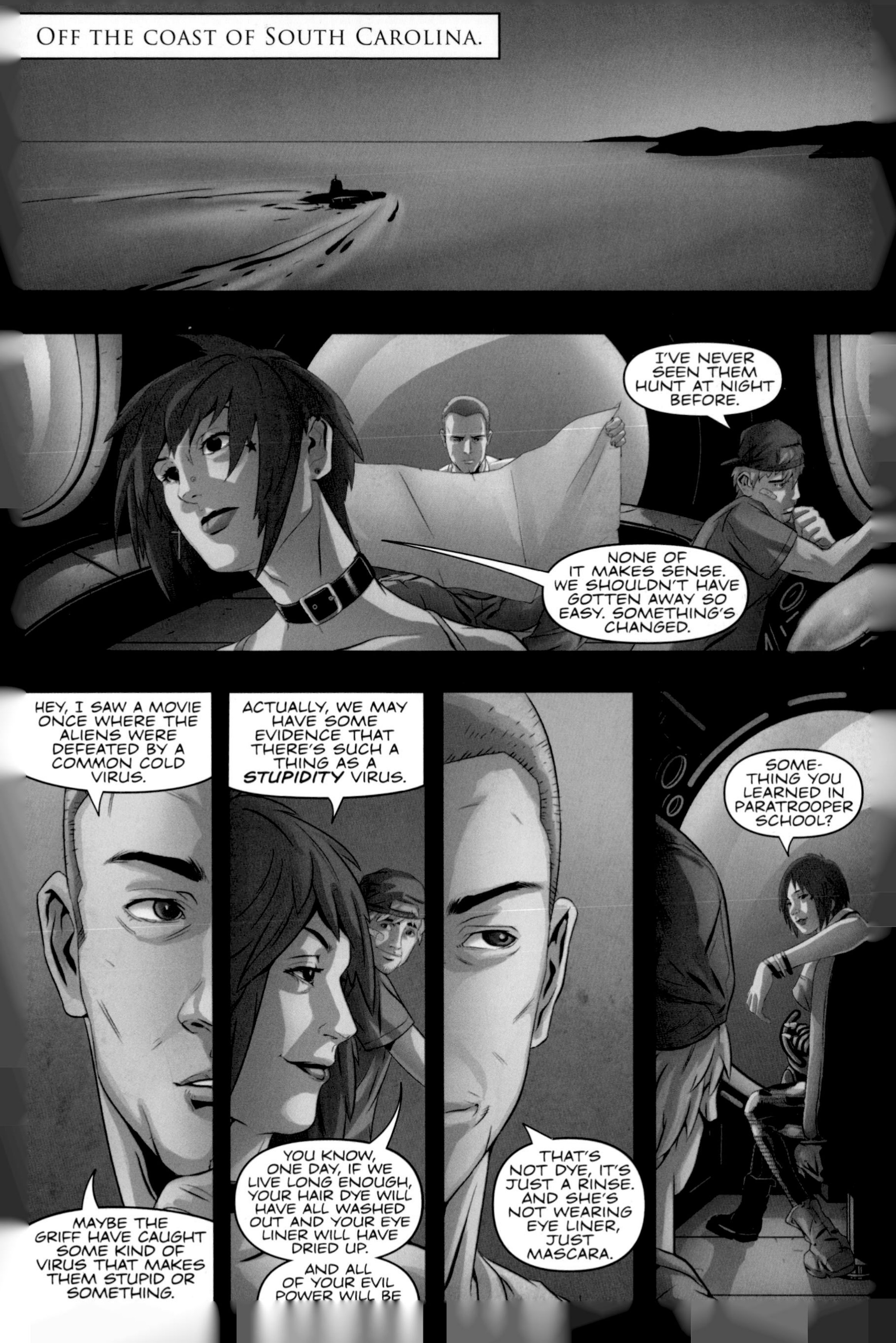
OFF THE COAST OF SOUTH CAROLINA.
I'VE NEVER SEEN THEM HUNT AT NIGHT BEFORE.
NONE OF IT MAKES SENSE. WE SHOULDN'T HAVE GOTTEN AWAY SO EASY. SOMETHING'S CHANGED.
HEY, I SAW A MOVIE ONCE WHERE THE ALIENS WERE DEFEATED BY A COMMON COLD VIRUS.
MAYBE THE GRIFF HAVE CAUGHT SOME KIND OF VIRUS THAT MAKES THEM STUPID OR SOMETHING.
ACTUALLY, WE MAY HAVE SOME EVIDENCE THAT THERE'S SUCH A THING AS A STUPIDITY VIRUS.
YOU KNOW, ONE DAY, IF WE LIVE LONG ENOUGH, YOUR HAIR DYE WILL HAVE ALL WASHED OUT AND YOUR EYE LINER WILL HAVE DRIED UP.
AND ALL OF YOUR EVIL POWER WILL BE
THAT'S NOT DYE, IT'S JUST A RINSE. AND SHE'S NOT WEARING EYE LINER, JUST MASCARA.
SOME-THING YOU LEARNED IN PARATROOPER SCHOOL?

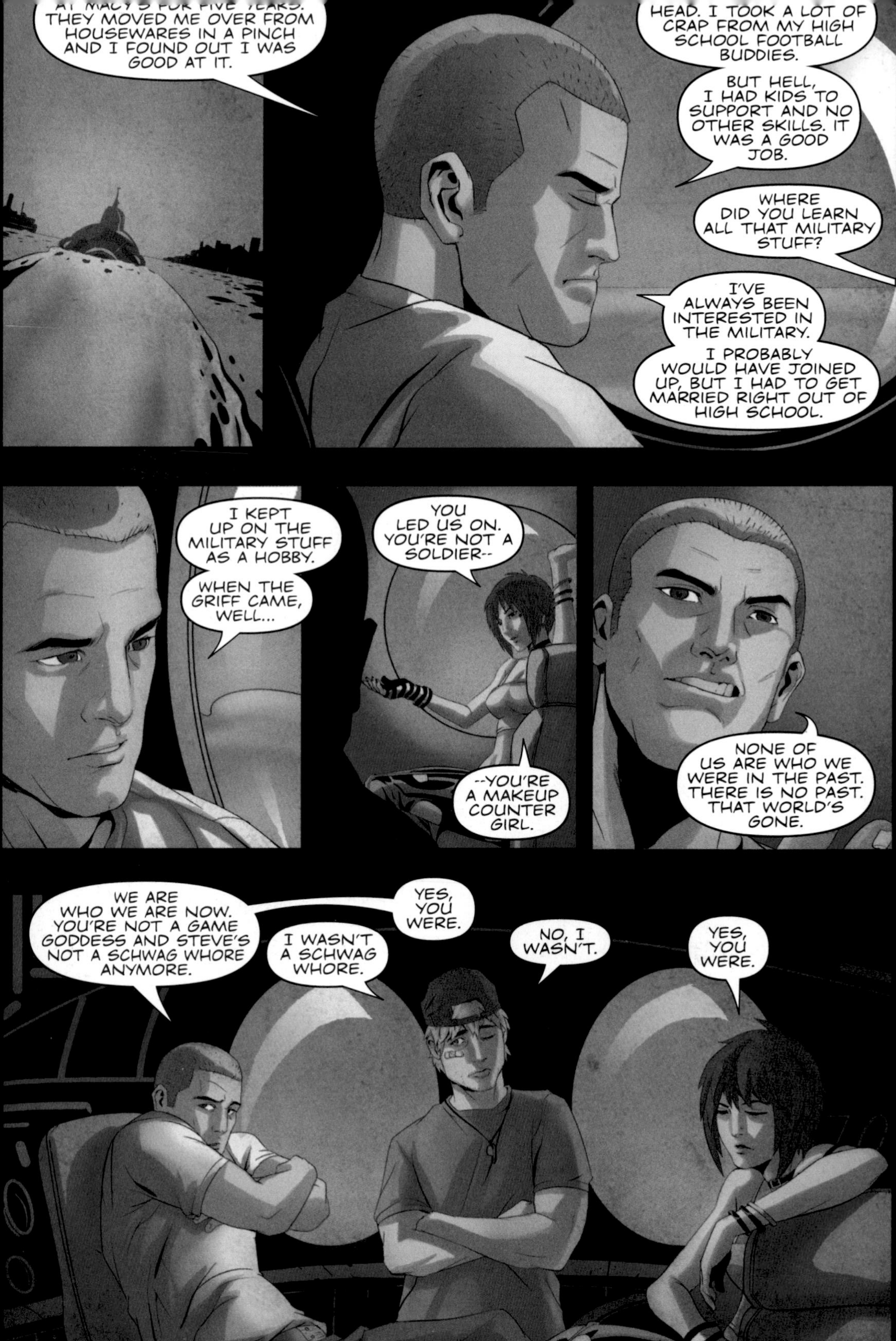

THEY MOVED ME OVER FROM HOUSEWARES IN A PINCH AND I FOUND OUT I WAS GOOD AT IT.
HEAD. I TOOK A LOT OF CRAP FROM MY HIGH SCHOOL FOOTBALL BUDDIES.
BUT HELL, I HAD KIDS TO SUPPORT AND NO OTHER SKILLS. IT WAS A GOOD JOB.
WHERE DID YOU LEARN ALL THAT MILITARY STUFF?
I'VE ALWAYS BEEN INTERESTED IN THE MILITARY.
I PROBABLY WOULD HAVE JOINED UP, BUT I HAD TO GET MARRIED RIGHT OUT OF HIGH SCHOOL.
I KEPT UP ON THE MILITARY STUFF AS A HOBBY.
WHEN THE GRIFF CAME, WELL...
YOU LED US ON. YOU'RE NOT A SOLDIER--
--YOU'RE A MAKEUP COUNTER GIRL.
NONE OF US ARE WHO WE WERE IN THE PAST. THERE IS NO PAST. THAT WORLD'S GONE.
WE ARE WHO WE ARE NOW. YOU'RE NOT A GAME GODDESS AND STEVE'S NOT A SCHWAG WHORE ANYMORE.
I WASN'T A SCHWAG WHORE.
YES, YOU WERE.
NO, I WASN'T.
YES, YOU WERE.

YES, I WAS.

WHEN I WENT BACK TO MY HOUSE TO LOOK FOR MY FAMILY AND COULDN'T FIND ENOUGH OF THEM TO BURY IN A COFFEE CAN...

WELL, I BECAME A SOLDIER. THAT'S WHO I NEED TO BE.

BUT IN AN EMERGENCY, YOU COULD STILL DO MY HIGHLIGHTS IF I NEEDED YOU TO.

WELL, CAPTAIN LANDCOMB, LET'S TRY THIS AGAIN. SEE IF WE CAN FIND SOME SUPPLIES AND GET BACK BEFORE DAWN.

I'LL COME WITH YOU.

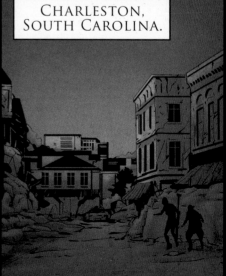

CHARLESTON, SOUTH CAROLINA.

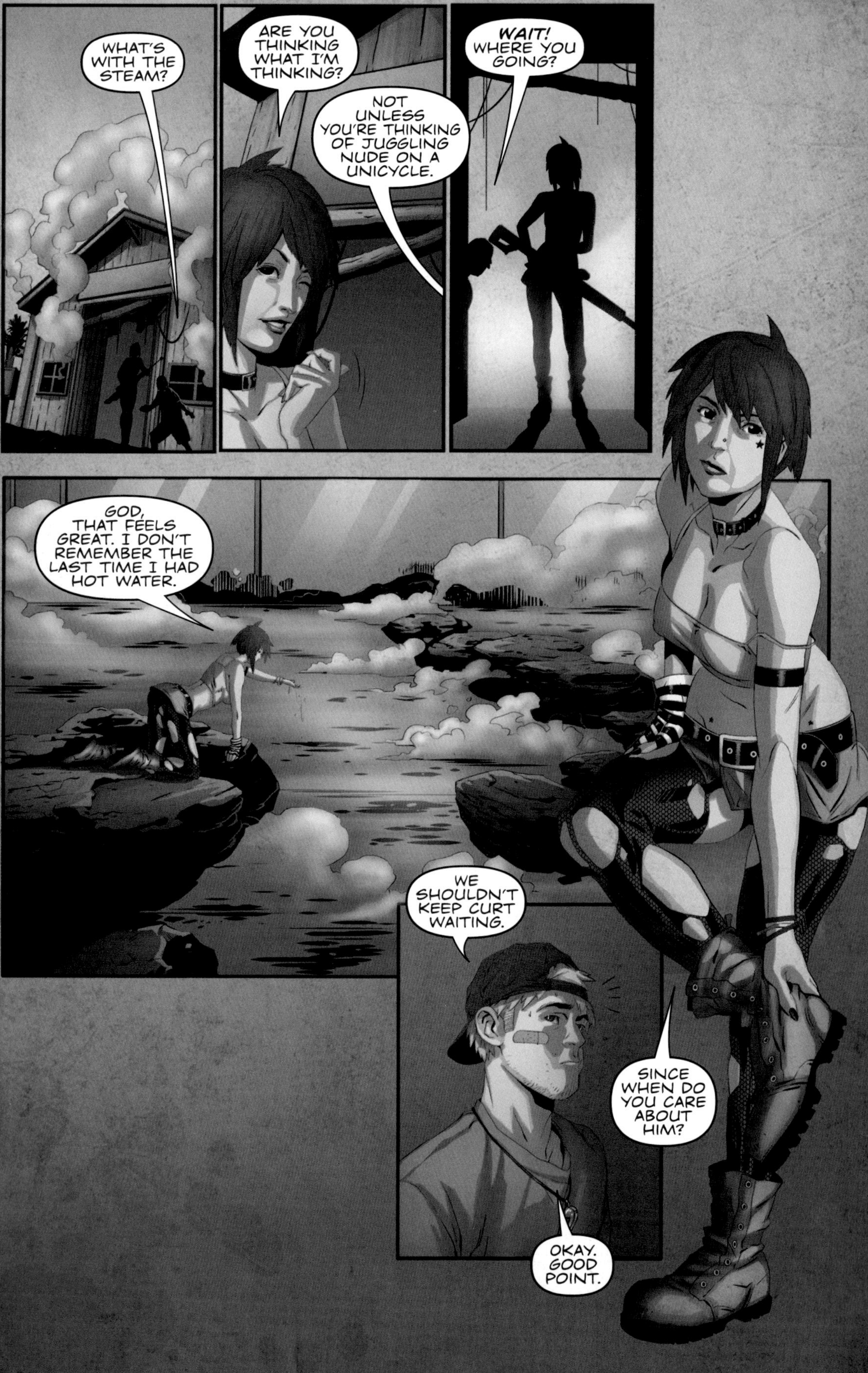
WHAT'S WITH THE STEAM?
ARE YOU THINKING WHAT I'M THINKING?
NOT UNLESS YOU'RE THINKING OF JUGGLING NUDE ON A UNICYCLE.
WAIT! WHERE YOU GOING?
GOD, THAT FEELS GREAT. I DON'T REMEMBER THE LAST TIME I HAD HOT WATER.
WE SHOULDN'T KEEP CURT WAITING.
SINCE WHEN DO YOU CARE ABOUT HIM?
OKAY. GOOD POINT.

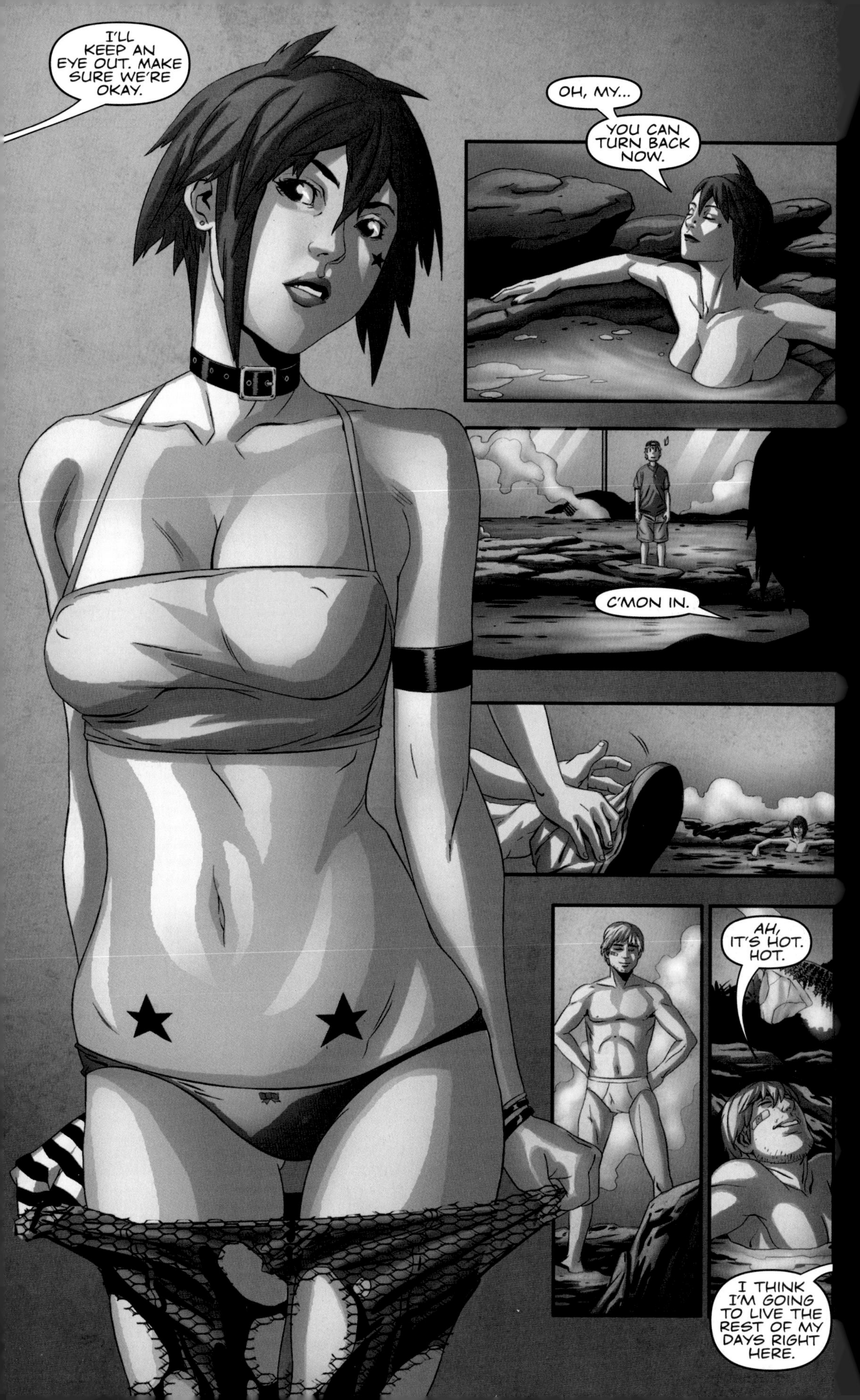
I'LL KEEP AN EYE OUT. MAKE SURE WE'RE OKAY.
OH, MY...
YOU CAN TURN BACK NOW.
C'MON IN.
AH, IT'S HOT. HOT.
I THINK I'M GOING TO LIVE THE REST OF MY DAYS RIGHT HERE.

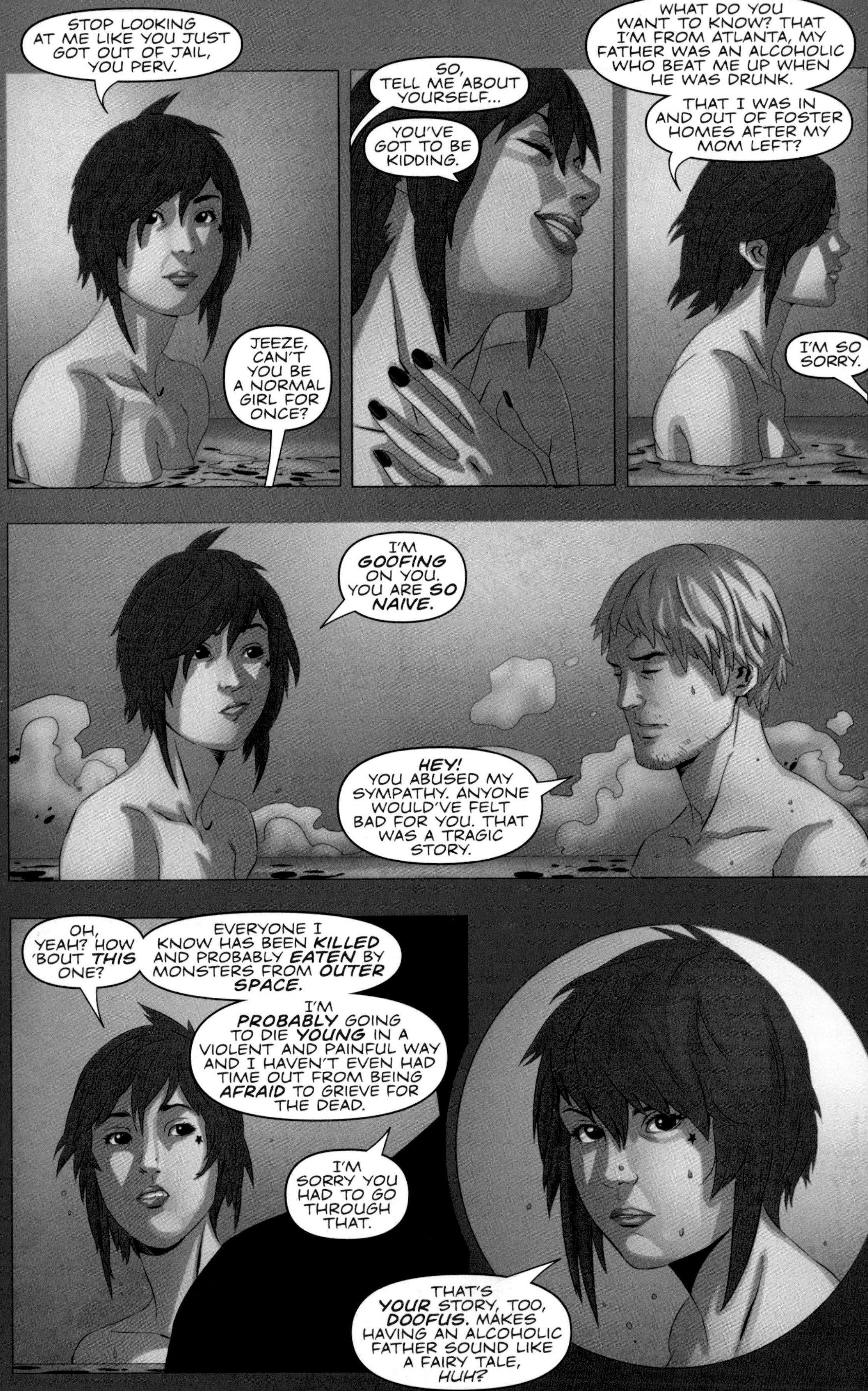

STOP LOOKING AT ME LIKE YOU JUST GOT OUT OF JAIL, YOU PERV.
JEEZE, CAN'T YOU BE A NORMAL GIRL FOR ONCE?
SO, TELL ME ABOUT YOURSELF...
YOU'VE GOT TO BE KIDDING.
WHAT DO YOU WANT TO KNOW? THAT I'M FROM ATLANTA, MY FATHER WAS AN ALCOHOLIC WHO BEAT ME UP WHEN HE WAS DRUNK.
THAT I WAS IN AND OUT OF FOSTER HOMES AFTER MY MOM LEFT?
I'M SO SORRY.
I'M **GOOFING** ON YOU. YOU ARE **SO NAIVE.**
HEY! YOU ABUSED MY SYMPATHY. ANYONE WOULD'VE FELT BAD FOR YOU. THAT WAS A TRAGIC STORY.
OH, YEAH? HOW 'BOUT **THIS** ONE?
EVERYONE I KNOW HAS BEEN **KILLED** AND PROBABLY **EATEN** BY MONSTERS FROM **OUTER SPACE.**
I'M **PROBABLY** GOING TO DIE **YOUNG** IN A VIOLENT AND PAINFUL WAY AND I HAVEN'T EVEN HAD TIME OUT FROM BEING **AFRAID** TO GRIEVE FOR THE DEAD.
I'M SORRY YOU HAD TO GO THROUGH THAT.
THAT'S **YOUR** STORY, TOO, **DOOFUS.** MAKES HAVING AN ALCOHOLIC FATHER SOUND LIKE A FAIRY TALE, **HUH?**

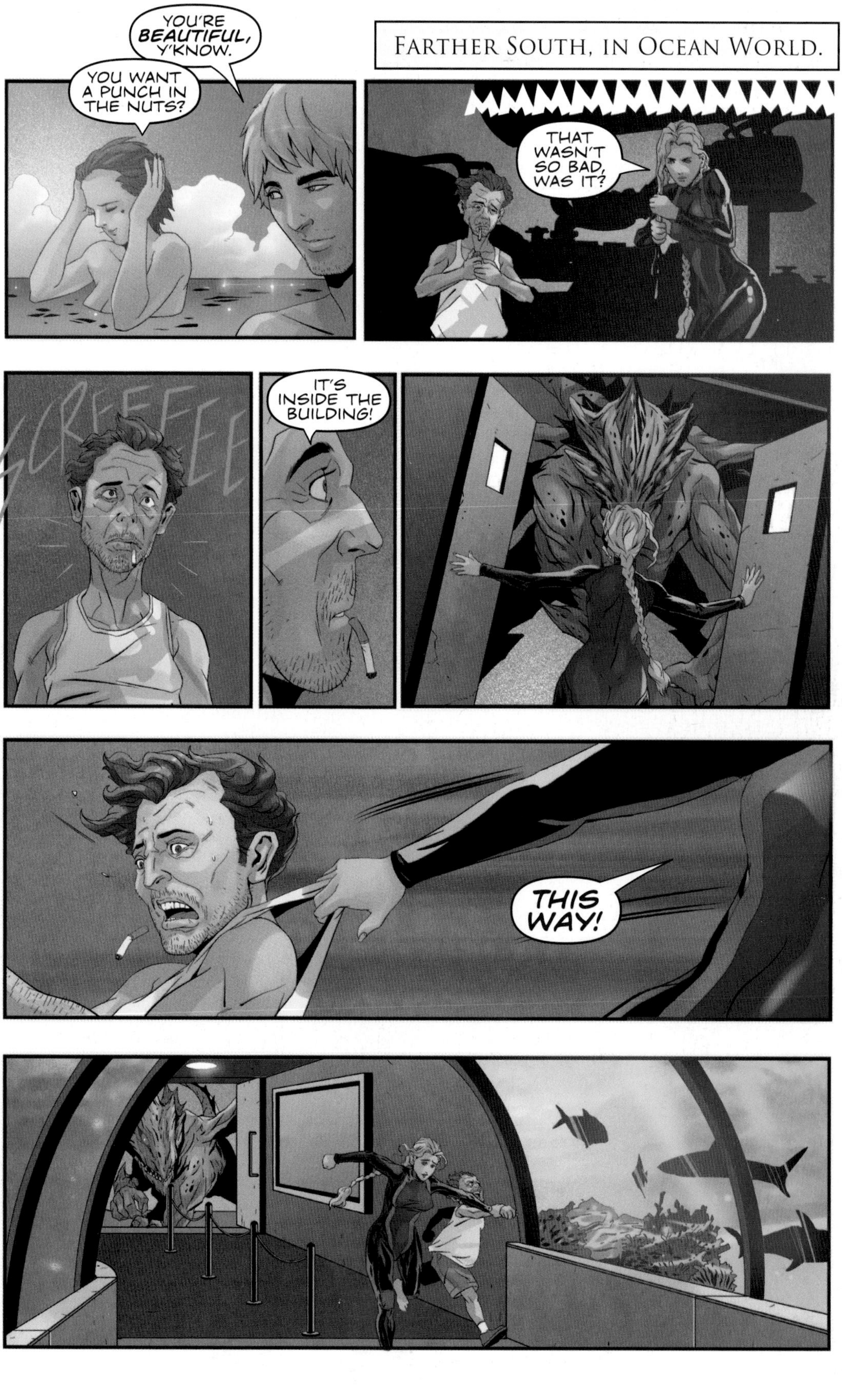

YOU'RE BEAUTIFUL, Y'KNOW.
YOU WANT A PUNCH IN THE NUTS?
FARTHER SOUTH, IN OCEAN WORLD.
MMMMMMMMMMMMM
THAT WASN'T SO BAD, WAS IT?
SCREEEEEE
IT'S INSIDE THE BUILDING!
THIS WAY!

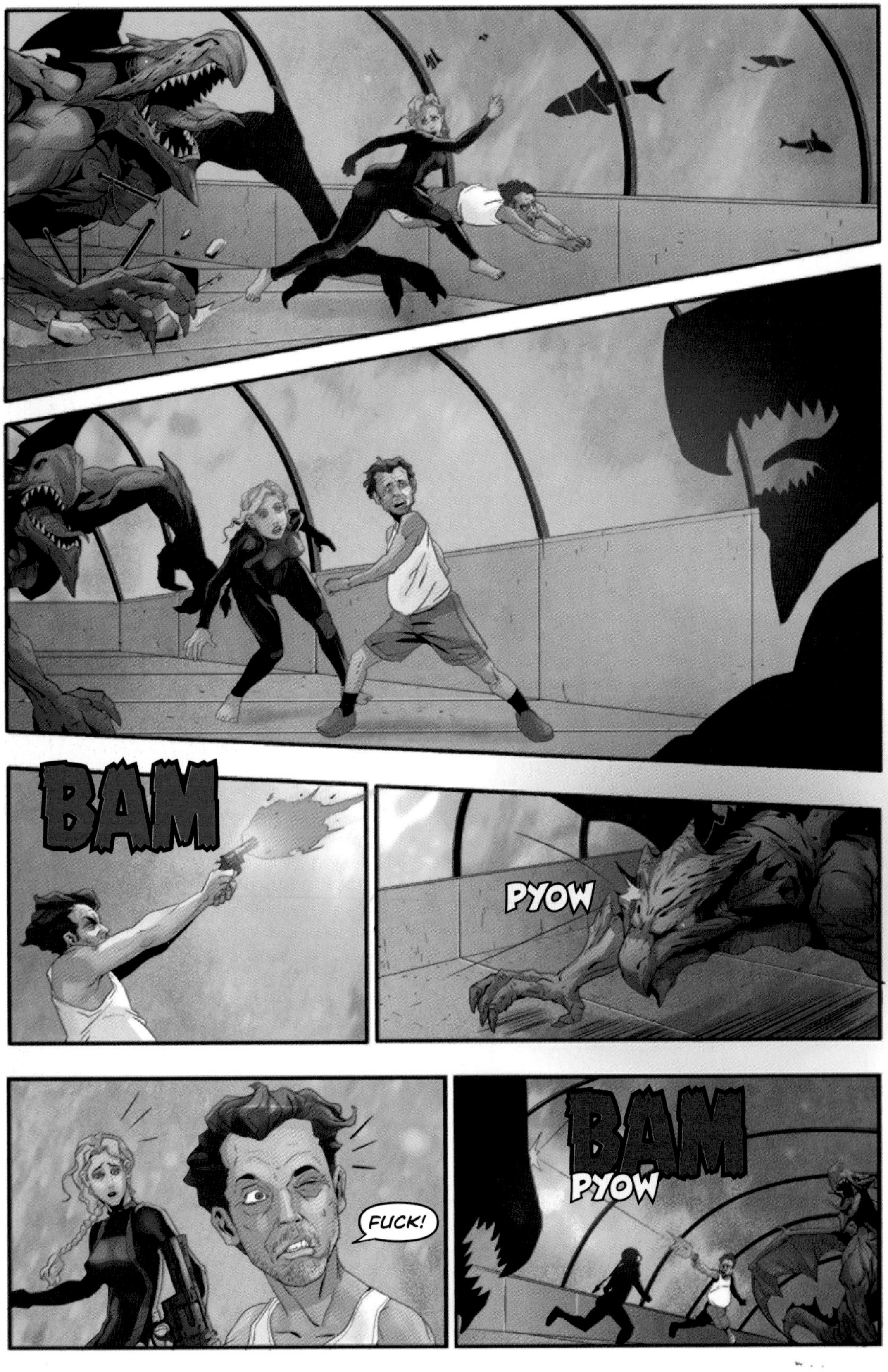
BAM
PYOW
FUCK!
BAM
PYOW

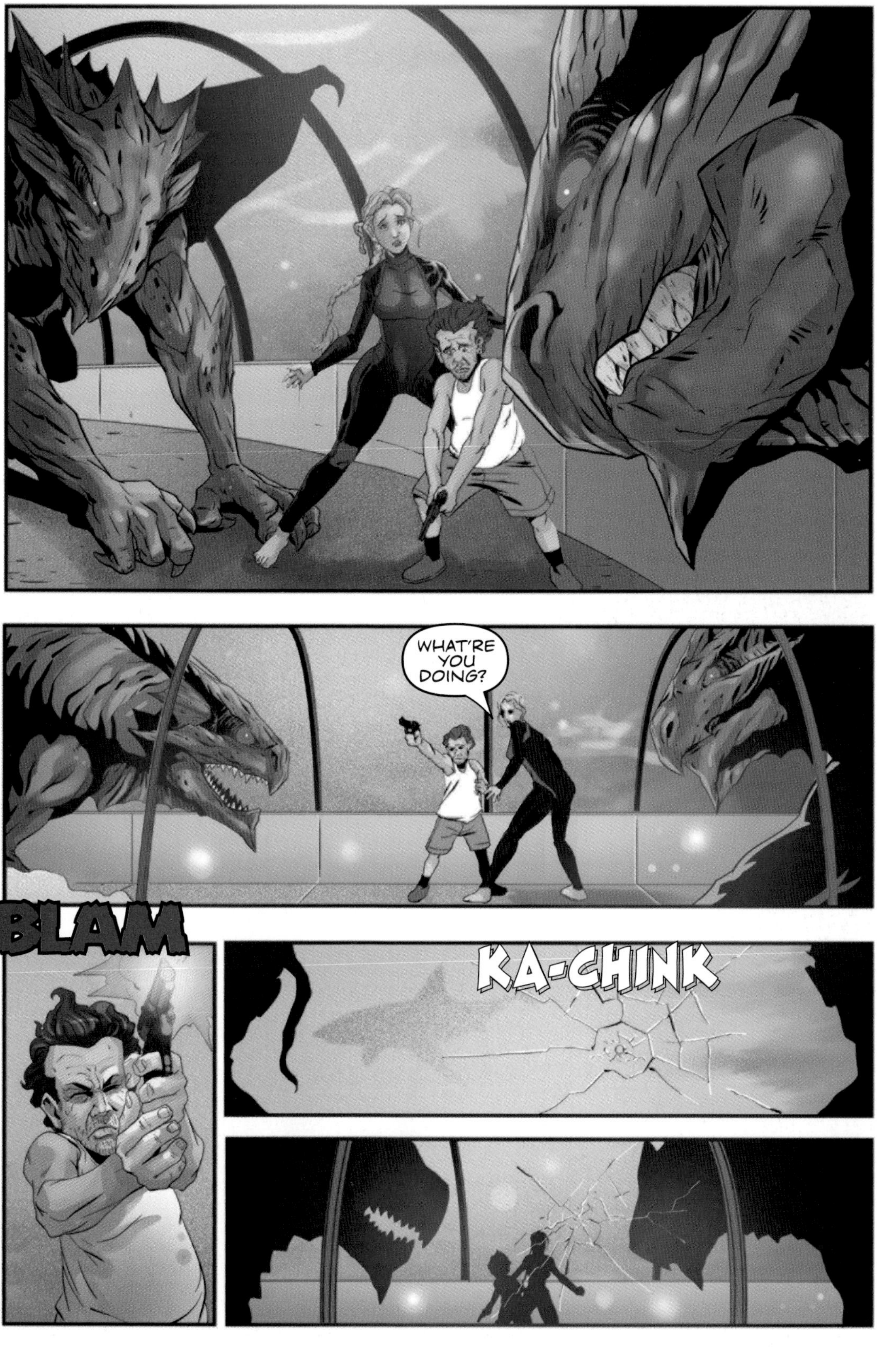
WHAT'RE YOU DOING?
BLAM
KA-CHINK

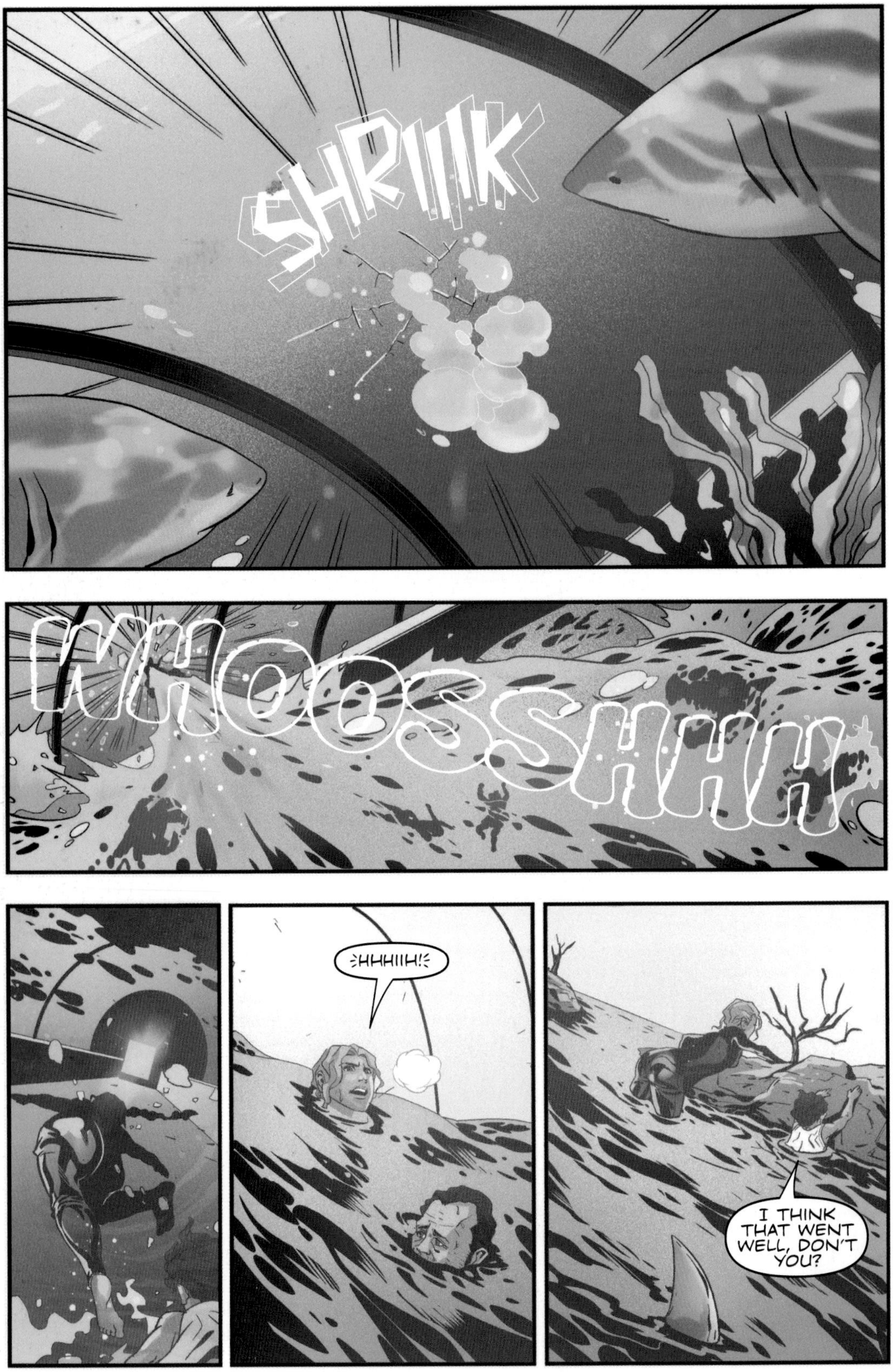
SHRIIIK
WHOOSSHHH
HHHIIH!
I THINK THAT WENT WELL, DON'T YOU?

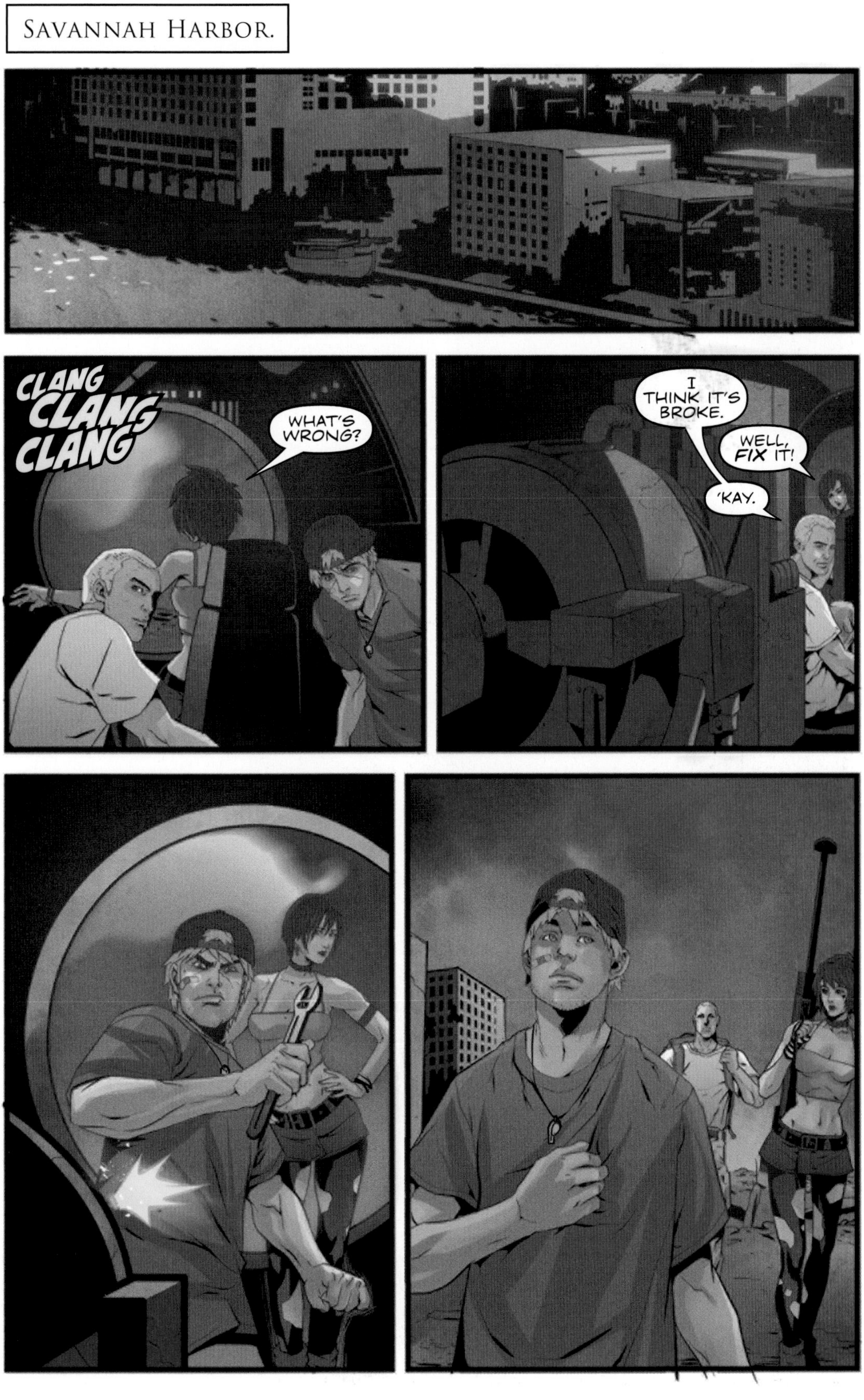
SAVANNAH HARBOR.
CLANG CLANG CLANG
WHAT'S WRONG?
I THINK IT'S BROKE.
WELL, FIX IT!
'KAY.

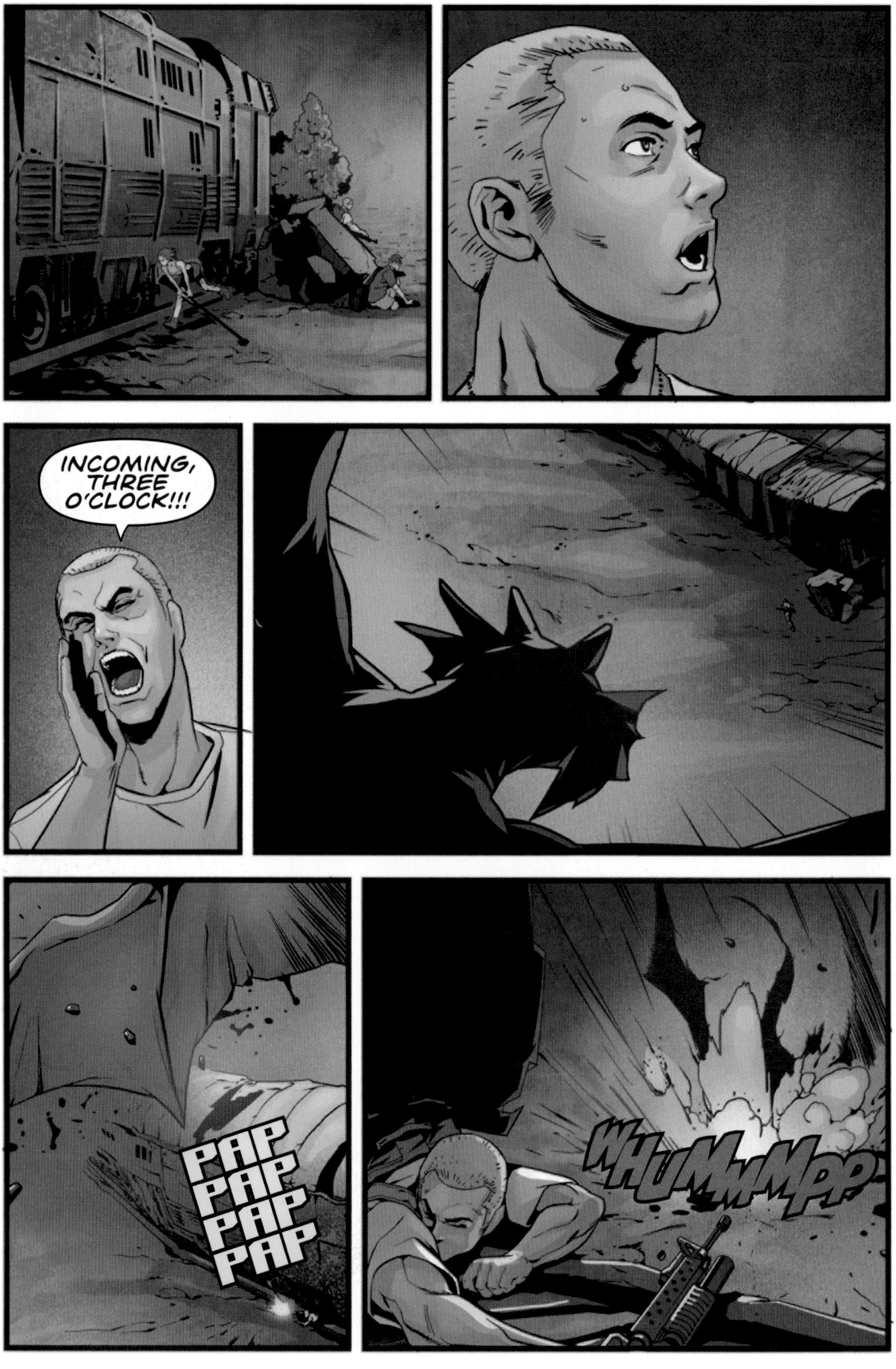
INCOMING, THREE O'CLOCK!!!
PAP PAP PAP PAP
WHUMMMPP

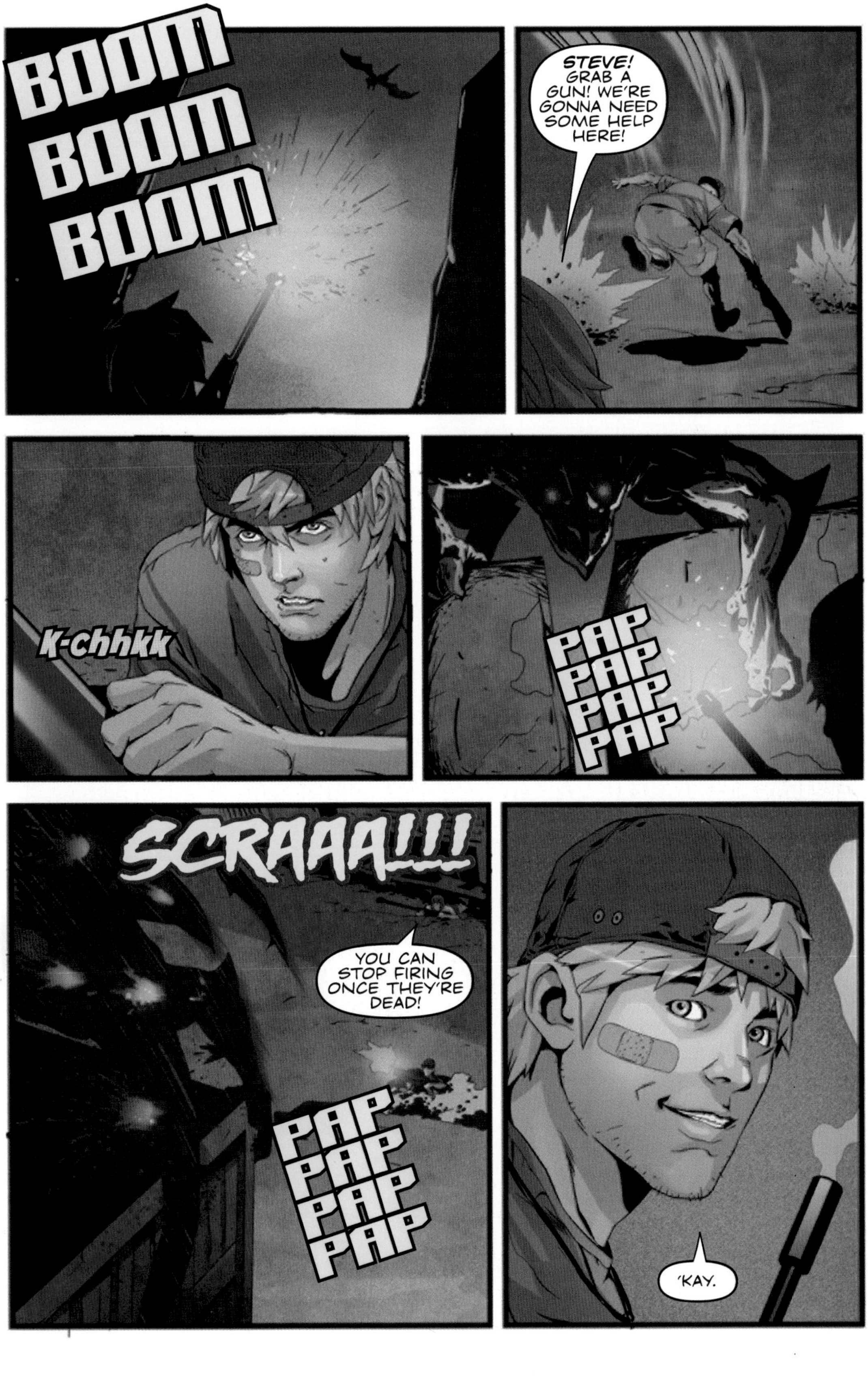
BOOM
BOOM
BOOM
STEVE! GRAB A GUN! WE'RE GONNA NEED SOME HELP HERE!
K-chhkk
PAP
PAP
PAP
PAP
SCRAAA!!!
YOU CAN STOP FIRING ONCE THEY'RE DEAD!
PAP
PAP
PAP
PAP
'KAY.

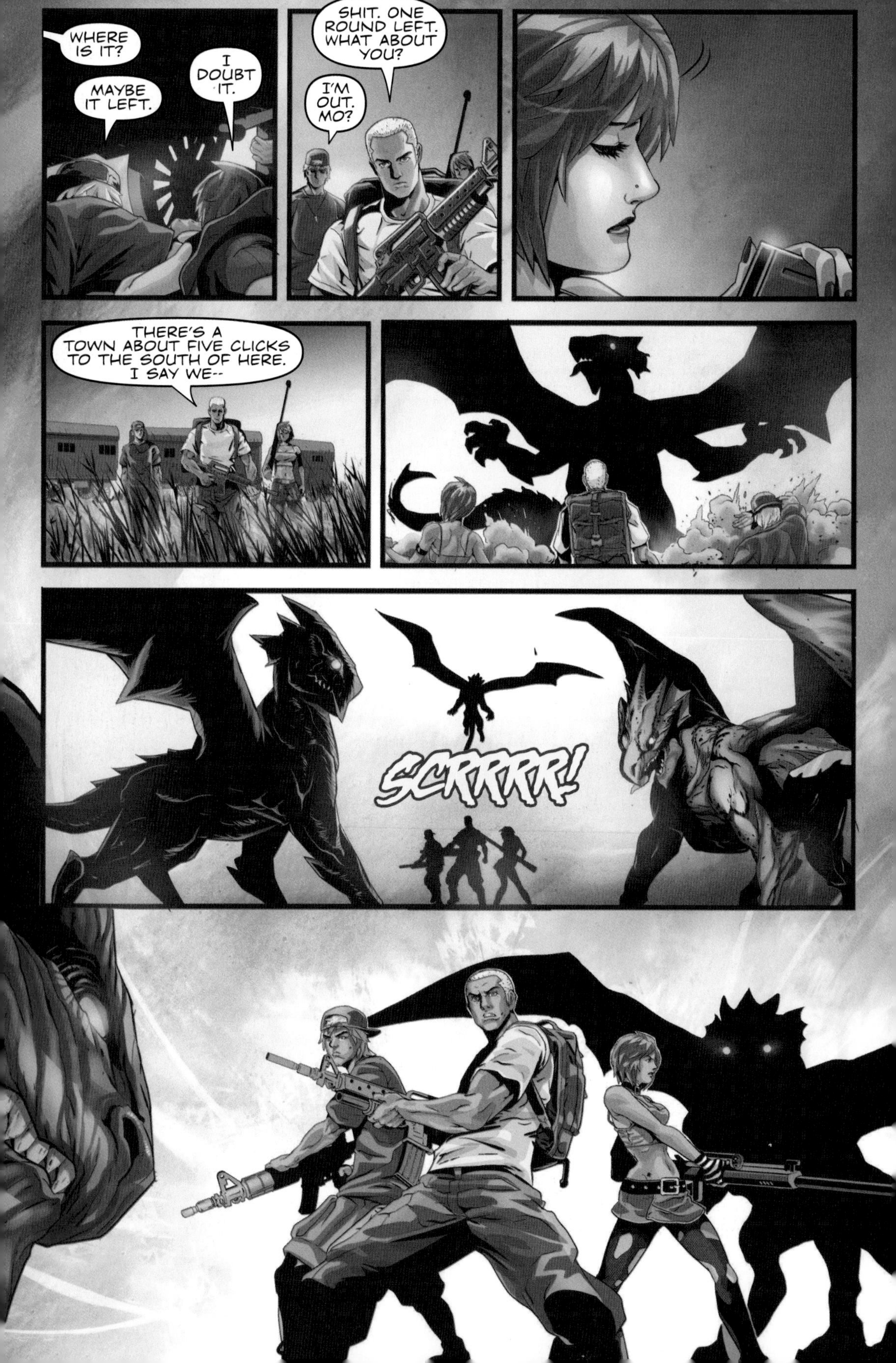
WHERE IS IT?
MAYBE IT LEFT.
I DOUBT IT.
SHIT. ONE ROUND LEFT. WHAT ABOUT YOU?
I'M OUT. MO?
THERE'S A TOWN ABOUT FIVE CLICKS TO THE SOUTH OF HERE. I SAY WE--
SCRRRR!

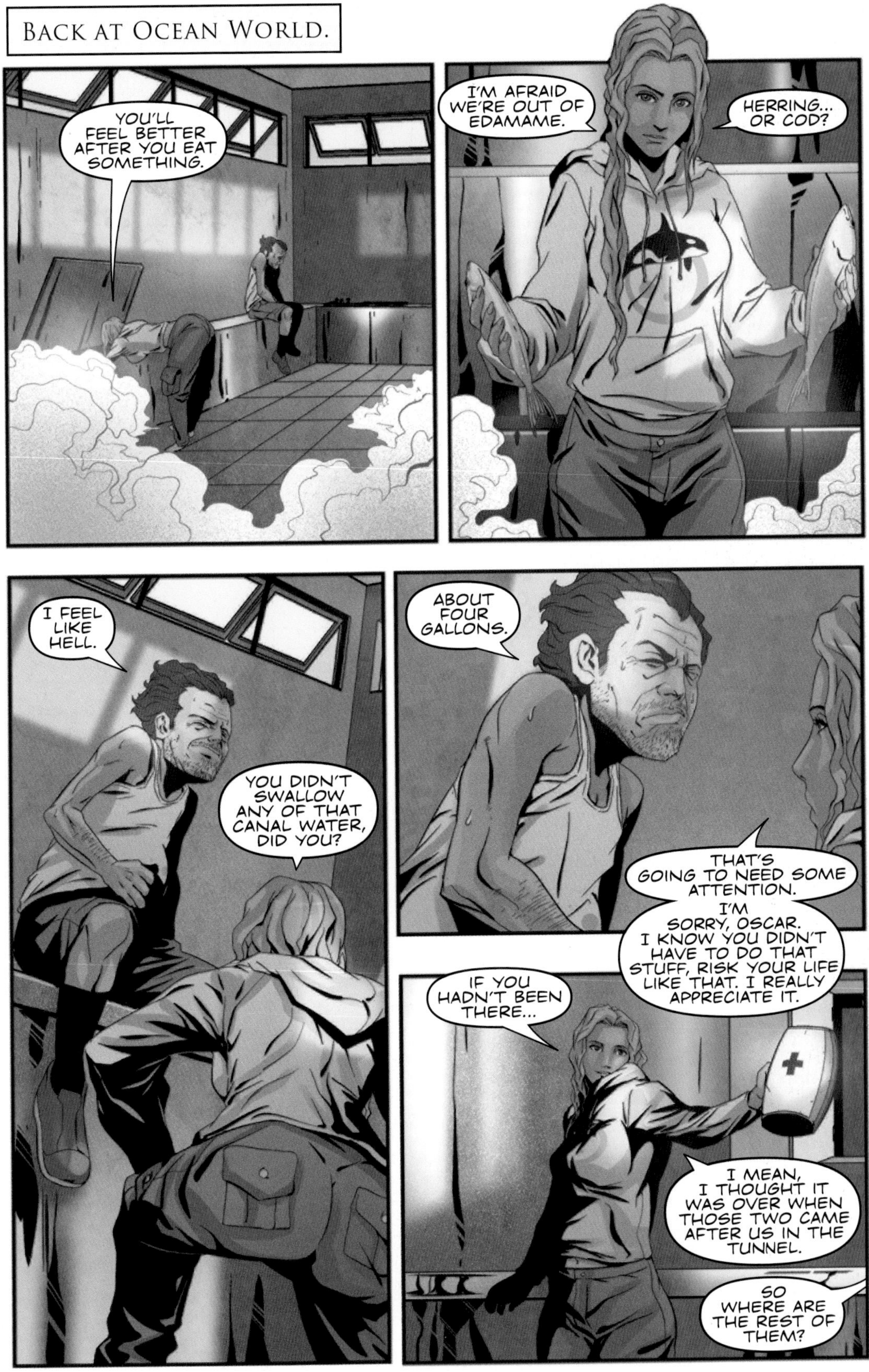
BACK AT OCEAN WORLD.
YOU'LL FEEL BETTER AFTER YOU EAT SOMETHING.
I'M AFRAID WE'RE OUT OF EDAMAME.
HERRING... OR COD?
I FEEL LIKE HELL.
YOU DIDN'T SWALLOW ANY OF THAT CANAL WATER, DID YOU?
ABOUT FOUR GALLONS.
THAT'S GOING TO NEED SOME ATTENTION.
I'M SORRY, OSCAR. I KNOW YOU DIDN'T HAVE TO DO THAT STUFF, RISK YOUR LIFE LIKE THAT. I REALLY APPRECIATE IT.
IF YOU HADN'T BEEN THERE...
I MEAN, I THOUGHT IT WAS OVER WHEN THOSE TWO CAME AFTER US IN THE TUNNEL.
SO WHERE ARE THE REST OF THEM?

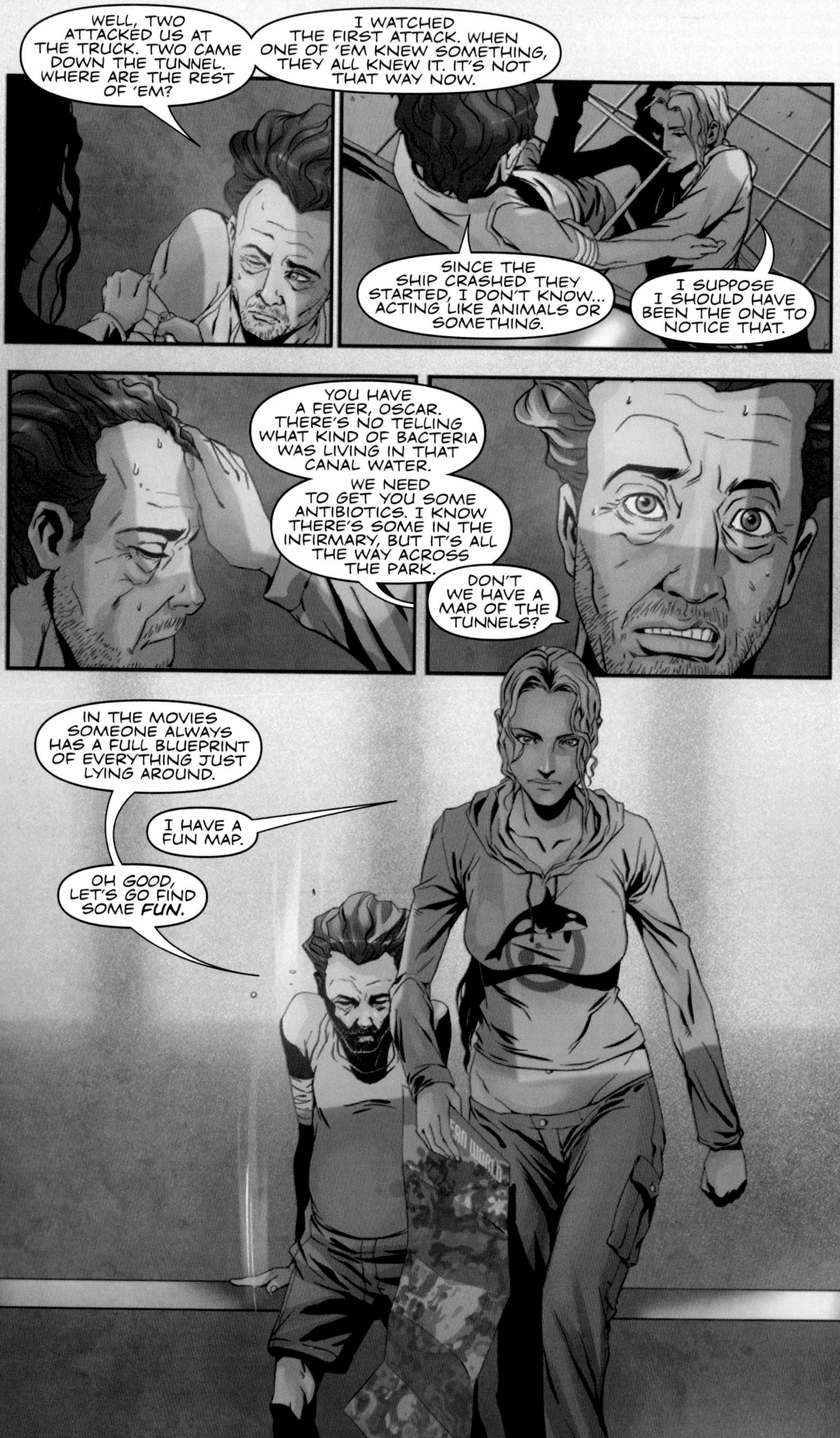
WELL, TWO ATTACKED US AT THE TRUCK. TWO CAME DOWN THE TUNNEL. WHERE ARE THE REST OF 'EM?
I WATCHED THE FIRST ATTACK. WHEN ONE OF 'EM KNEW SOMETHING, THEY ALL KNEW IT. IT'S NOT THAT WAY NOW.
SINCE THE SHIP CRASHED THEY STARTED, I DON'T KNOW... ACTING LIKE ANIMALS OR SOMETHING.
I SUPPOSE I SHOULD HAVE BEEN THE ONE TO NOTICE THAT.
YOU HAVE A FEVER, OSCAR. THERE'S NO TELLING WHAT KIND OF BACTERIA WAS LIVING IN THAT CANAL WATER.
WE NEED TO GET YOU SOME ANTIBIOTICS. I KNOW THERE'S SOME IN THE INFIRMARY, BUT IT'S ALL THE WAY ACROSS THE PARK.
DON'T WE HAVE A MAP OF THE TUNNELS?
IN THE MOVIES SOMEONE ALWAYS HAS A FULL BLUEPRINT OF EVERYTHING JUST LYING AROUND.
I HAVE A FUN MAP.
OH GOOD, LET'S GO FIND SOME FUN.

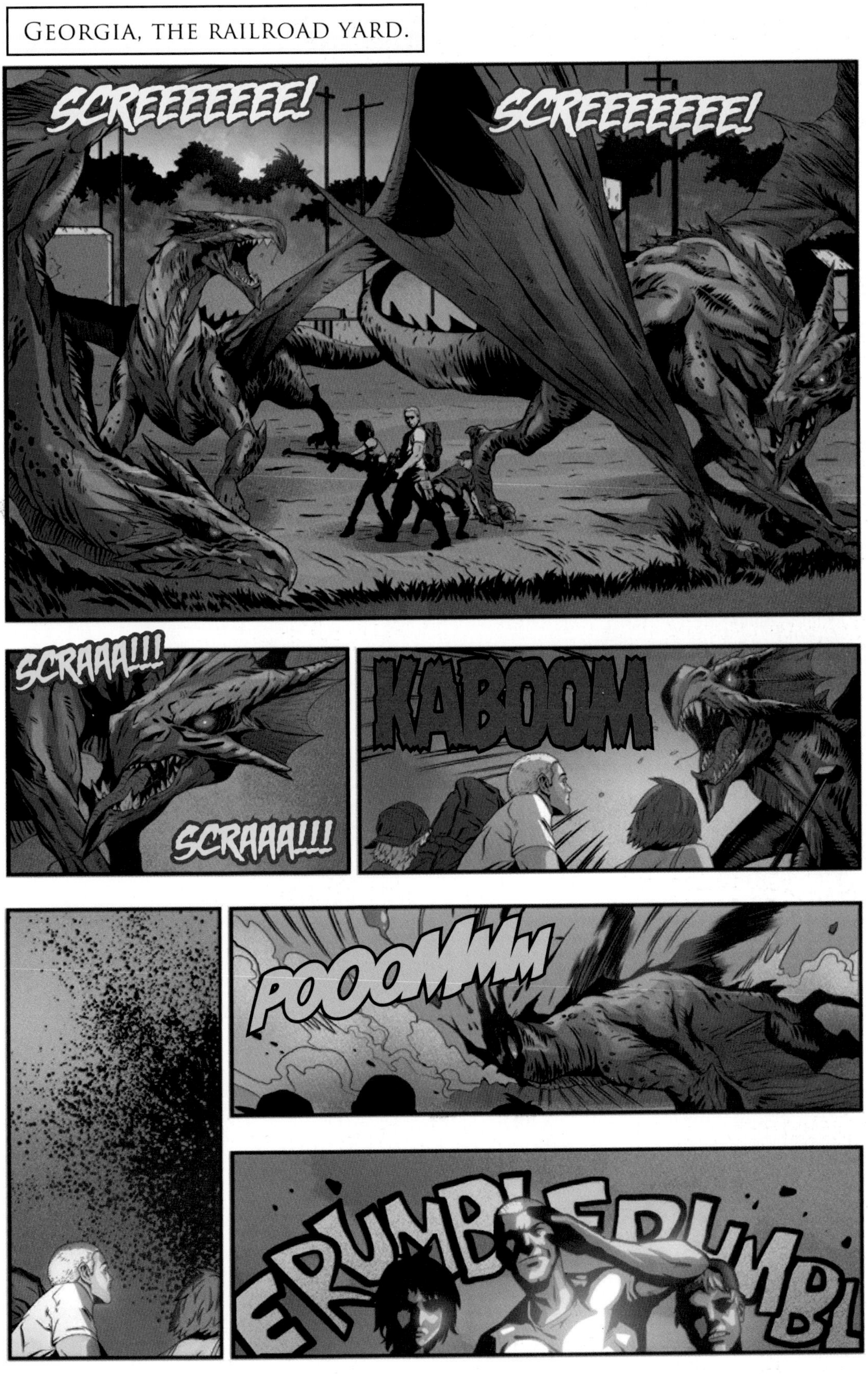
GEORGIA, THE RAILROAD YARD.
SCREEEEEEEE!
SCREEEEEEEE!
SCRAAA!!!
SCRAAA!!!
KABOOM
POOOMMM

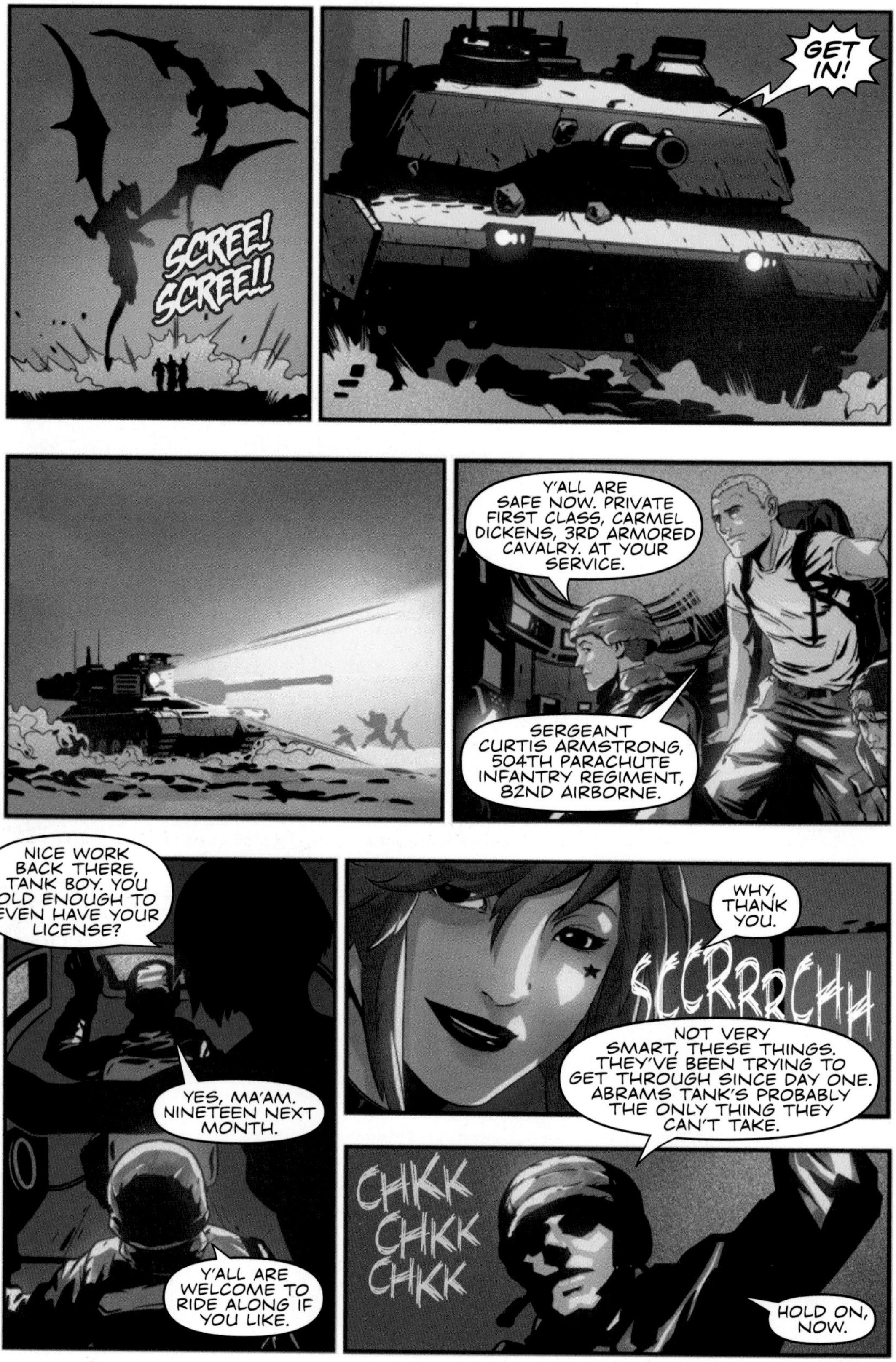
SCREE! SCREE!!
GET IN!
Y'ALL ARE SAFE NOW. PRIVATE FIRST CLASS, CARMEL DICKENS, 3RD ARMORED CAVALRY. AT YOUR SERVICE.
SERGEANT CURTIS ARMSTRONG, 504TH PARACHUTE INFANTRY REGIMENT, 82ND AIRBORNE.
NICE WORK BACK THERE, TANK BOY. YOU OLD ENOUGH TO EVEN HAVE YOUR LICENSE?
YES, MA'AM. NINETEEN NEXT MONTH.
Y'ALL ARE WELCOME TO RIDE ALONG IF YOU LIKE.
WHY, THANK YOU.
SCCRRRCHH
NOT VERY SMART, THESE THINGS. THEY'VE BEEN TRYING TO GET THROUGH SINCE DAY ONE. ABRAMS TANK'S PROBABLY THE ONLY THING THEY CAN'T TAKE.
CHKK CHKK CHKK
HOLD ON, NOW.

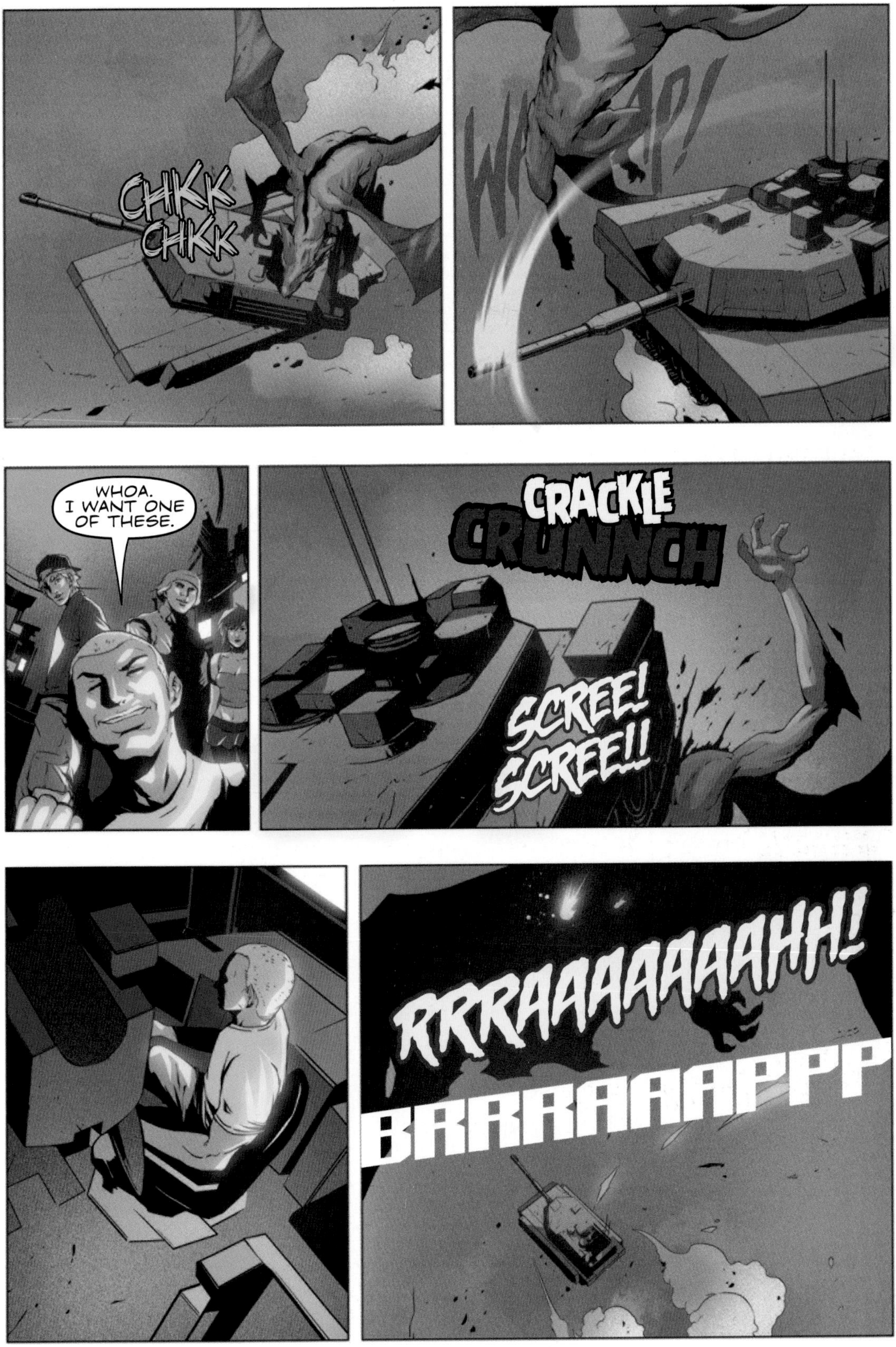
CHKK
CHKK
WHOA. I WANT ONE OF THESE.
CRACKLE
CRUNNCH
SCREE!
SCREE!!
RRRAAAAAAAHH!
BRRRAAAAPPP

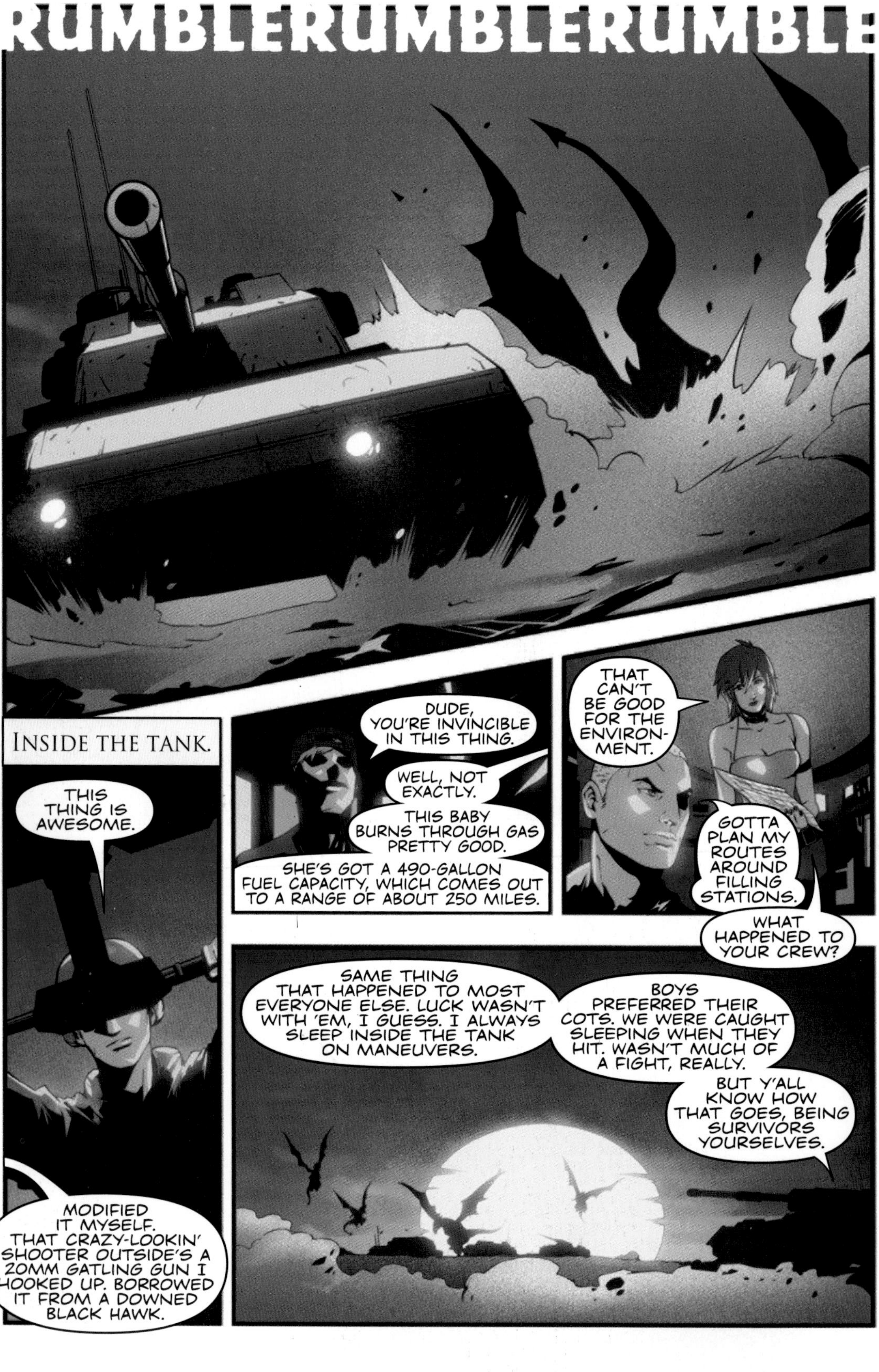
RUMBLERUMBLERUMBLE
INSIDE THE TANK.
THIS THING IS AWESOME.
DUDE, YOU'RE INVINCIBLE IN THIS THING.
WELL, NOT EXACTLY.
THIS BABY BURNS THROUGH GAS PRETTY GOOD.
SHE'S GOT A 490-GALLON FUEL CAPACITY, WHICH COMES OUT TO A RANGE OF ABOUT 250 MILES.
THAT CAN'T BE GOOD FOR THE ENVIRON-MENT.
GOTTA PLAN MY ROUTES AROUND FILLING STATIONS.
WHAT HAPPENED TO YOUR CREW?
SAME THING THAT HAPPENED TO MOST EVERYONE ELSE. LUCK WASN'T WITH 'EM, I GUESS. I ALWAYS SLEEP INSIDE THE TANK ON MANEUVERS.
BOYS PREFERRED THEIR COTS. WE WERE CAUGHT SLEEPING WHEN THEY HIT. WASN'T MUCH OF A FIGHT, REALLY.
BUT Y'ALL KNOW HOW THAT GOES, BEING SURVIVORS YOURSELVES.
MODIFIED IT MYSELF. THAT CRAZY-LOOKIN' SHOOTER OUTSIDE'S A 20MM GATLING GUN I HOOKED UP. BORROWED IT FROM A DOWNED BLACK HAWK.

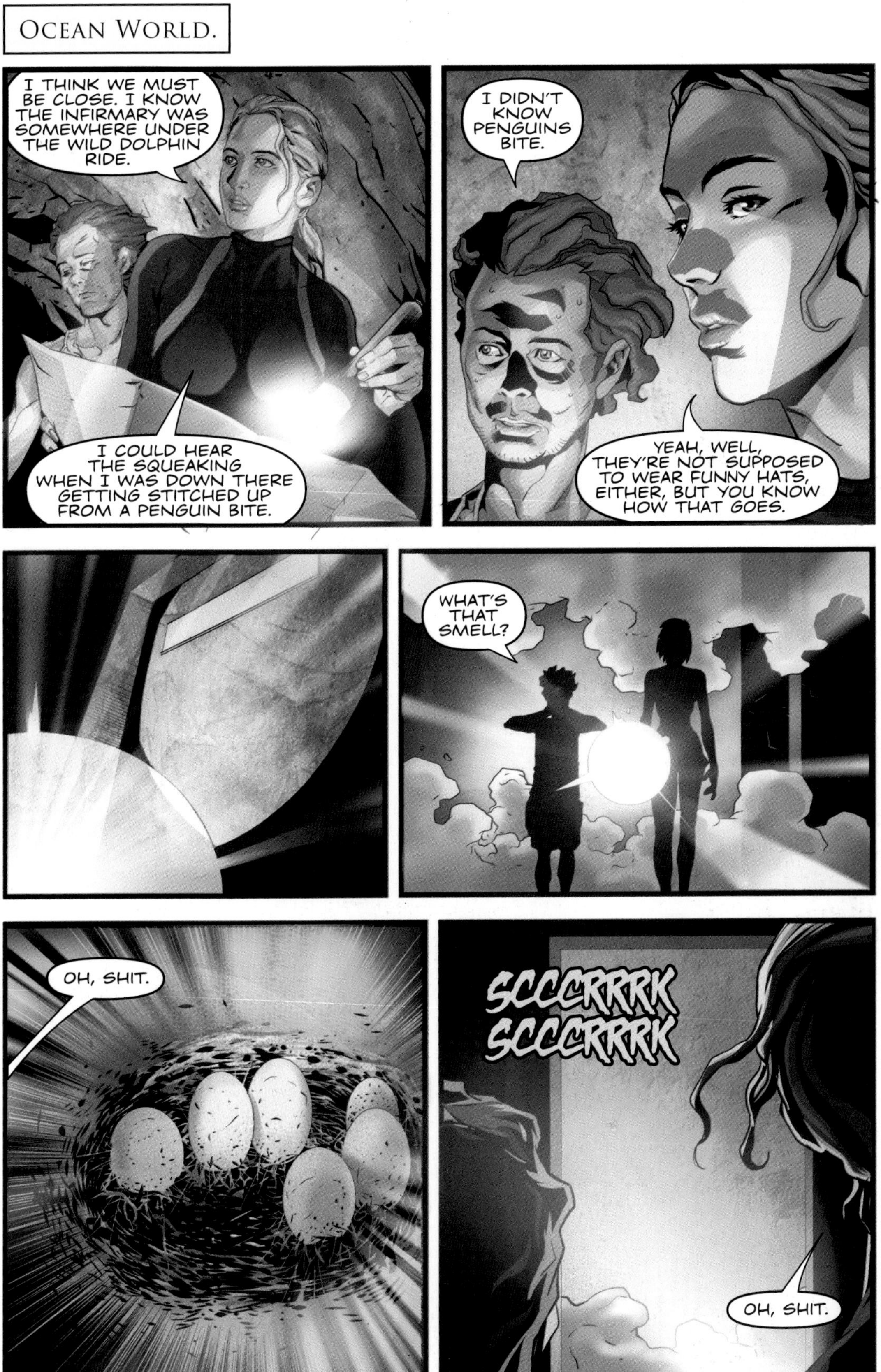
OCEAN WORLD.
I THINK WE MUST BE CLOSE. I KNOW THE INFIRMARY WAS SOMEWHERE UNDER THE WILD DOLPHIN RIDE.
I COULD HEAR THE SQUEAKING WHEN I WAS DOWN THERE GETTING STITCHED UP FROM A PENGUIN BITE.
I DIDN'T KNOW PENGUINS BITE.
YEAH, WELL, THEY'RE NOT SUPPOSED TO WEAR FUNNY HATS, EITHER, BUT YOU KNOW HOW THAT GOES.
WHAT'S THAT SMELL?
OH, SHIT.
SCCCRRRK
SCCCRRRK
OH, SHIT.

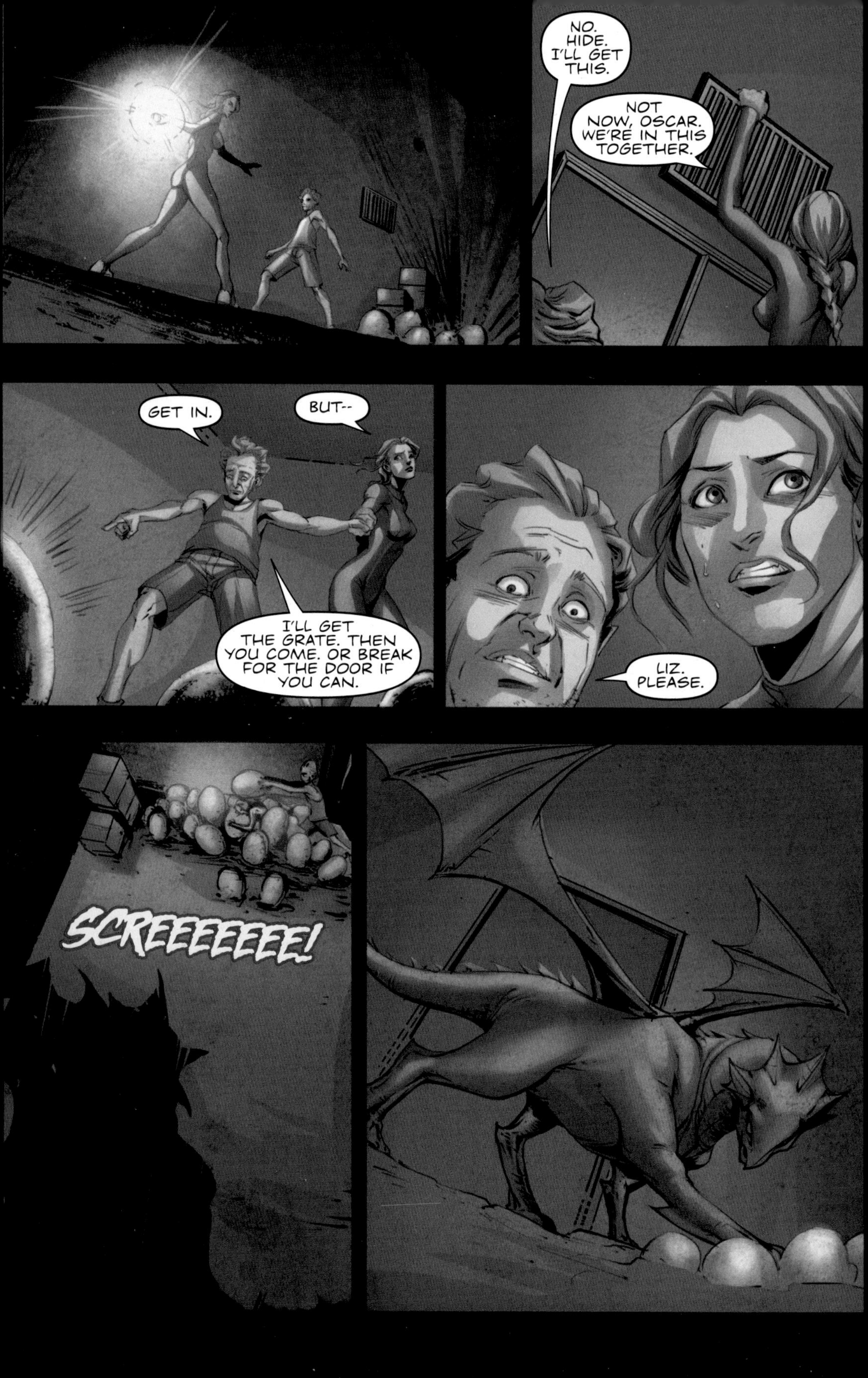
NO. HIDE. I'LL GET THIS.
NOT NOW, OSCAR. WE'RE IN THIS TOGETHER.
GET IN.
BUT--
I'LL GET THE GRATE. THEN YOU COME. OR BREAK FOR THE DOOR IF YOU CAN.
LIZ. PLEASE.
SCREEEEEEEE!

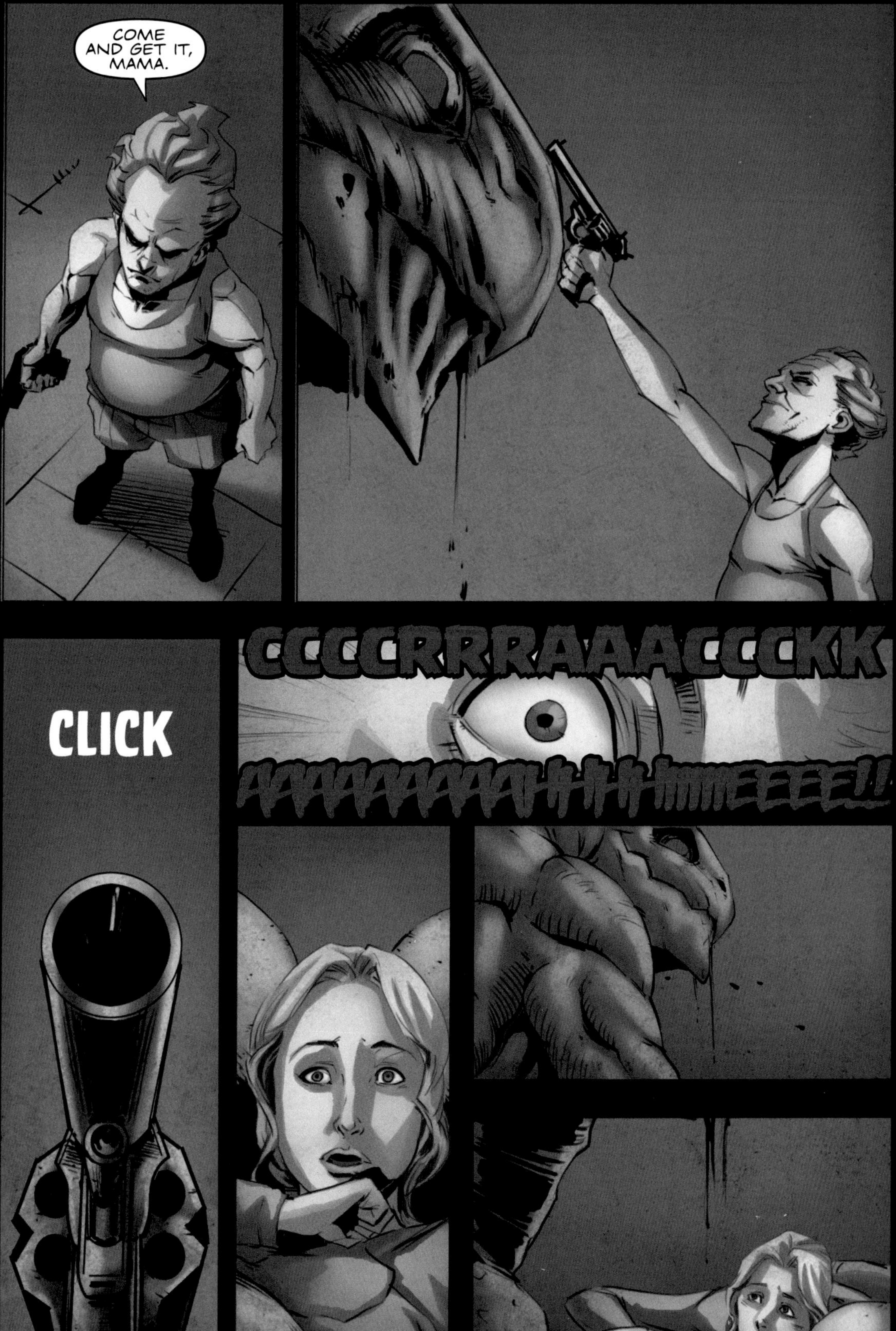
COME AND GET IT, MAMA.
CLICK
CCCCRRRAAACCCCKK
AAAAAAAAAAHHHHHHHEEEEE!!

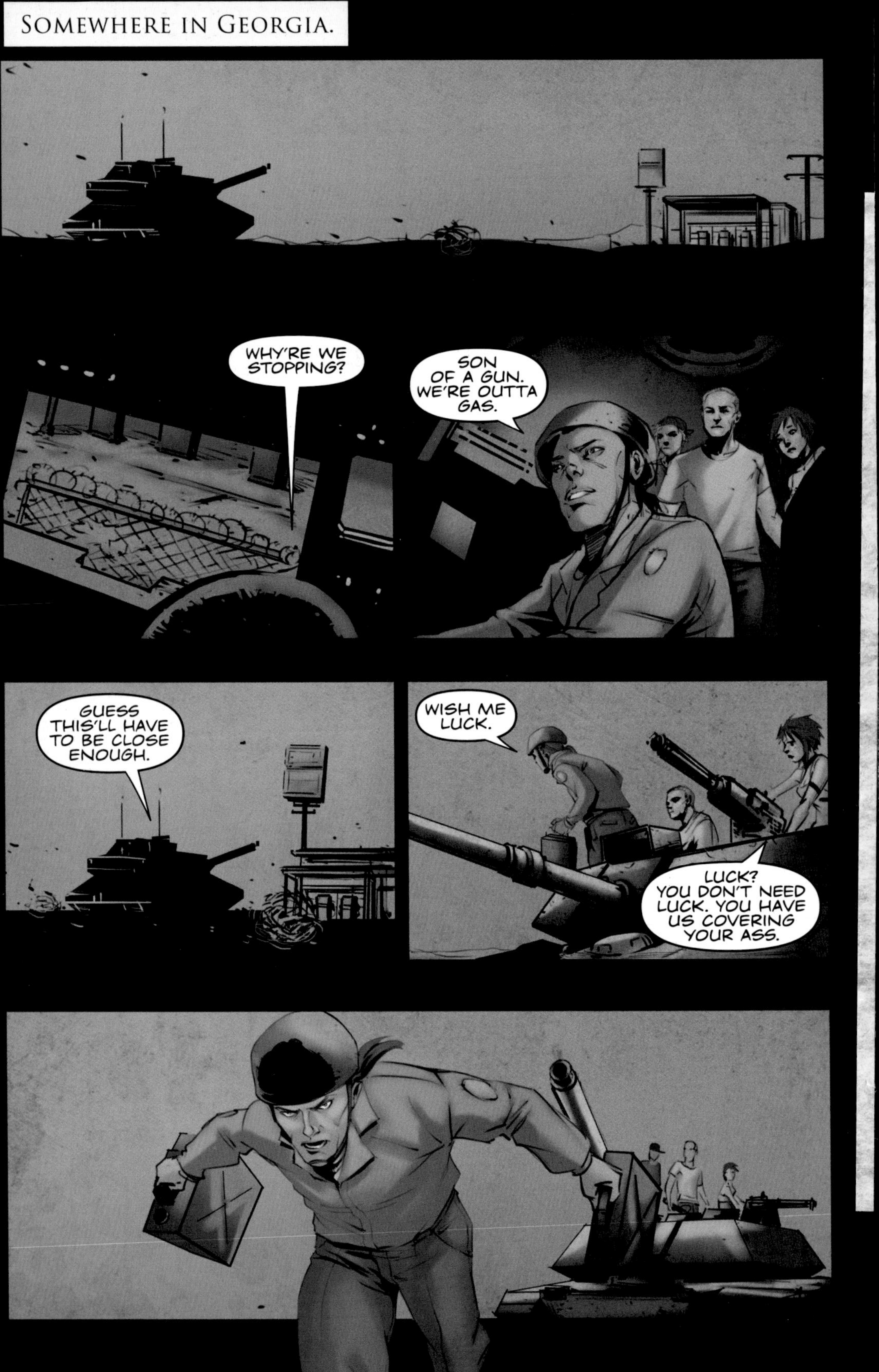
SOMEWHERE IN GEORGIA.
WHY'RE WE STOPPING?
SON OF A GUN. WE'RE OUTTA GAS.
GUESS THIS'LL HAVE TO BE CLOSE ENOUGH.
WISH ME LUCK.
LUCK? YOU DON'T NEED LUCK. YOU HAVE US COVERING YOUR ASS.

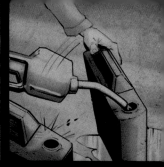

BOOM

SCREEEEEEE!

BRAAAP

AAAHHHH!!!

C'MON...
C'MON...

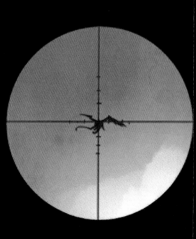

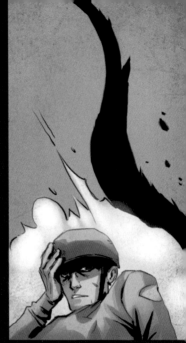

HURRY!

SCREE!
SCREE!!

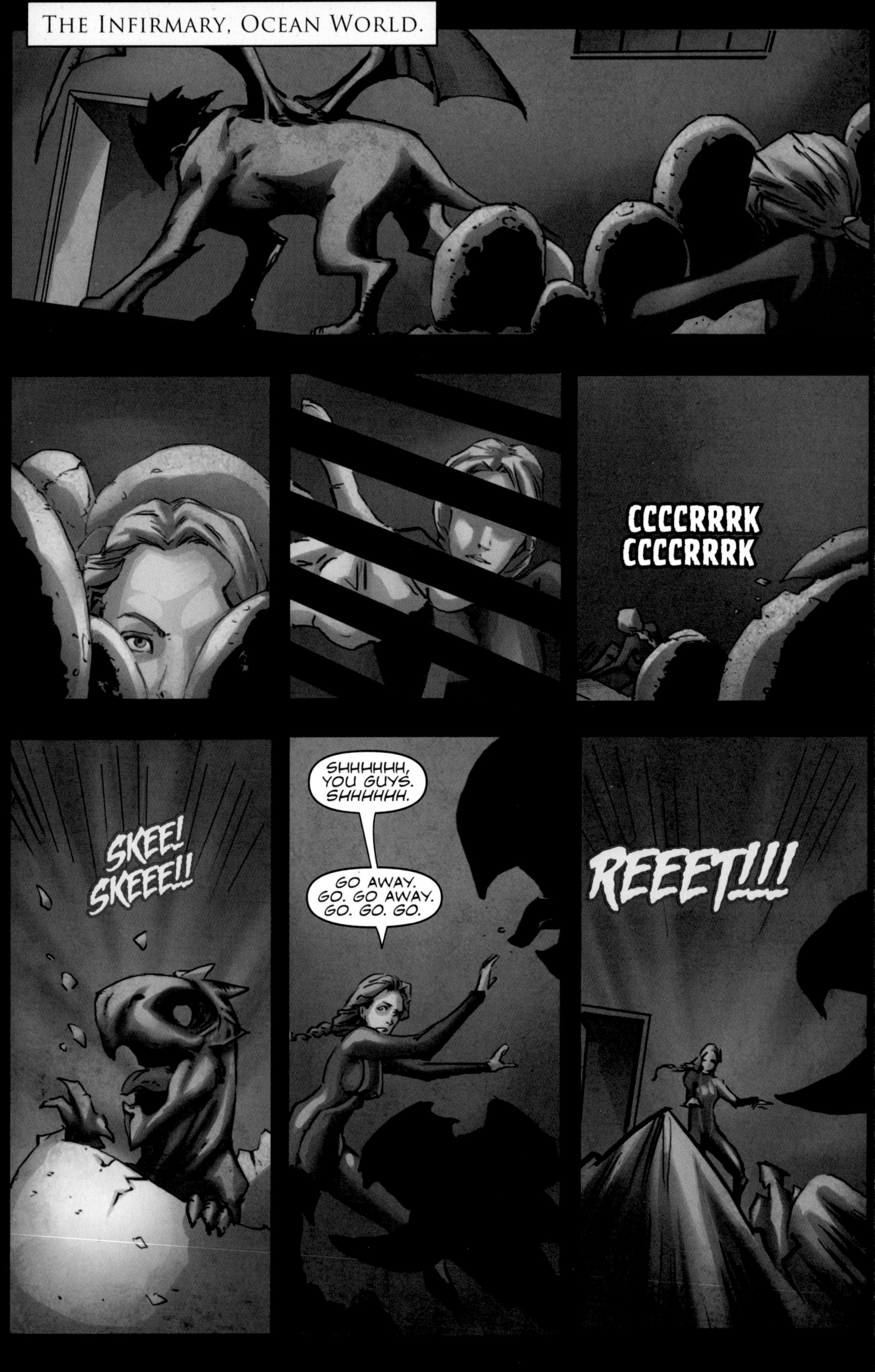
THE INFIRMARY, OCEAN WORLD.
CCCCRRRK
CCCCRRRK
SKEE! SKEEE!!
SHHHHHH, YOU GUYS. SHHHHHH.
GO AWAY. GO. GO AWAY. GO. GO. GO.
REEET!!!

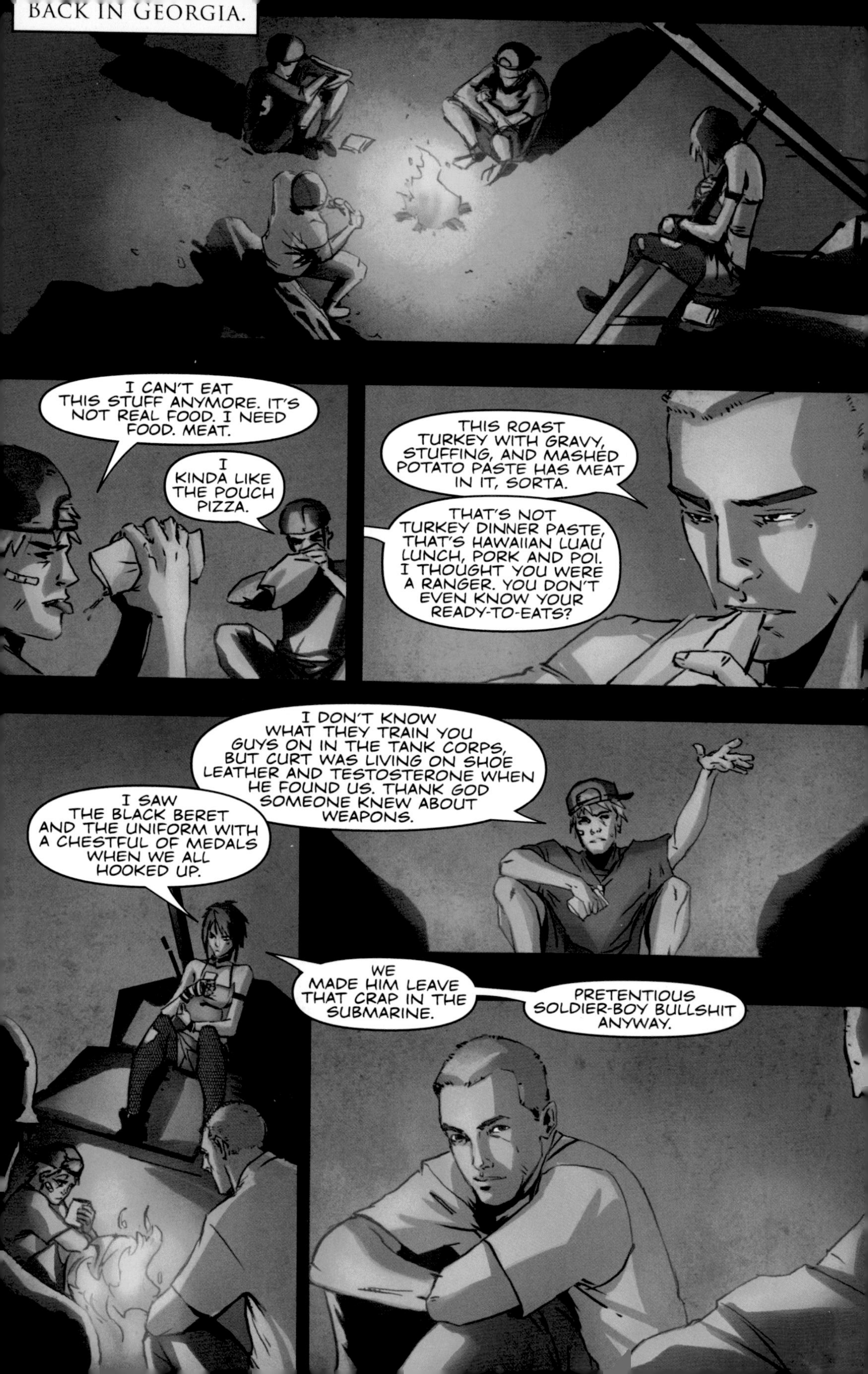
BACK IN GEORGIA.
I CAN'T EAT THIS STUFF ANYMORE. IT'S NOT REAL FOOD. I NEED FOOD. MEAT.
I KINDA LIKE THE POUCH PIZZA.
THIS ROAST TURKEY WITH GRAVY, STUFFING, AND MASHED POTATO PASTE HAS MEAT IN IT, SORTA.
THAT'S NOT TURKEY DINNER PASTE, THAT'S HAWAIIAN LUAU LUNCH, PORK AND POI. I THOUGHT YOU WERE A RANGER. YOU DON'T EVEN KNOW YOUR READY-TO-EATS?
I DON'T KNOW WHAT THEY TRAIN YOU GUYS ON IN THE TANK CORPS, BUT CURT WAS LIVING ON SHOE LEATHER AND TESTOSTERONE WHEN HE FOUND US. THANK GOD SOMEONE KNEW ABOUT WEAPONS.
I SAW THE BLACK BERET AND THE UNIFORM WITH A CHESTFUL OF MEDALS WHEN WE ALL HOOKED UP.
WE MADE HIM LEAVE THAT CRAP IN THE SUBMARINE.
PRETENTIOUS SOLDIER-BOY BULLSHIT ANYWAY.

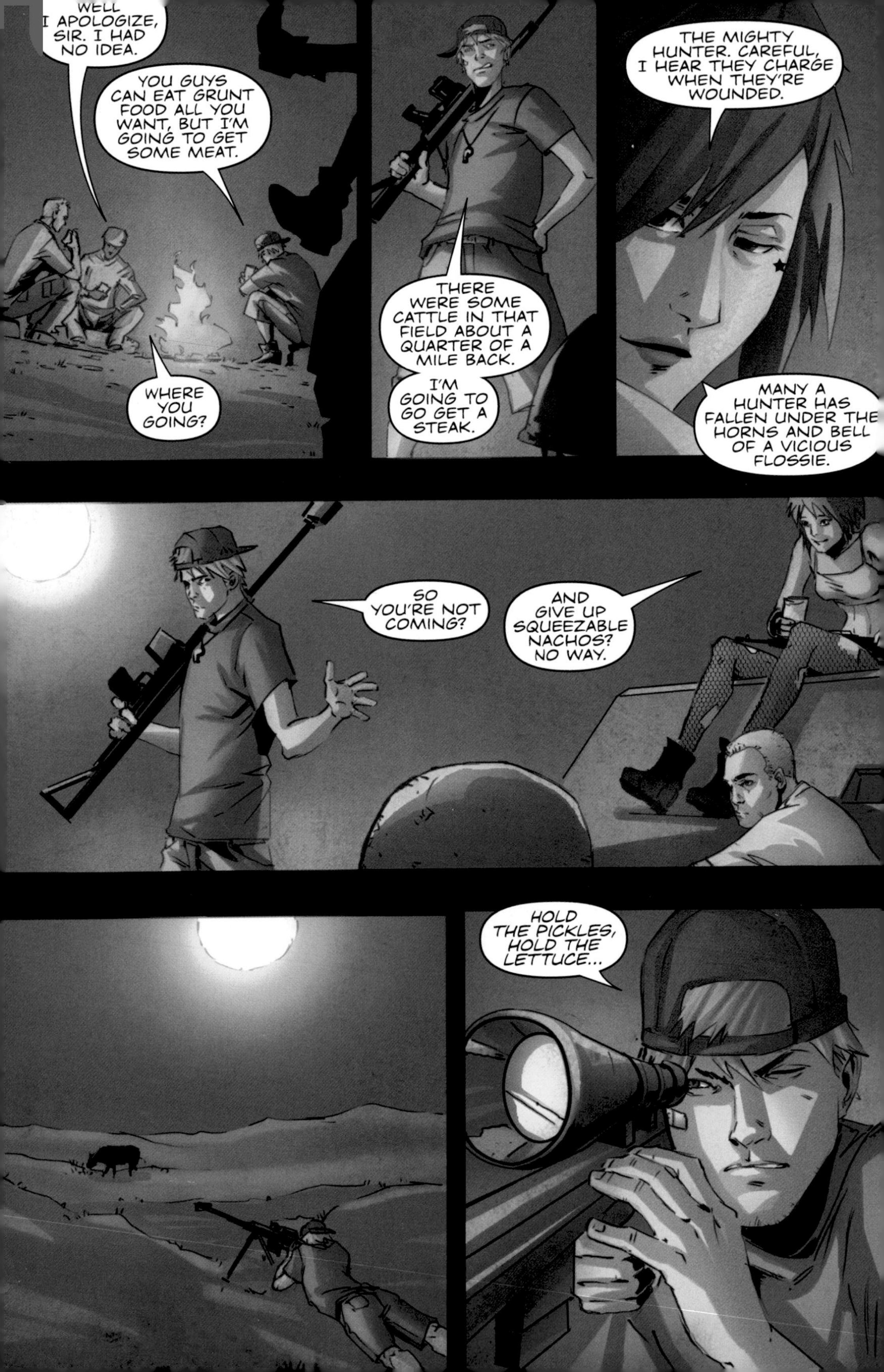
WELL I APOLOGIZE, SIR. I HAD NO IDEA.
YOU GUYS CAN EAT GRUNT FOOD ALL YOU WANT, BUT I'M GOING TO GET SOME MEAT.
WHERE YOU GOING?
THERE WERE SOME CATTLE IN THAT FIELD ABOUT A QUARTER OF A MILE BACK.
I'M GOING TO GO GET A STEAK.
THE MIGHTY HUNTER. CAREFUL, I HEAR THEY CHARGE WHEN THEY'RE WOUNDED.
MANY A HUNTER HAS FALLEN UNDER THE HORNS AND BELL OF A VICIOUS FLOSSIE.
SO YOU'RE NOT COMING?
AND GIVE UP SQUEEZABLE NACHOS? NO WAY.
HOLD THE PICKLES, HOLD THE LETTUCE...

SIGH...

MY COW,
YOU BASTARD.
MY COW.

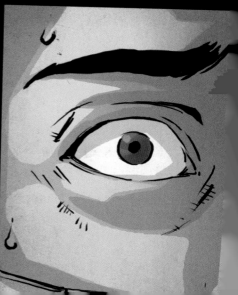

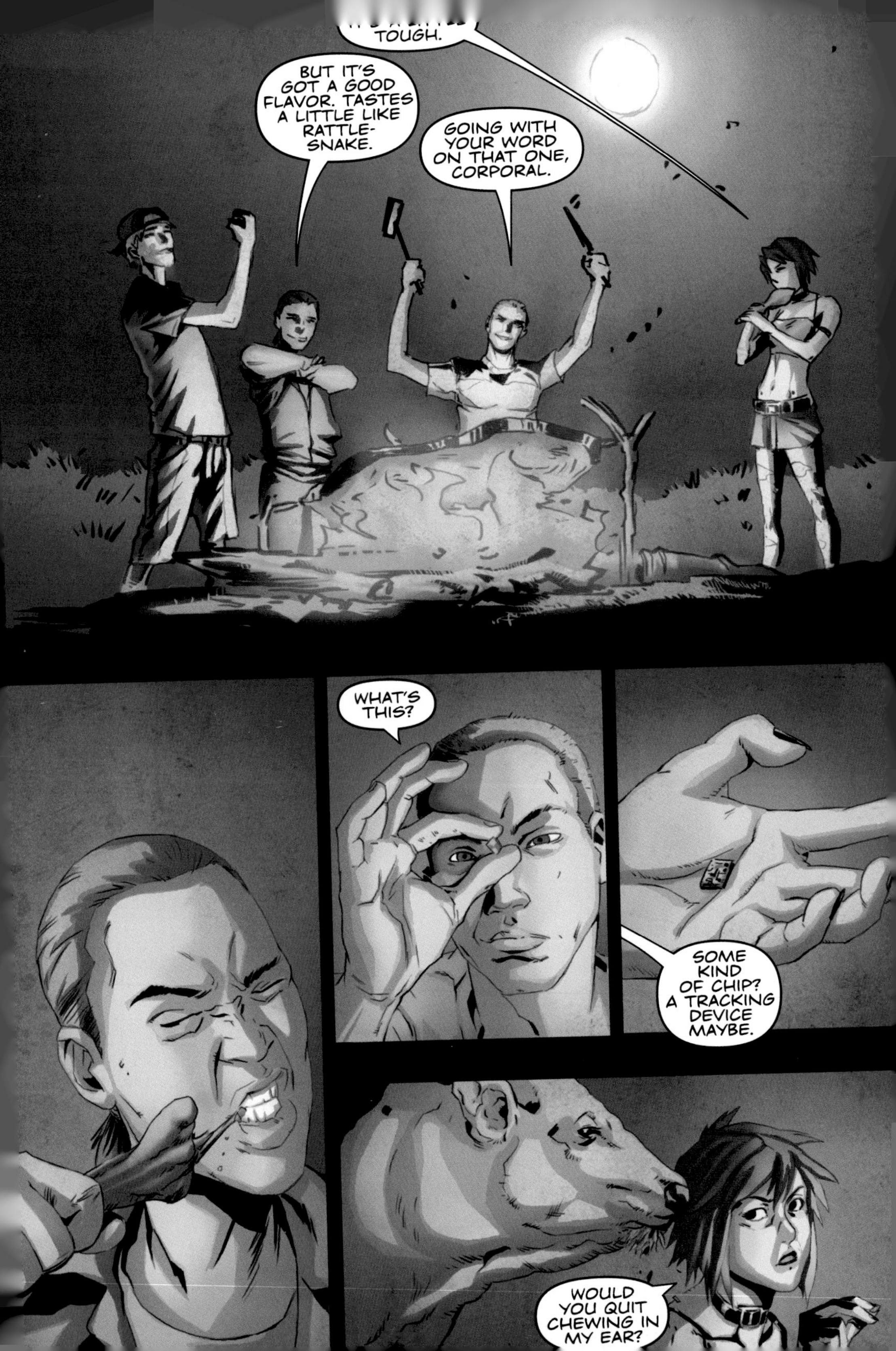
TOUGH.
BUT IT'S GOT A GOOD FLAVOR. TASTES A LITTLE LIKE RATTLE-SNAKE.
GOING WITH YOUR WORD ON THAT ONE, CORPORAL.
WHAT'S THIS?
SOME KIND OF CHIP? A TRACKING DEVICE MAYBE.
WOULD YOU QUIT CHEWING IN MY EAR?

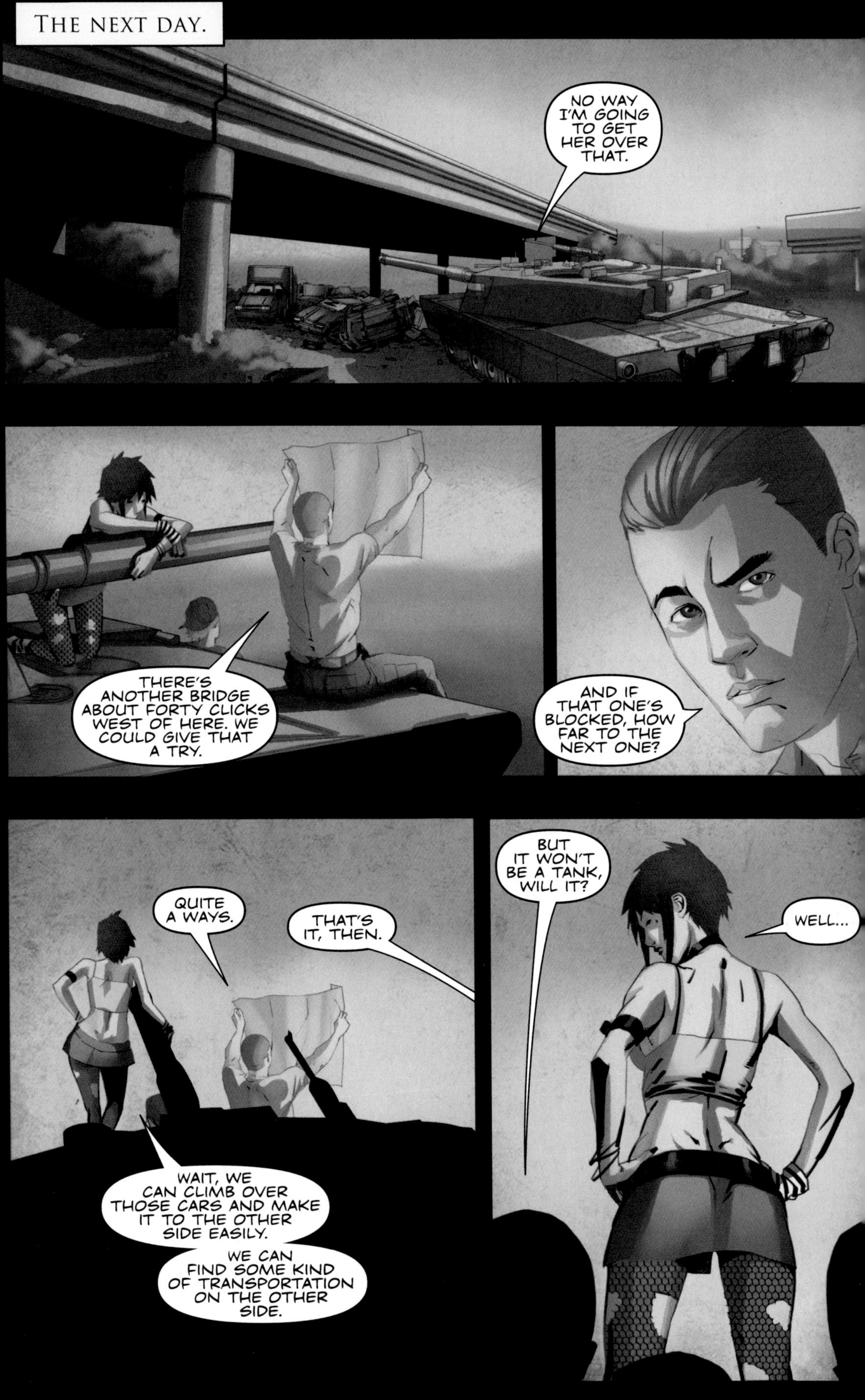
THE NEXT DAY.
NO WAY I'M GOING TO GET HER OVER THAT.
THERE'S ANOTHER BRIDGE ABOUT FORTY CLICKS WEST OF HERE. WE COULD GIVE THAT A TRY.
AND IF THAT ONE'S BLOCKED, HOW FAR TO THE NEXT ONE?
QUITE A WAYS.
THAT'S IT, THEN.
WAIT, WE CAN CLIMB OVER THOSE CARS AND MAKE IT TO THE OTHER SIDE EASILY.
WE CAN FIND SOME KIND OF TRANSPORTATION ON THE OTHER SIDE.
BUT IT WON'T BE A TANK, WILL IT?
WELL...

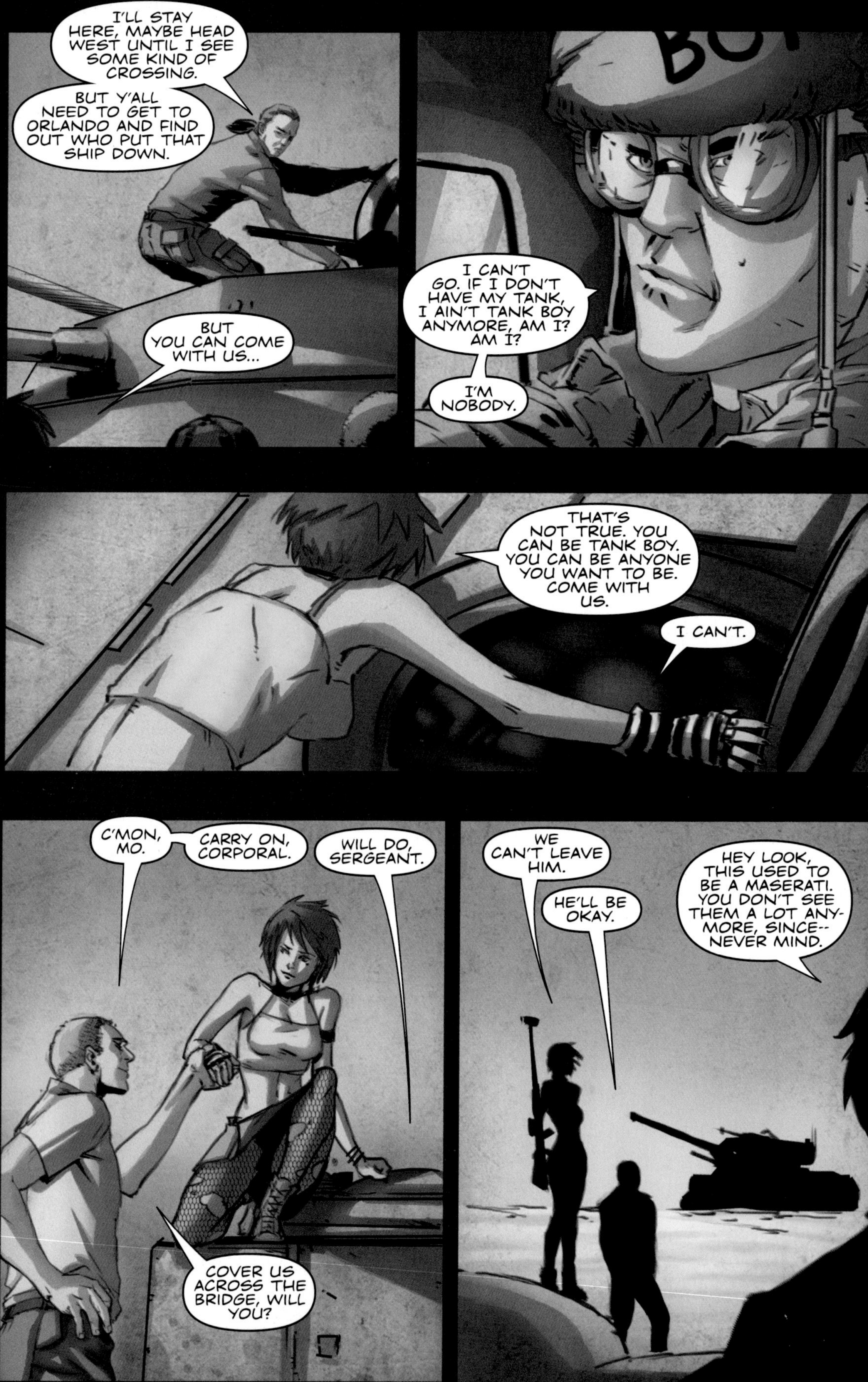
I'LL STAY HERE, MAYBE HEAD WEST UNTIL I SEE SOME KIND OF CROSSING.
BUT Y'ALL NEED TO GET TO ORLANDO AND FIND OUT WHO PUT THAT SHIP DOWN.
BUT YOU CAN COME WITH US...
BOY
I CAN'T GO. IF I DON'T HAVE MY TANK, I AIN'T TANK BOY ANYMORE, AM I? AM I?
I'M NOBODY.
THAT'S NOT TRUE. YOU CAN BE TANK BOY. YOU CAN BE ANYONE YOU WANT TO BE. COME WITH US.
I CAN'T.
C'MON, MO.
CARRY ON, CORPORAL.
WILL DO, SERGEANT.
COVER US ACROSS THE BRIDGE, WILL YOU?
WE CAN'T LEAVE HIM.
HE'LL BE OKAY.
HEY LOOK, THIS USED TO BE A MASERATI. YOU DON'T SEE THEM A LOT ANY-MORE, SINCE-- NEVER MIND.

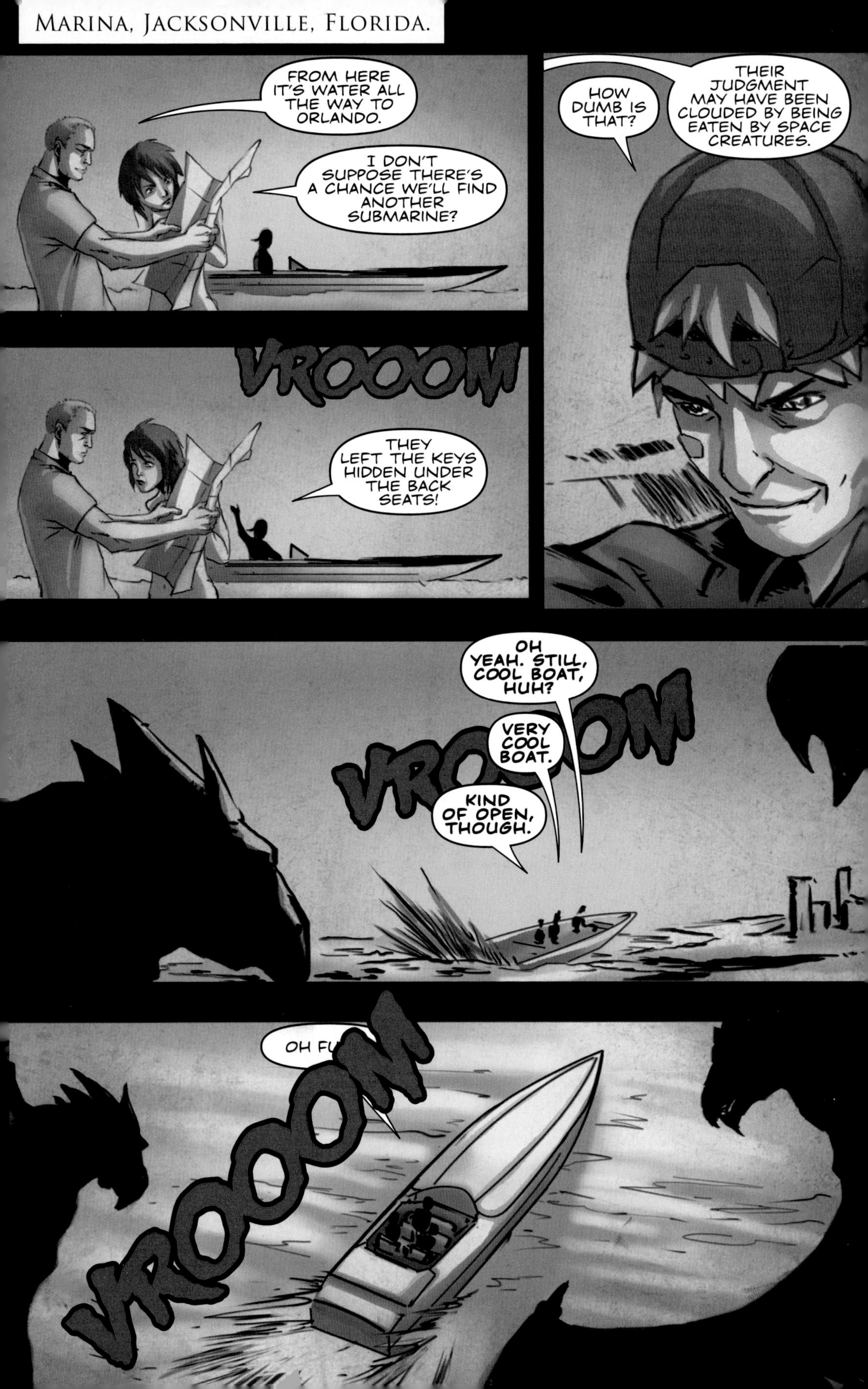

MARINA, JACKSONVILLE, FLORIDA.
FROM HERE IT'S WATER ALL THE WAY TO ORLANDO.
I DON'T SUPPOSE THERE'S A CHANCE WE'LL FIND ANOTHER SUBMARINE?
HOW DUMB IS THAT?
THEIR JUDGMENT MAY HAVE BEEN CLOUDED BY BEING EATEN BY SPACE CREATURES.
VROOOM
THEY LEFT THE KEYS HIDDEN UNDER THE BACK SEATS!
VROOOM
OH YEAH. STILL, COOL BOAT, HUH?
VERY COOL BOAT.
KIND OF OPEN, THOUGH.
OH FU
VROOOOM

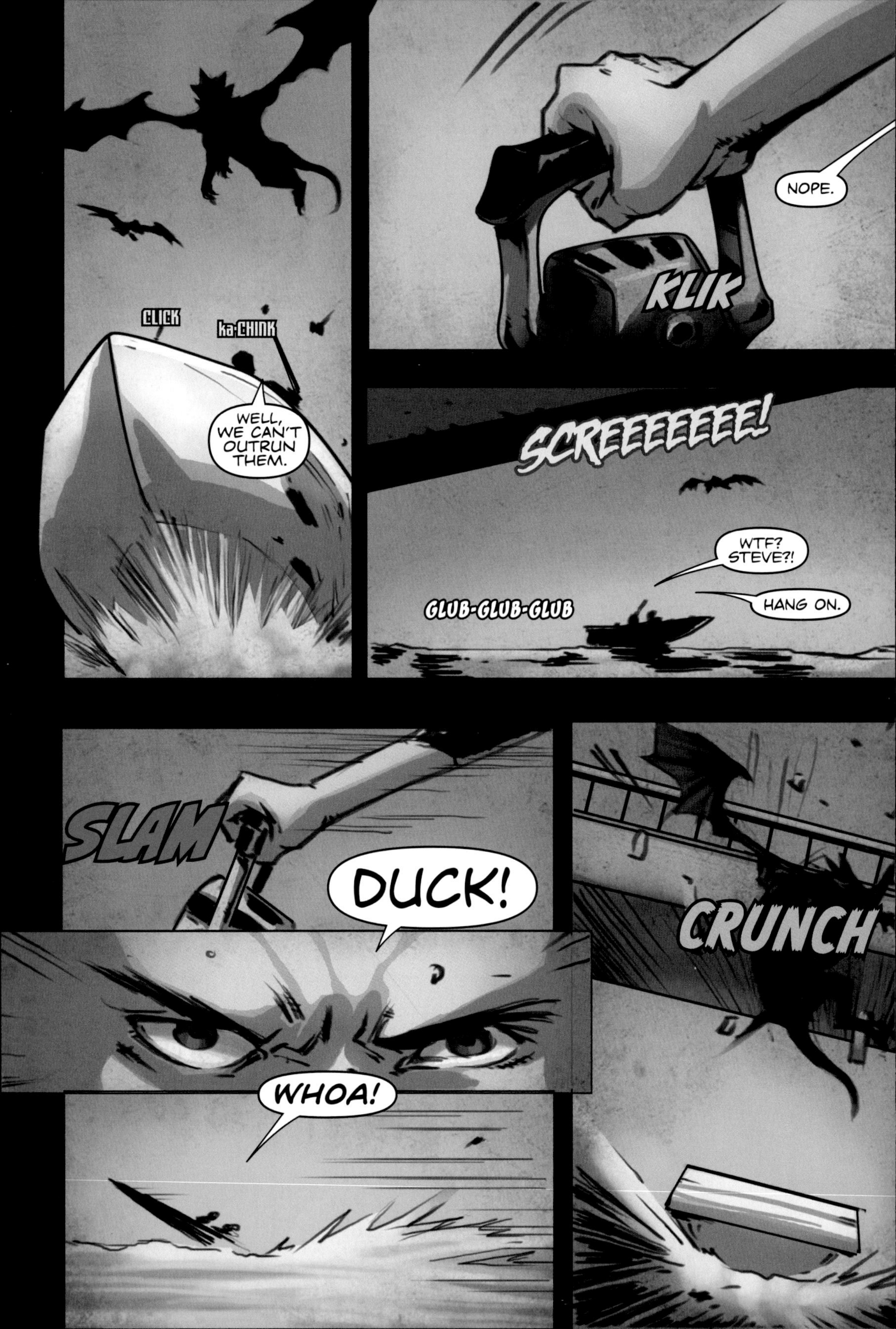
CLICK
KA-CHINK
WELL, WE CAN'T OUTRUN THEM.
NOPE.
KLIK
SCREEEEEEEE!
WTF? STEVE?!
GLUB-GLUB-GLUB
HANG ON.
SLAM
DUCK!
CRUNCH
WHOA!

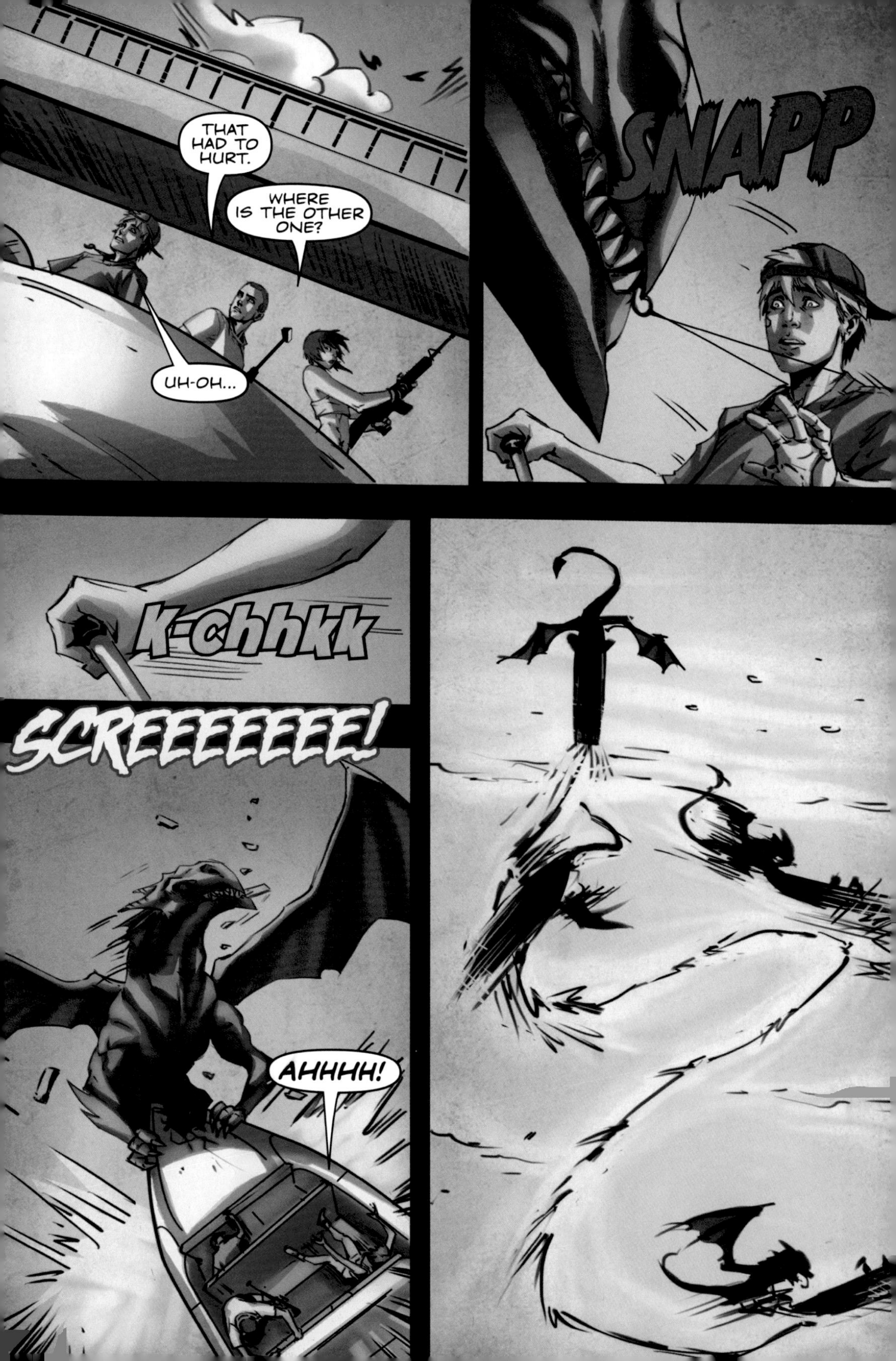
THAT HAD TO HURT.
WHERE IS THE OTHER ONE?
UH-OH...
SNAPP
K-CHHKK
SCREEEEEEEE!
AHHHH!

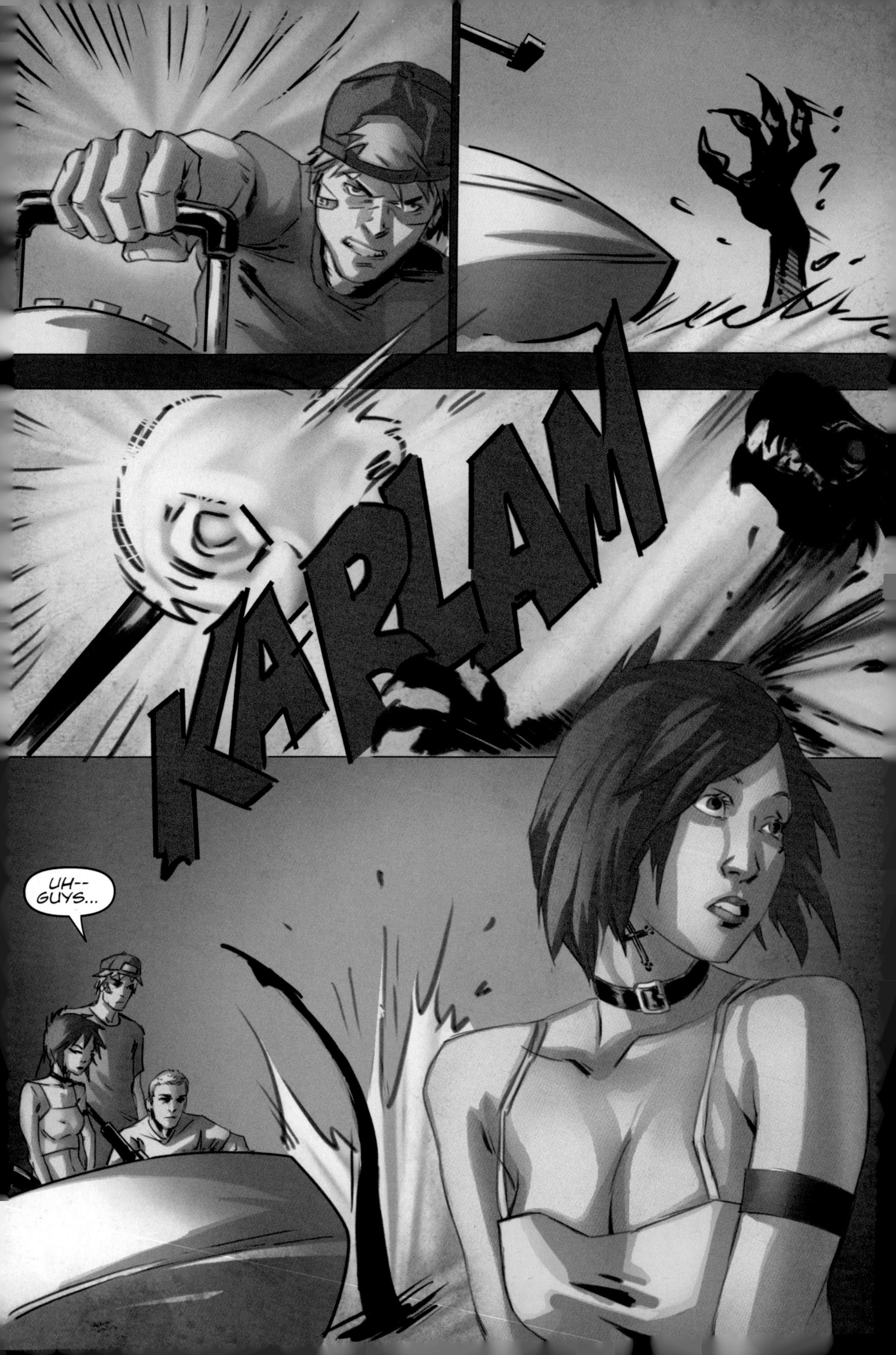
KARLAM
UH-- GUYS...

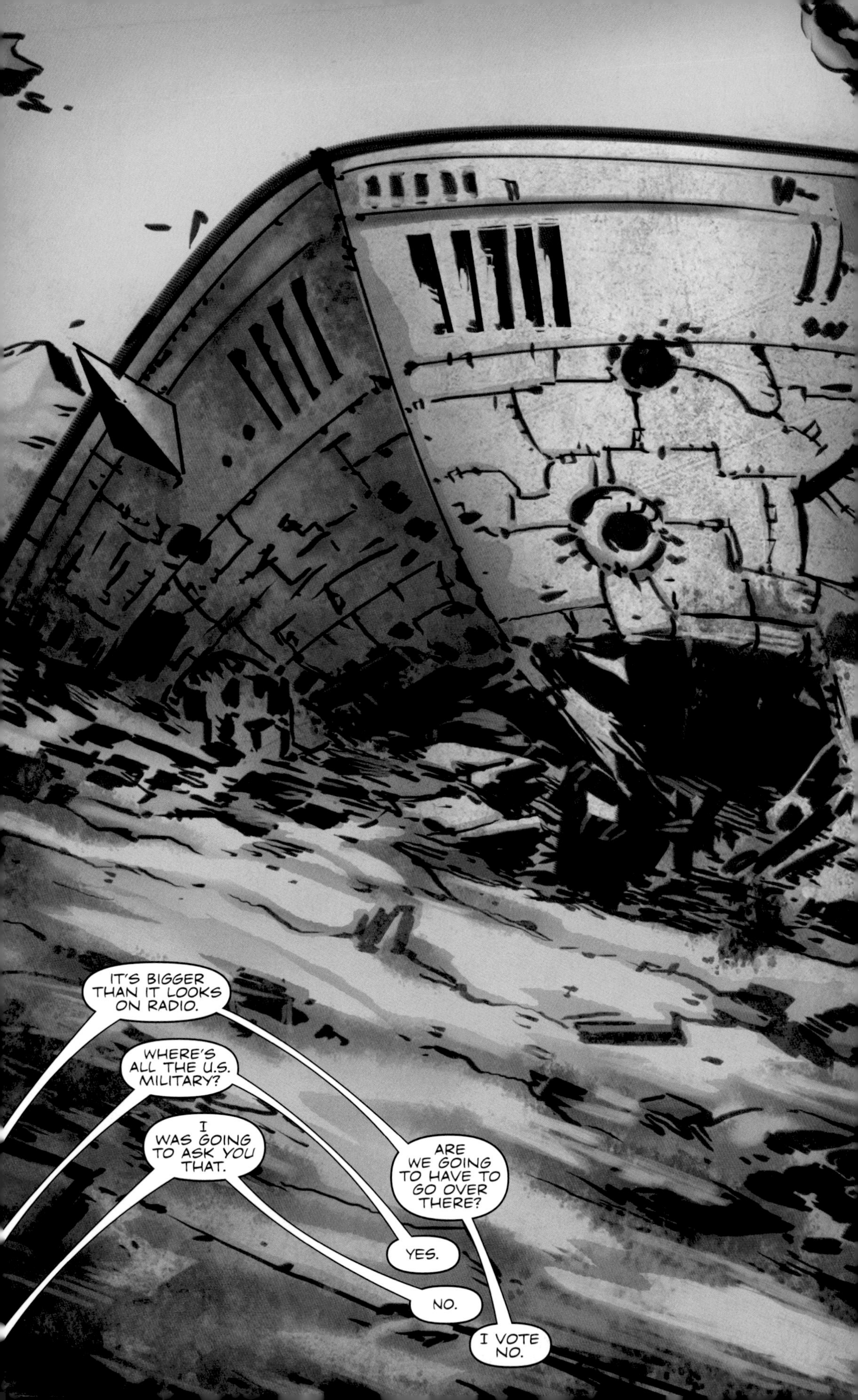
IT'S BIGGER THAN IT LOOKS ON RADIO.
WHERE'S ALL THE U.S. MILITARY?
I WAS GOING TO ASK YOU THAT.
ARE WE GOING TO HAVE TO GO OVER THERE?
YES.
NO.
I VOTE NO.

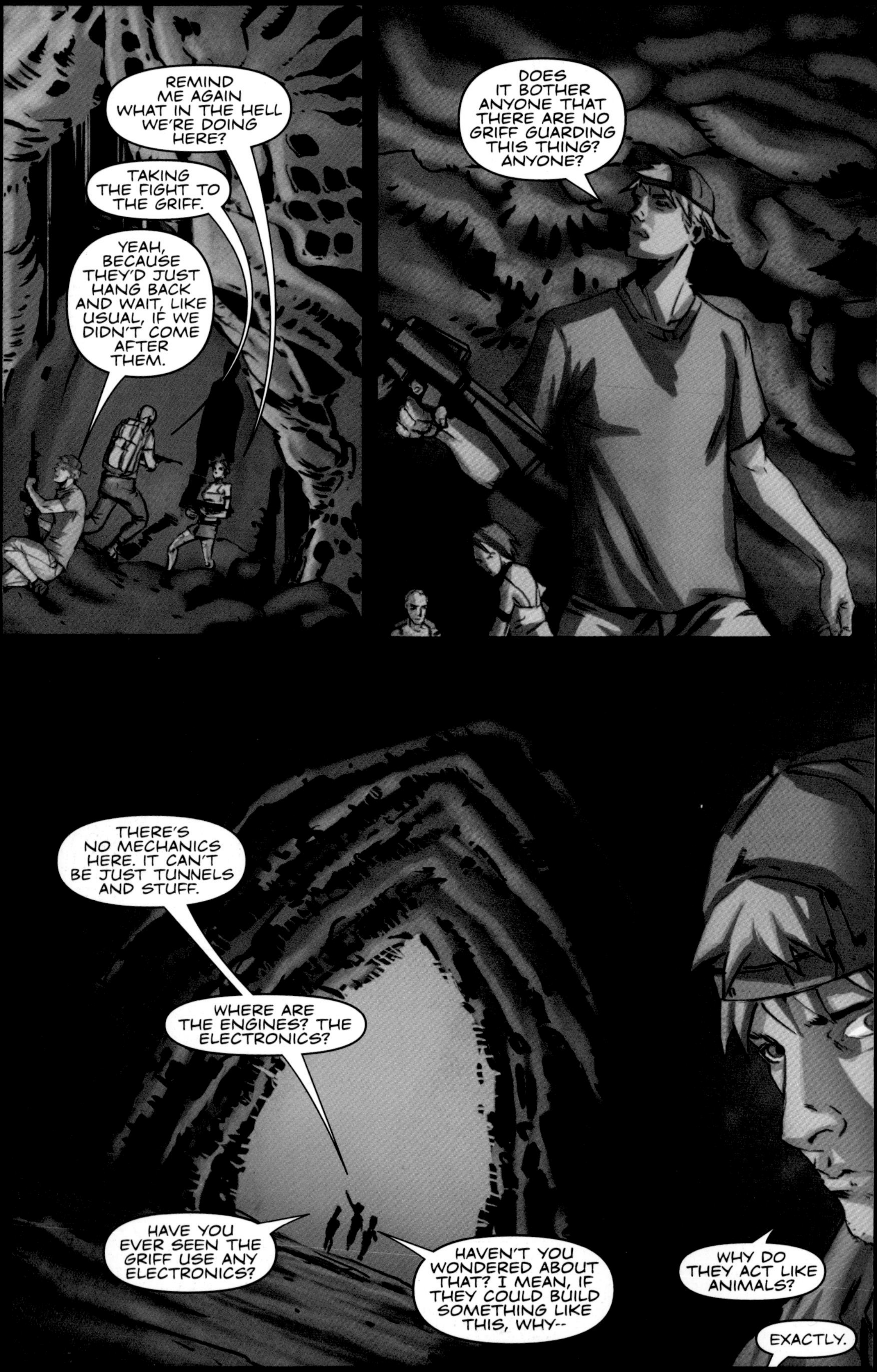
REMIND ME AGAIN WHAT IN THE HELL WE'RE DOING HERE?
TAKING THE FIGHT TO THE GRIFF.
YEAH, BECAUSE THEY'D JUST HANG BACK AND WAIT, LIKE USUAL, IF WE DIDN'T COME AFTER THEM.
DOES IT BOTHER ANYONE THAT THERE ARE NO GRIFF GUARDING THIS THING? ANYONE?
THERE'S NO MECHANICS HERE. IT CAN'T BE JUST TUNNELS AND STUFF.
WHERE ARE THE ENGINES? THE ELECTRONICS?
HAVE YOU EVER SEEN THE GRIFF USE ANY ELECTRONICS?
HAVEN'T YOU WONDERED ABOUT THAT? I MEAN, IF THEY COULD BUILD SOMETHING LIKE THIS, WHY--
WHY DO THEY ACT LIKE ANIMALS?
EXACTLY.

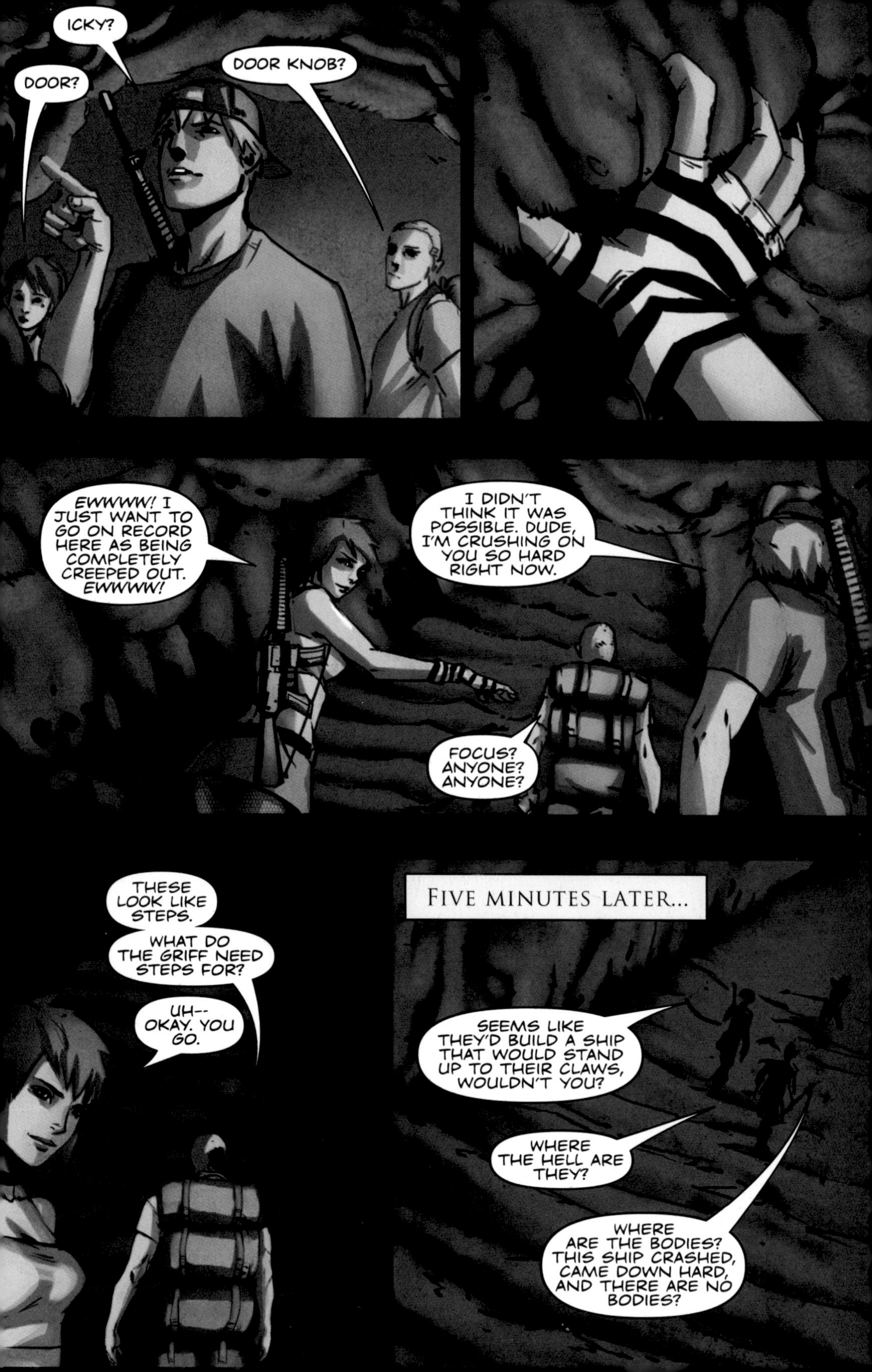
ICKY?
DOOR?
DOOR KNOB?
EWWWW! I JUST WANT TO GO ON RECORD HERE AS BEING COMPLETELY CREEPED OUT. EWWWW!
I DIDN'T THINK IT WAS POSSIBLE. DUDE, I'M CRUSHING ON YOU SO HARD RIGHT NOW.
FOCUS? ANYONE? ANYONE?
THESE LOOK LIKE STEPS.
WHAT DO THE GRIFF NEED STEPS FOR?
UH-- OKAY. YOU GO.
FIVE MINUTES LATER...
SEEMS LIKE THEY'D BUILD A SHIP THAT WOULD STAND UP TO THEIR CLAWS, WOULDN'T YOU?
WHERE THE HELL ARE THEY?
WHERE ARE THE BODIES? THIS SHIP CRASHED, CAME DOWN HARD, AND THERE ARE NO BODIES?

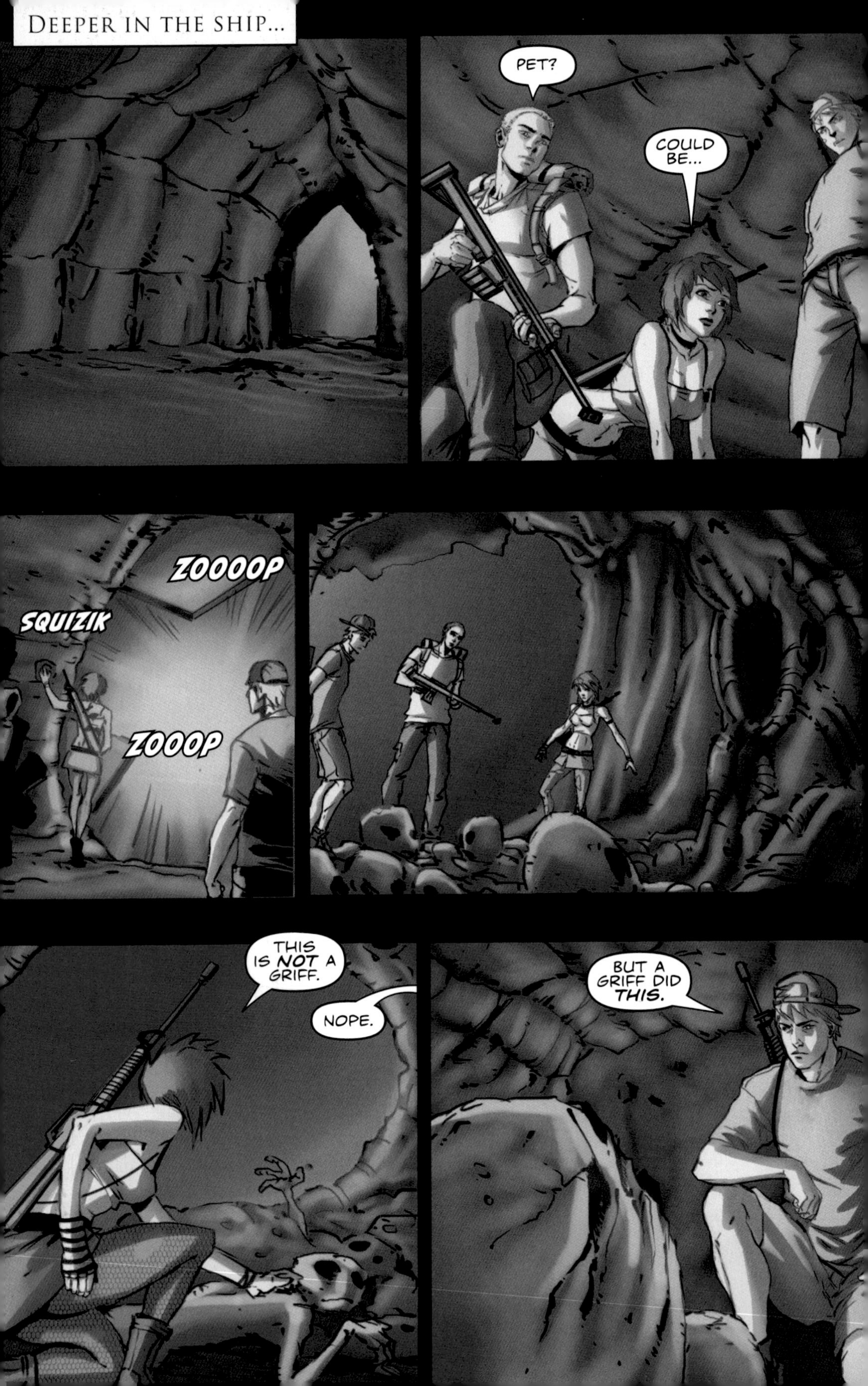
DEEPER IN THE SHIP...
PET?
COULD BE...
SQUIZIK
ZOOOOP
ZOOOP
THIS IS NOT A GRIFF.
NOPE.
BUT A GRIFF DID THIS.

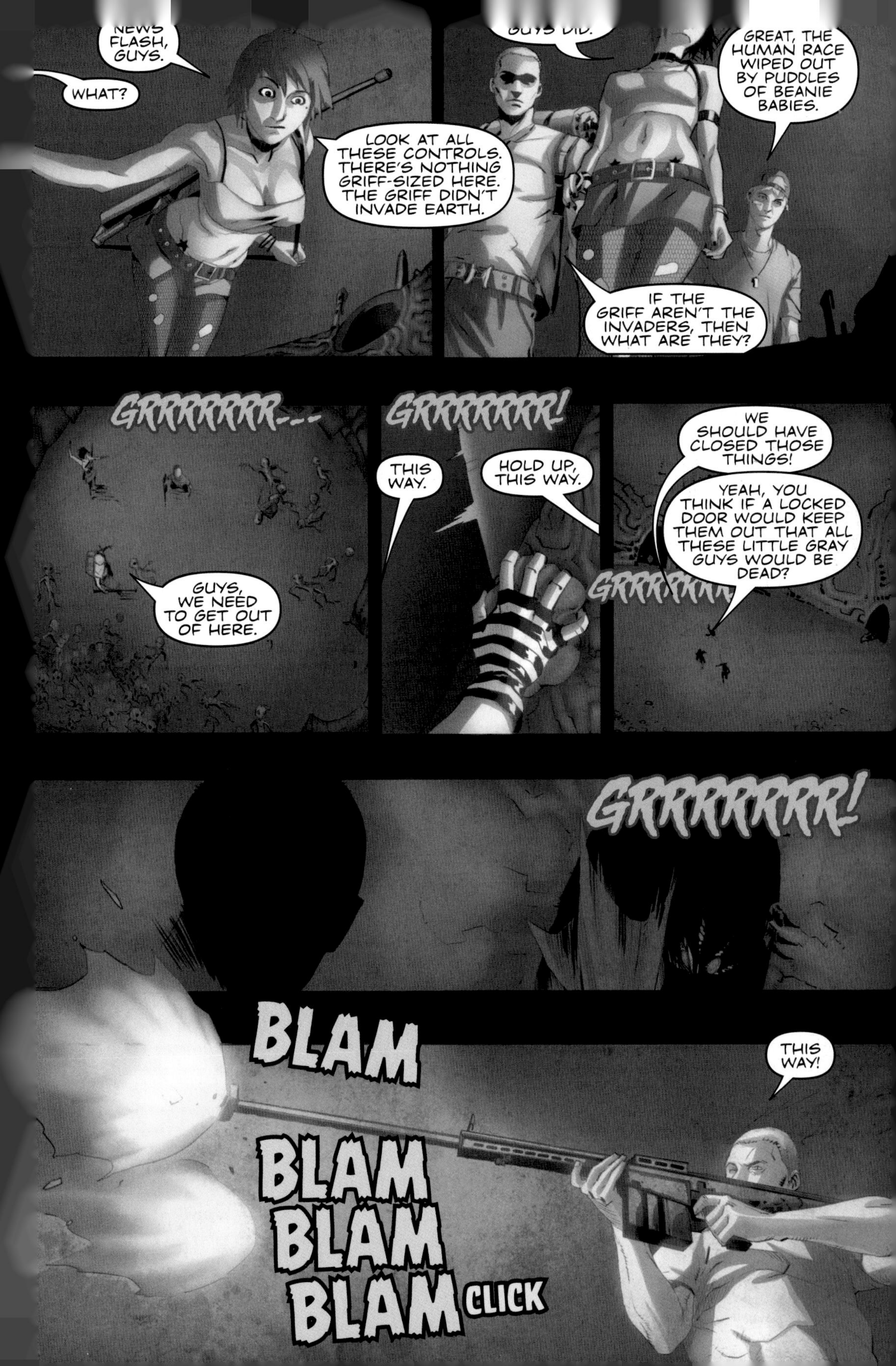
NEWS FLASH, GUYS.
WHAT?
LOOK AT ALL THESE CONTROLS. THERE'S NOTHING GRIFF-SIZED HERE. THE GRIFF DIDN'T INVADE EARTH.
GUYS DID.
GREAT, THE HUMAN RACE WIPED OUT BY PUDDLES OF BEANIE BABIES.
IF THE GRIFF AREN'T THE INVADERS, THEN WHAT ARE THEY?
GRRRRRRR- - -
GUYS, WE NEED TO GET OUT OF HERE.
GRRRRRRR!
THIS WAY.
HOLD UP, THIS WAY.
WE SHOULD HAVE CLOSED THOSE THINGS!
YEAH, YOU THINK IF A LOCKED DOOR WOULD KEEP THEM OUT THAT ALL THESE LITTLE GRAY GUYS WOULD BE DEAD?
GRRRRRRR!
BLAM
THIS WAY!
BLAM
BLAM
BLAM CLICK

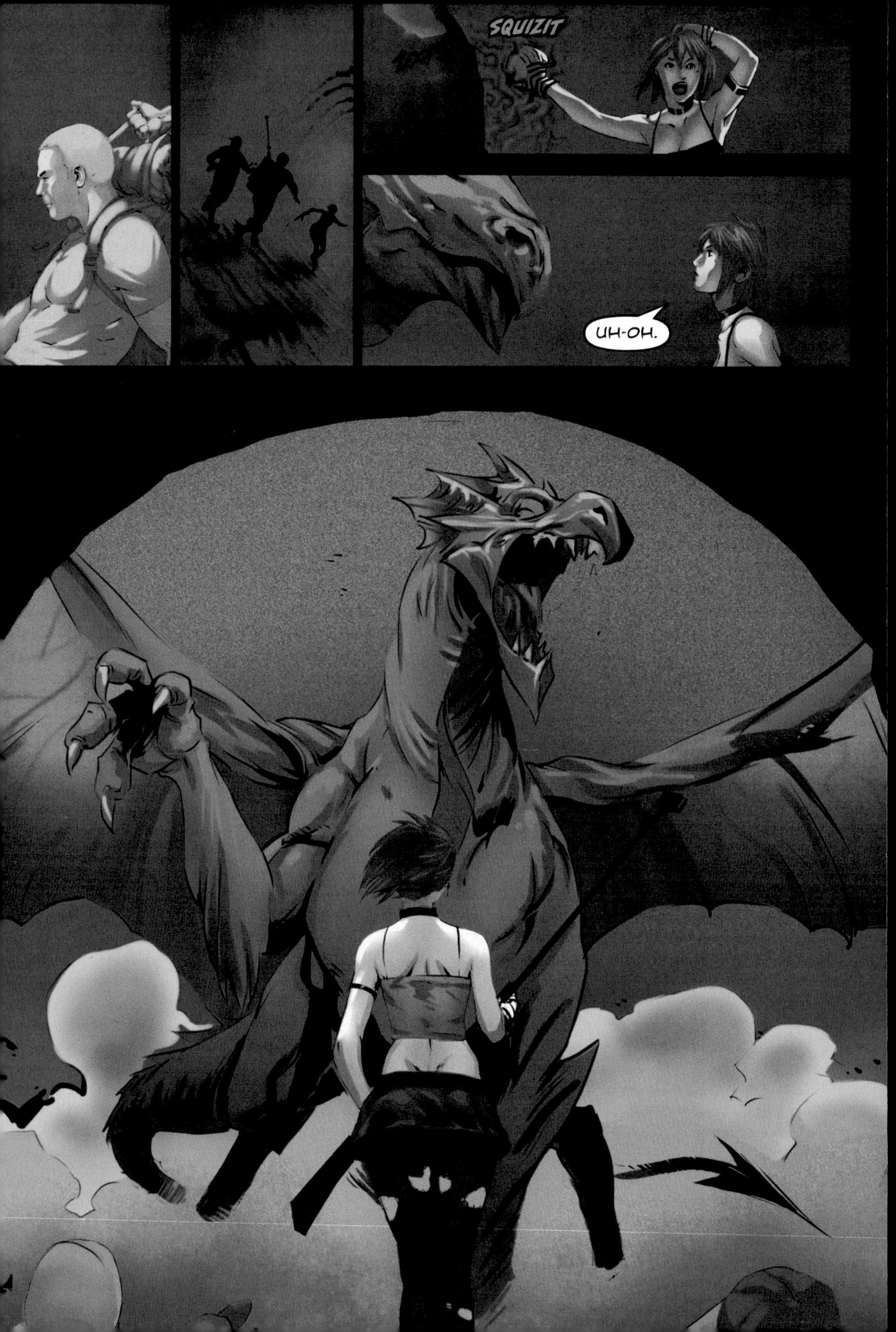
SQUIZIT
UH-OH.

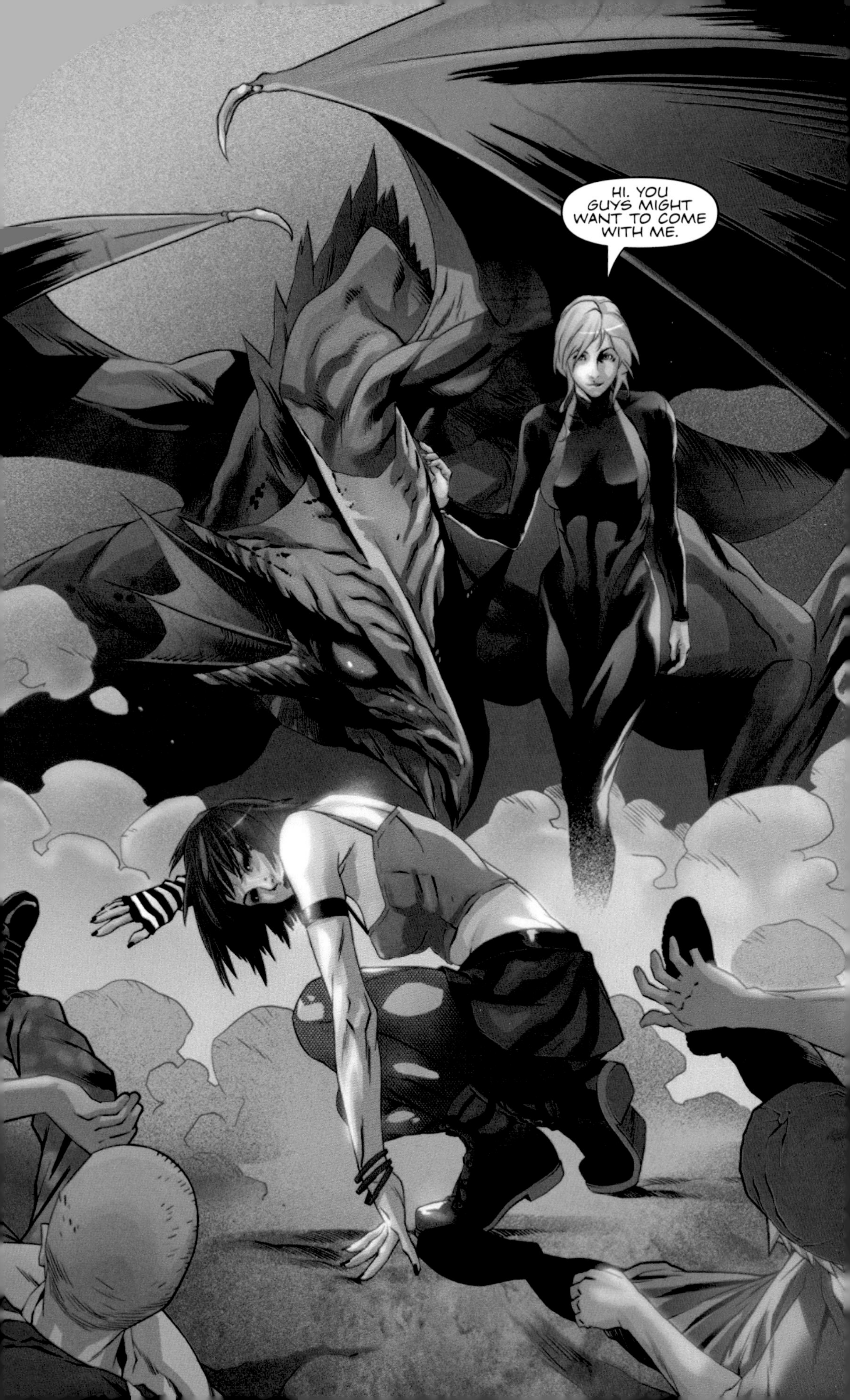
HI. YOU GUYS MIGHT WANT TO COME WITH ME.

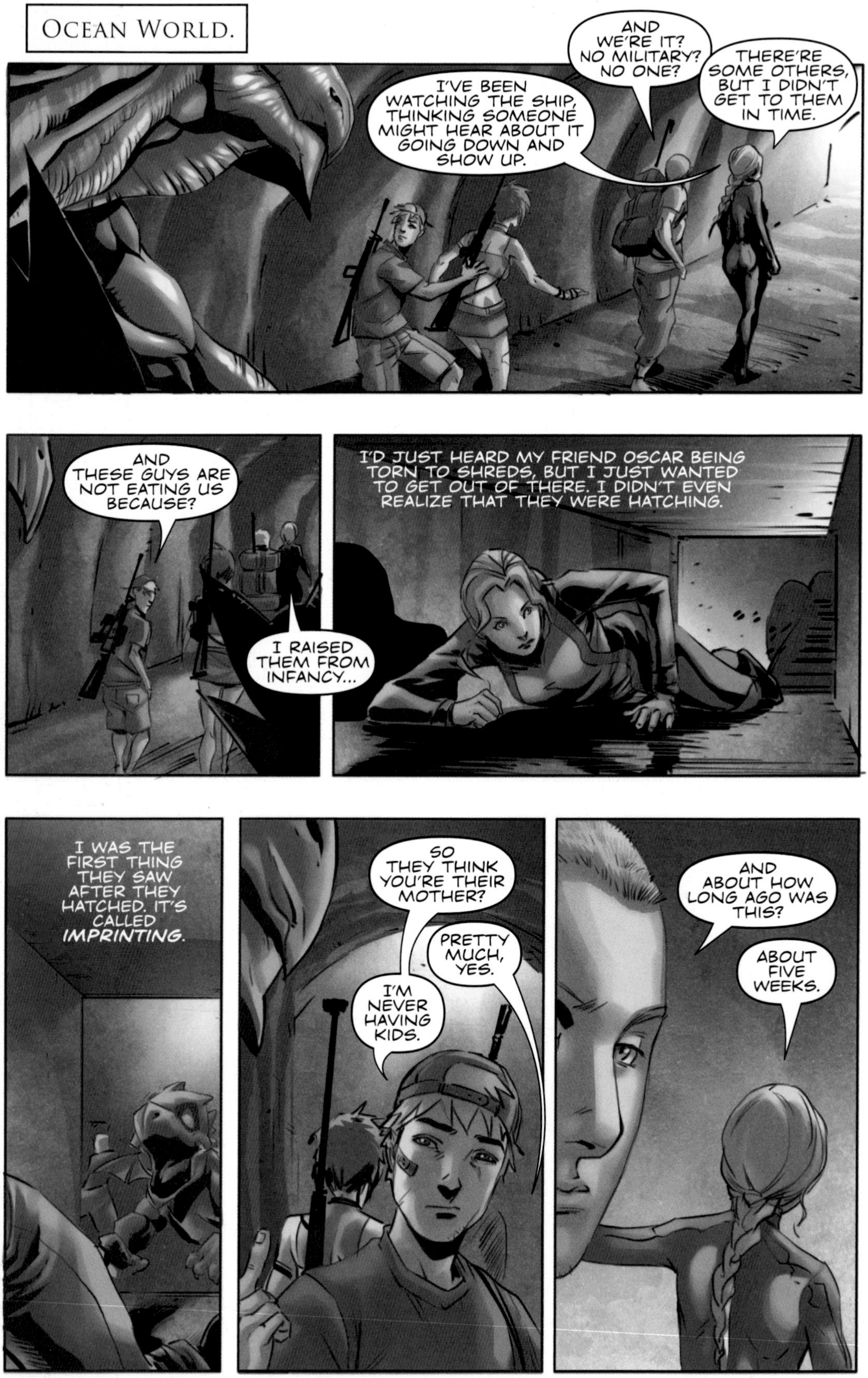
OCEAN WORLD.
I'VE BEEN WATCHING THE SHIP, THINKING SOMEONE MIGHT HEAR ABOUT IT GOING DOWN AND SHOW UP.
AND WE'RE IT? NO MILITARY? NO ONE?
THERE'RE SOME OTHERS, BUT I DIDN'T GET TO THEM IN TIME.
AND THESE GUYS ARE NOT EATING US BECAUSE?
I RAISED THEM FROM INFANCY...
I'D JUST HEARD MY FRIEND OSCAR BEING TORN TO SHREDS, BUT I JUST WANTED TO GET OUT OF THERE. I DIDN'T EVEN REALIZE THAT THEY WERE HATCHING.
I WAS THE FIRST THING THEY SAW AFTER THEY HATCHED. IT'S CALLED *IMPRINTING*.
SO THEY THINK YOU'RE THEIR MOTHER?
PRETTY MUCH, YES.
I'M NEVER HAVING KIDS.
AND ABOUT HOW LONG AGO WAS THIS?
ABOUT FIVE WEEKS.

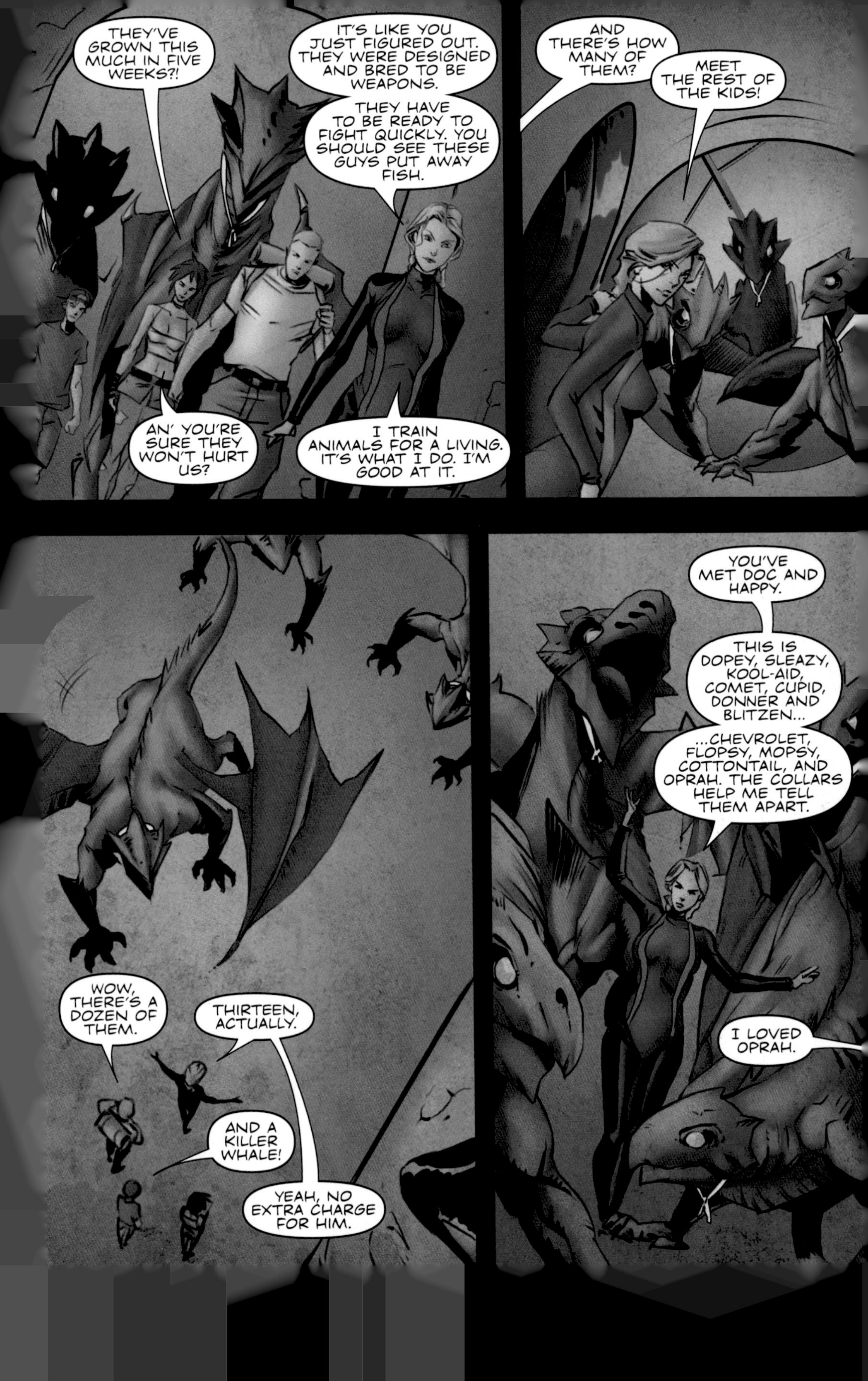
THEY'VE GROWN THIS MUCH IN FIVE WEEKS?!
IT'S LIKE YOU JUST FIGURED OUT. THEY WERE DESIGNED AND BRED TO BE WEAPONS.
THEY HAVE TO BE READY TO FIGHT QUICKLY. YOU SHOULD SEE THESE GUYS PUT AWAY FISH.
AN' YOU'RE SURE THEY WON'T HURT US?
I TRAIN ANIMALS FOR A LIVING. IT'S WHAT I DO. I'M GOOD AT IT.
AND THERE'S HOW MANY OF THEM?
MEET THE REST OF THE KIDS!
WOW, THERE'S A DOZEN OF THEM.
THIRTEEN, ACTUALLY.
AND A KILLER WHALE!
YEAH, NO EXTRA CHARGE FOR HIM.
YOU'VE MET DOC AND HAPPY.
THIS IS DOPEY, SLEAZY, KOOL-AID, COMET, CUPID, DONNER AND BLITZEN...
...CHEVROLET, FLOPSY, MOPSY, COTTONTAIL, AND OPRAH. THE COLLARS HELP ME TELL THEM APART.
I LOVED OPRAH.

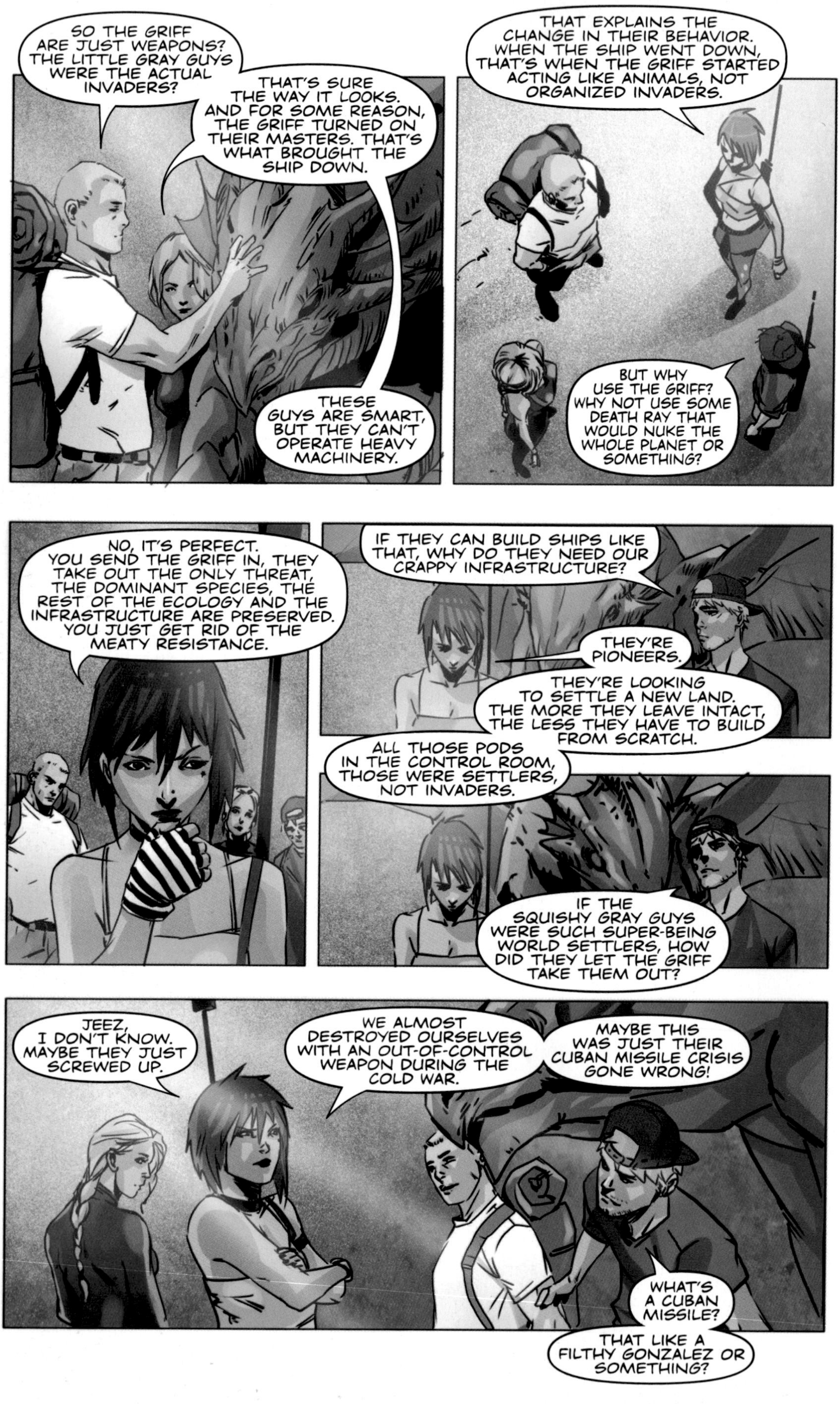
SO THE GRIFF ARE JUST WEAPONS? THE LITTLE GRAY GUYS WERE THE ACTUAL INVADERS?
THAT'S SURE THE WAY IT LOOKS. AND FOR SOME REASON, THE GRIFF TURNED ON THEIR MASTERS. THAT'S WHAT BROUGHT THE SHIP DOWN.
THESE GUYS ARE SMART, BUT THEY CAN'T OPERATE HEAVY MACHINERY.
THAT EXPLAINS THE CHANGE IN THEIR BEHAVIOR. WHEN THE SHIP WENT DOWN, THAT'S WHEN THE GRIFF STARTED ACTING LIKE ANIMALS, NOT ORGANIZED INVADERS.
BUT WHY USE THE GRIFF? WHY NOT USE SOME DEATH RAY THAT WOULD NUKE THE WHOLE PLANET OR SOMETHING?
NO, IT'S PERFECT. YOU SEND THE GRIFF IN, THEY TAKE OUT THE ONLY THREAT, THE DOMINANT SPECIES, THE REST OF THE ECOLOGY AND THE INFRASTRUCTURE ARE PRESERVED. YOU JUST GET RID OF THE MEATY RESISTANCE.
IF THEY CAN BUILD SHIPS LIKE THAT, WHY DO THEY NEED OUR CRAPPY INFRASTRUCTURE?
THEY'RE PIONEERS.
THEY'RE LOOKING TO SETTLE A NEW LAND. THE MORE THEY LEAVE INTACT, THE LESS THEY HAVE TO BUILD FROM SCRATCH.
ALL THOSE PODS IN THE CONTROL ROOM, THOSE WERE SETTLERS, NOT INVADERS.
IF THE SQUISHY GRAY GUYS WERE SUCH SUPER-BEING WORLD SETTLERS, HOW DID THEY LET THE GRIFF TAKE THEM OUT?
JEEZ, I DON'T KNOW. MAYBE THEY JUST SCREWED UP.
WE ALMOST DESTROYED OURSELVES WITH AN OUT-OF-CONTROL WEAPON DURING THE COLD WAR.
MAYBE THIS WAS JUST THEIR CUBAN MISSILE CRISIS GONE WRONG!
WHAT'S A CUBAN MISSILE?
THAT LIKE A FILTHY GONZALEZ OR SOMETHING?

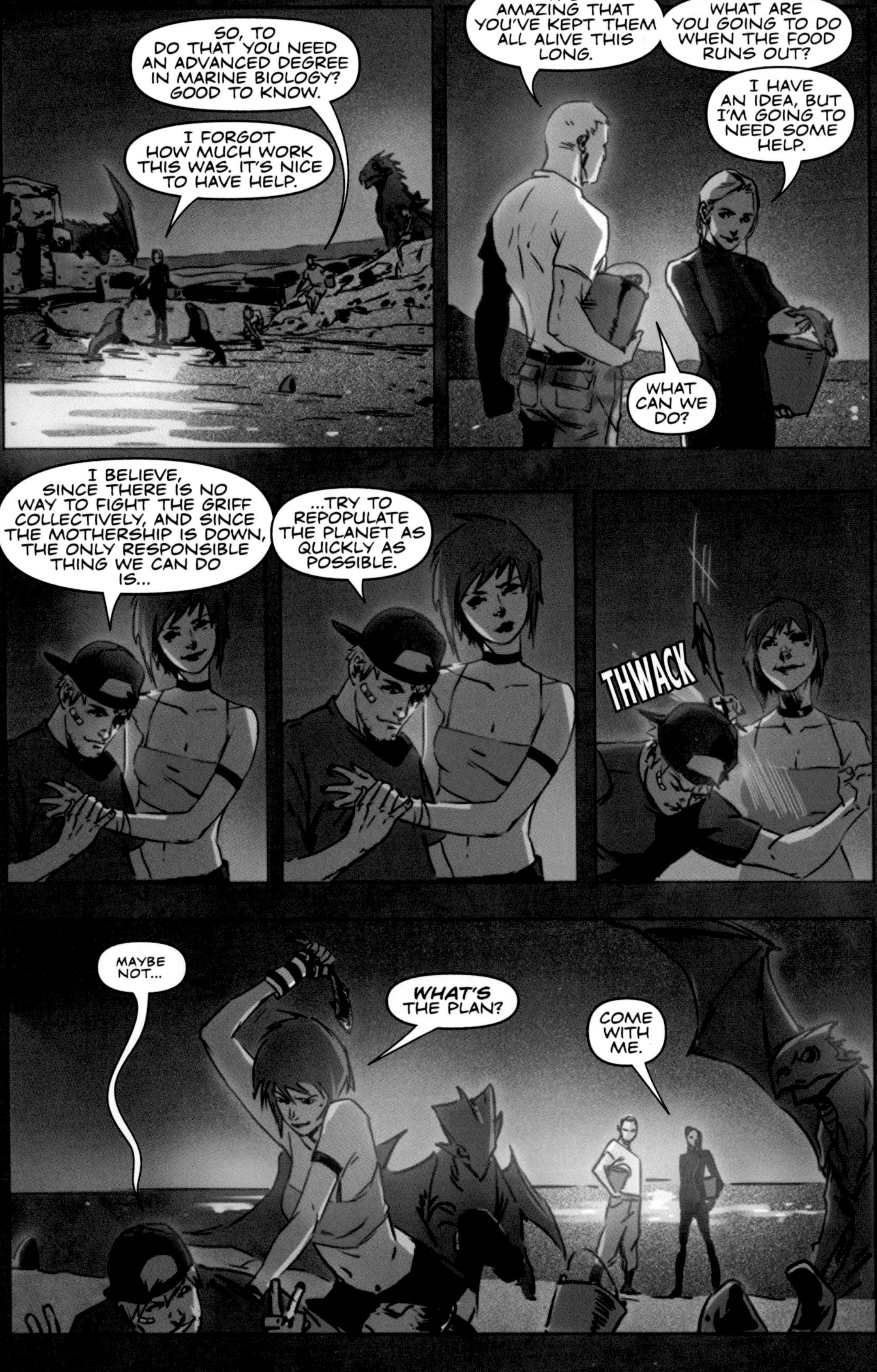
SO, TO DO THAT YOU NEED AN ADVANCED DEGREE IN MARINE BIOLOGY? GOOD TO KNOW.
I FORGOT HOW MUCH WORK THIS WAS. IT'S NICE TO HAVE HELP.
IT'S AMAZING THAT YOU'VE KEPT THEM ALL ALIVE THIS LONG.
WHAT ARE YOU GOING TO DO WHEN THE FOOD RUNS OUT?
I HAVE AN IDEA, BUT I'M GOING TO NEED SOME HELP.
WHAT CAN WE DO?
I BELIEVE, SINCE THERE IS NO WAY TO FIGHT THE GRIFF COLLECTIVELY, AND SINCE THE MOTHERSHIP IS DOWN, THE ONLY RESPONSIBLE THING WE CAN DO IS...
...TRY TO REPOPULATE THE PLANET AS QUICKLY AS POSSIBLE.
THWACK
MAYBE NOT...
WHAT'S THE PLAN?
COME WITH ME.

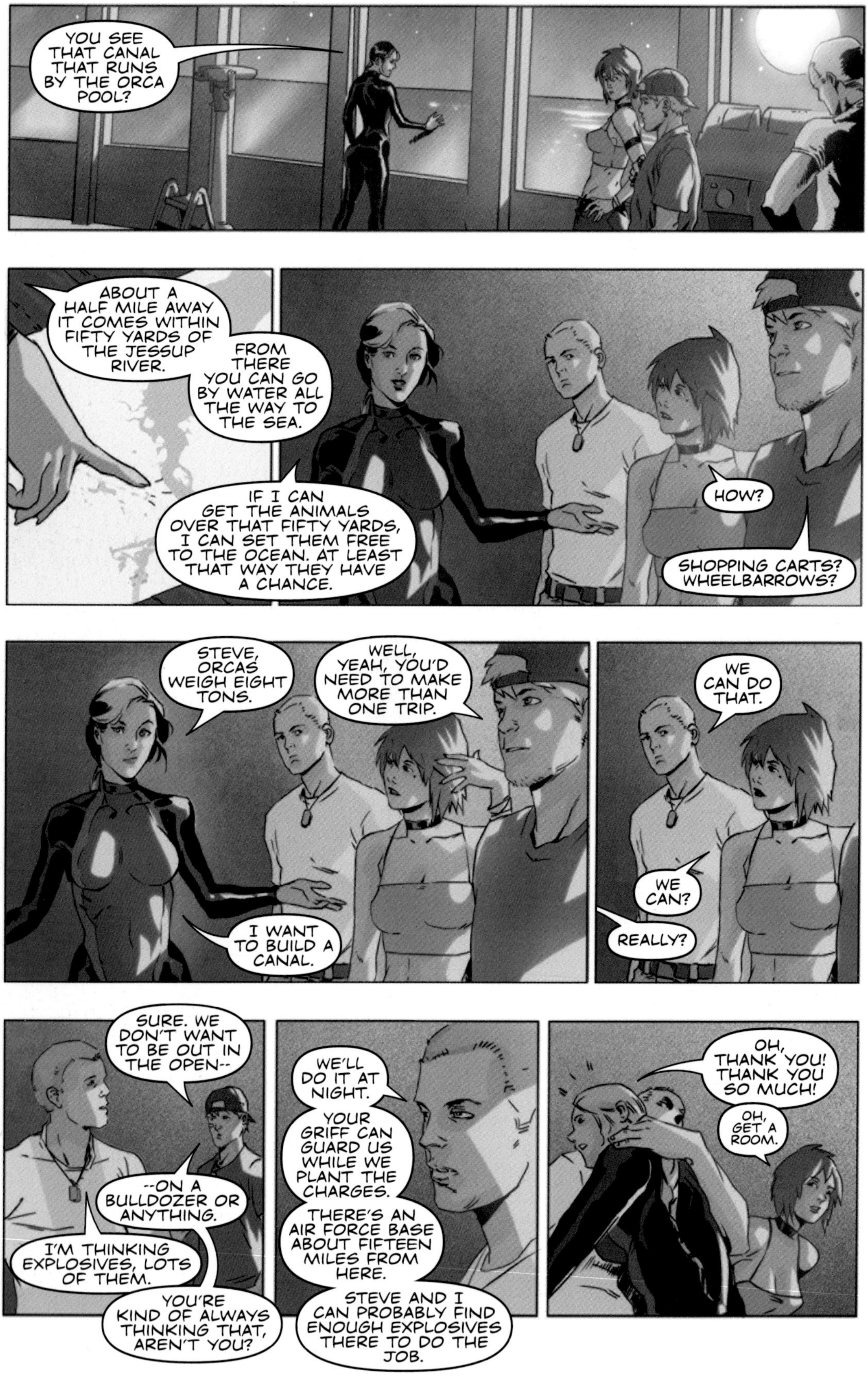
YOU SEE THAT CANAL THAT RUNS BY THE ORCA POOL?
ABOUT A HALF MILE AWAY IT COMES WITHIN FIFTY YARDS OF THE JESSUP RIVER.
FROM THERE YOU CAN GO BY WATER ALL THE WAY TO THE SEA.
IF I CAN GET THE ANIMALS OVER THAT FIFTY YARDS, I CAN SET THEM FREE TO THE OCEAN. AT LEAST THAT WAY THEY HAVE A CHANCE.
HOW?
SHOPPING CARTS? WHEELBARROWS?
STEVE, ORCAS WEIGH EIGHT TONS.
WELL, YEAH, YOU'D NEED TO MAKE MORE THAN ONE TRIP.
I WANT TO BUILD A CANAL.
WE CAN DO THAT.
WE CAN?
REALLY?
SURE. WE DON'T WANT TO BE OUT IN THE OPEN--
--ON A BULLDOZER OR ANYTHING.
I'M THINKING EXPLOSIVES, LOTS OF THEM.
YOU'RE KIND OF ALWAYS THINKING THAT, AREN'T YOU?
WE'LL DO IT AT NIGHT.
YOUR GRIFF CAN GUARD US WHILE WE PLANT THE CHARGES.
THERE'S AN AIR FORCE BASE ABOUT FIFTEEN MILES FROM HERE.
STEVE AND I CAN PROBABLY FIND ENOUGH EXPLOSIVES THERE TO DO THE JOB.
OH, THANK YOU! THANK YOU SO MUCH!
OH, GET A ROOM.

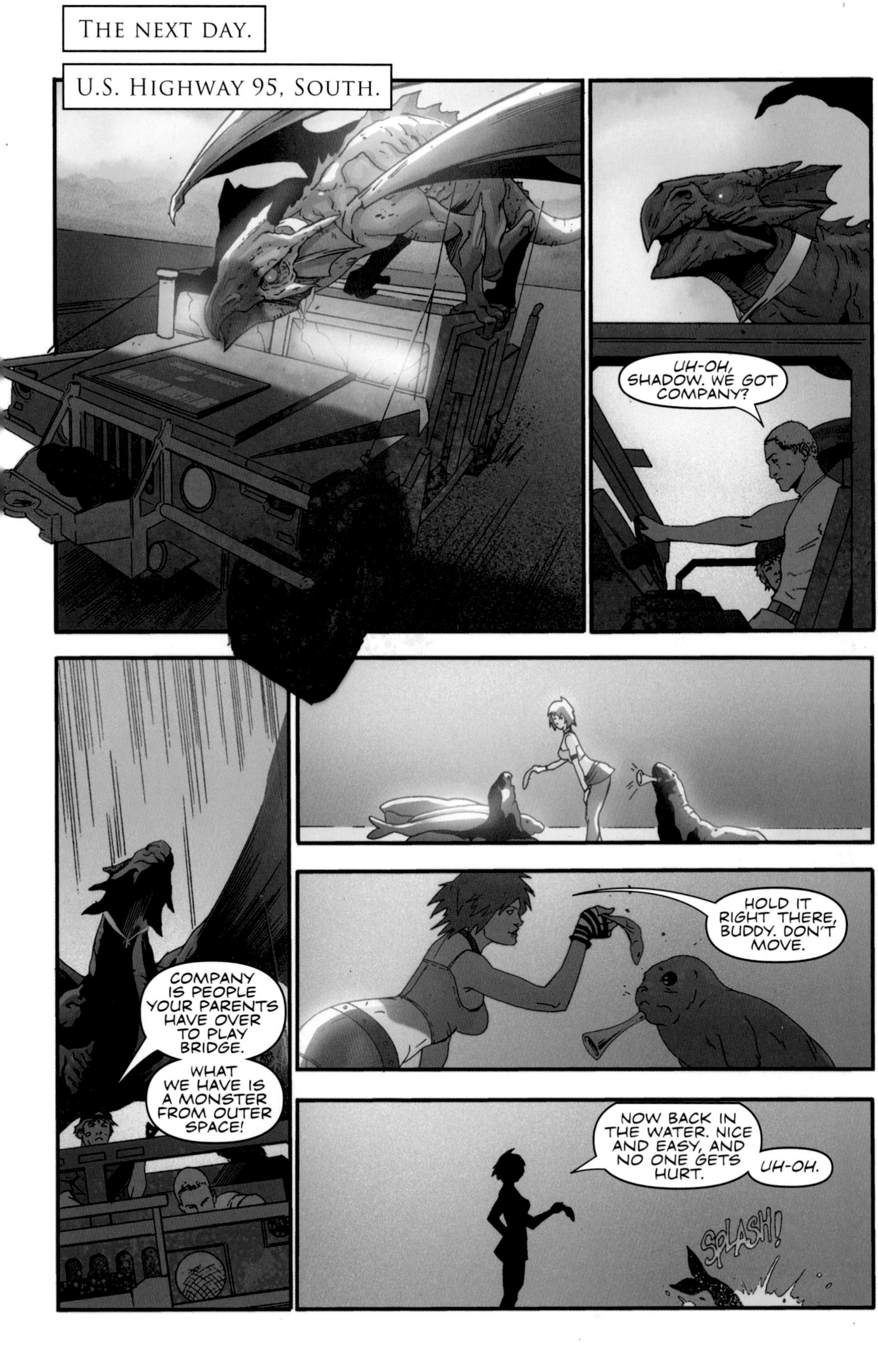
THE NEXT DAY.
U.S. HIGHWAY 95, SOUTH.
UH-OH, SHADOW. WE GOT COMPANY?
COMPANY IS PEOPLE YOUR PARENTS HAVE OVER TO PLAY BRIDGE.
WHAT WE HAVE IS A MONSTER FROM OUTER SPACE!
HOLD IT RIGHT THERE, BUDDY. DON'T MOVE.
NOW BACK IN THE WATER. NICE AND EASY, AND NO ONE GETS HURT.
UH-OH.
SPLASH!

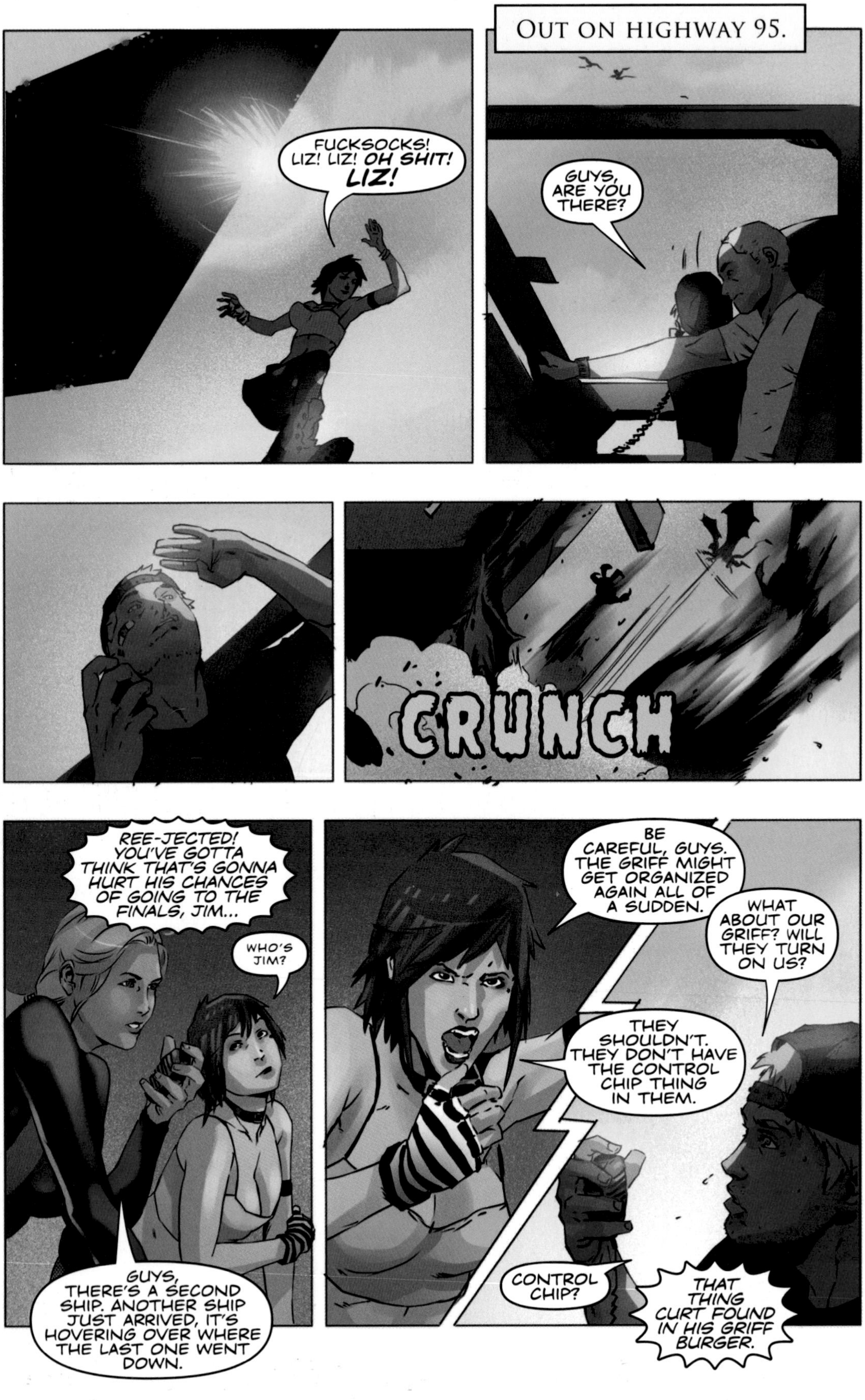
FUCKSOCKS! LIZ! LIZ! OH SHIT! LIZ!
OUT ON HIGHWAY 95.
GUYS, ARE YOU THERE?
CRUNCH
REE-JECTED! YOU'VE GOTTA THINK THAT'S GONNA HURT HIS CHANCES OF GOING TO THE FINALS, JIM...
WHO'S JIM?
GUYS, THERE'S A SECOND SHIP. ANOTHER SHIP JUST ARRIVED, IT'S HOVERING OVER WHERE THE LAST ONE WENT DOWN.
BE CAREFUL, GUYS. THE GRIFF MIGHT GET ORGANIZED AGAIN ALL OF A SUDDEN.
WHAT ABOUT OUR GRIFF? WILL THEY TURN ON US?
THEY SHOULDN'T. THEY DON'T HAVE THE CONTROL CHIP THING IN THEM.
CONTROL CHIP?
THAT THING CURT FOUND IN HIS GRIFF BURGER.

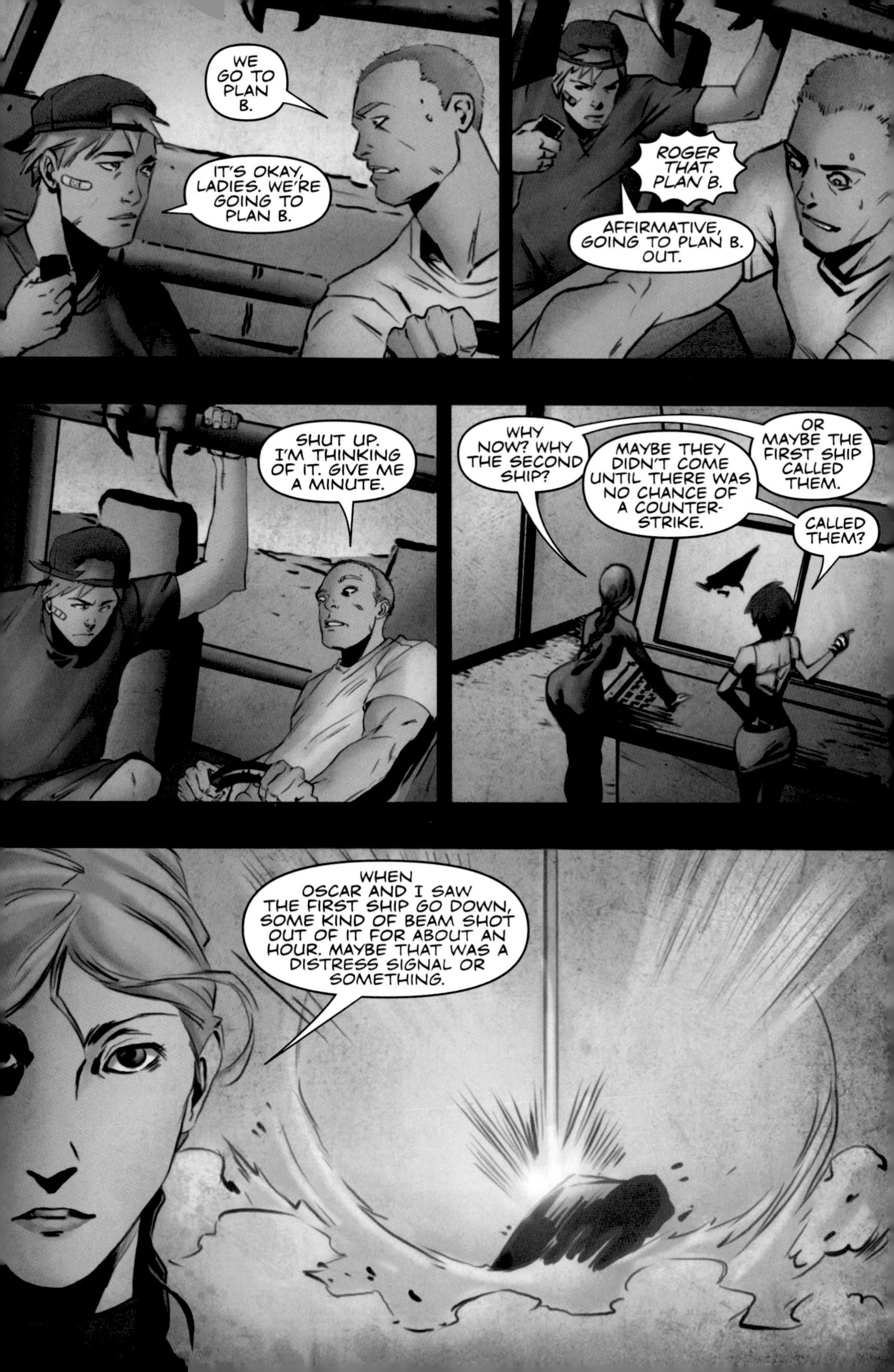
WE GO TO PLAN B.
IT'S OKAY, LADIES. WE'RE GOING TO PLAN B.
ROGER THAT. PLAN B.
AFFIRMATIVE, GOING TO PLAN B. OUT.
SHUT UP. I'M THINKING OF IT. GIVE ME A MINUTE.
WHY NOW? WHY THE SECOND SHIP?
MAYBE THEY DIDN'T COME UNTIL THERE WAS NO CHANCE OF A COUNTER-STRIKE.
OR MAYBE THE FIRST SHIP CALLED THEM.
CALLED THEM?
WHEN OSCAR AND I SAW THE FIRST SHIP GO DOWN, SOME KIND OF BEAM SHOT OUT OF IT FOR ABOUT AN HOUR. MAYBE THAT WAS A DISTRESS SIGNAL OR SOMETHING.

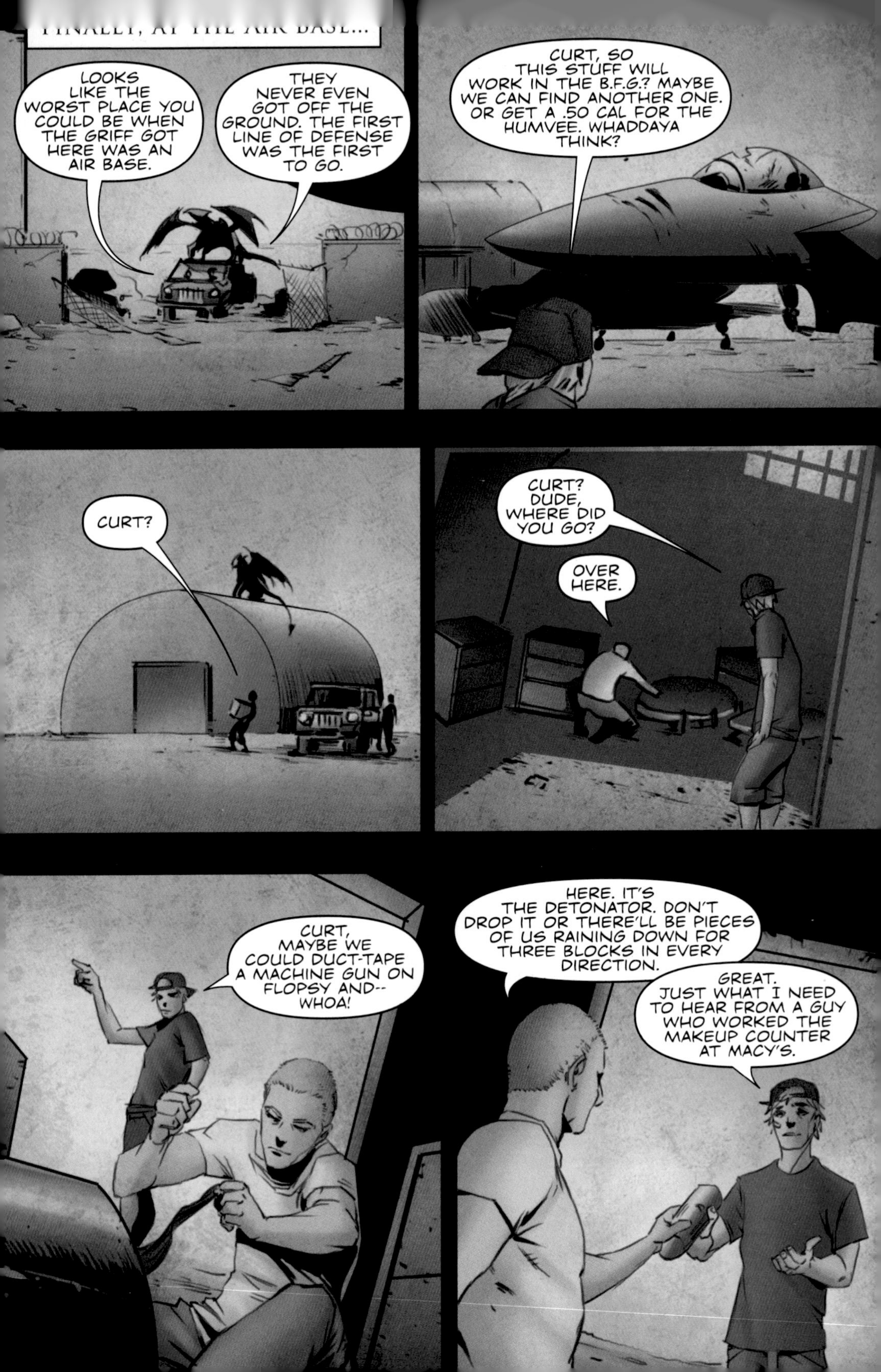
FINALLY, AT THE AIR BASE...
LOOKS LIKE THE WORST PLACE YOU COULD BE WHEN THE GRIFF GOT HERE WAS AN AIR BASE.
THEY NEVER EVEN GOT OFF THE GROUND. THE FIRST LINE OF DEFENSE WAS THE FIRST TO GO.
CURT, SO THIS STUFF WILL WORK IN THE B.F.G.? MAYBE WE CAN FIND ANOTHER ONE. OR GET A .50 CAL FOR THE HUMVEE. WHADDAYA THINK?
CURT?
CURT? DUDE, WHERE DID YOU GO?
OVER HERE.
CURT, MAYBE WE COULD DUCT-TAPE A MACHINE GUN ON FLOPSY AND-- WHOA!
HERE. IT'S THE DETONATOR. DON'T DROP IT OR THERE'LL BE PIECES OF US RAINING DOWN FOR THREE BLOCKS IN EVERY DIRECTION.
GREAT. JUST WHAT I NEED TO HEAR FROM A GUY WHO WORKED THE MAKEUP COUNTER AT MACY'S.

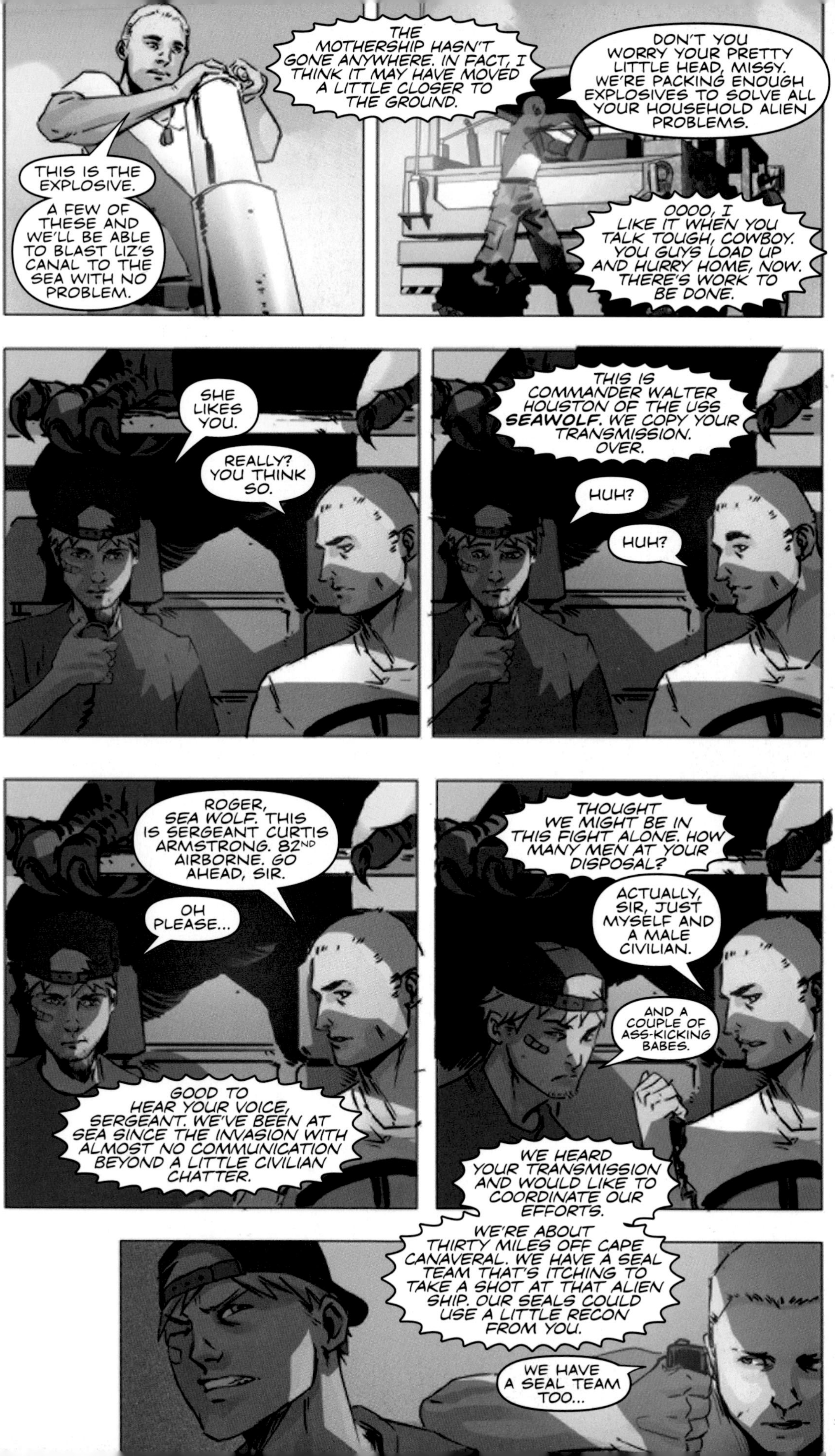
THIS IS THE EXPLOSIVE.
A FEW OF THESE AND WE'LL BE ABLE TO BLAST LIZ'S CANAL TO THE SEA WITH NO PROBLEM.
THE MOTHERSHIP HASN'T GONE ANYWHERE. IN FACT, I THINK IT MAY HAVE MOVED A LITTLE CLOSER TO THE GROUND.
DON'T YOU WORRY YOUR PRETTY LITTLE HEAD, MISSY. WE'RE PACKING ENOUGH EXPLOSIVES TO SOLVE ALL YOUR HOUSEHOLD ALIEN PROBLEMS.
OOOO, I LIKE IT WHEN YOU TALK TOUGH, COWBOY. YOU GUYS LOAD UP AND HURRY HOME, NOW. THERE'S WORK TO BE DONE.
SHE LIKES YOU.
REALLY? YOU THINK SO.
THIS IS COMMANDER WALTER HOUSTON OF THE USS SEAWOLF. WE COPY YOUR TRANSMISSION. OVER.
HUH?
HUH?
ROGER, SEA WOLF. THIS IS SERGEANT CURTIS ARMSTRONG. 82ND AIRBORNE. GO AHEAD, SIR.
OH PLEASE...
GOOD TO HEAR YOUR VOICE, SERGEANT. WE'VE BEEN AT SEA SINCE THE INVASION WITH ALMOST NO COMMUNICATION BEYOND A LITTLE CIVILIAN CHATTER.
THOUGHT WE MIGHT BE IN THIS FIGHT ALONE. HOW MANY MEN AT YOUR DISPOSAL?
ACTUALLY, SIR, JUST MYSELF AND A MALE CIVILIAN.
AND A COUPLE OF ASS-KICKING BABES.
WE HEARD YOUR TRANSMISSION AND WOULD LIKE TO COORDINATE OUR EFFORTS.
WE'RE ABOUT THIRTY MILES OFF CAPE CANAVERAL. WE HAVE A SEAL TEAM THAT'S ITCHING TO TAKE A SHOT AT THAT ALIEN SHIP. OUR SEALS COULD USE A LITTLE RECON FROM YOU.
WE HAVE A SEAL TEAM TOO...

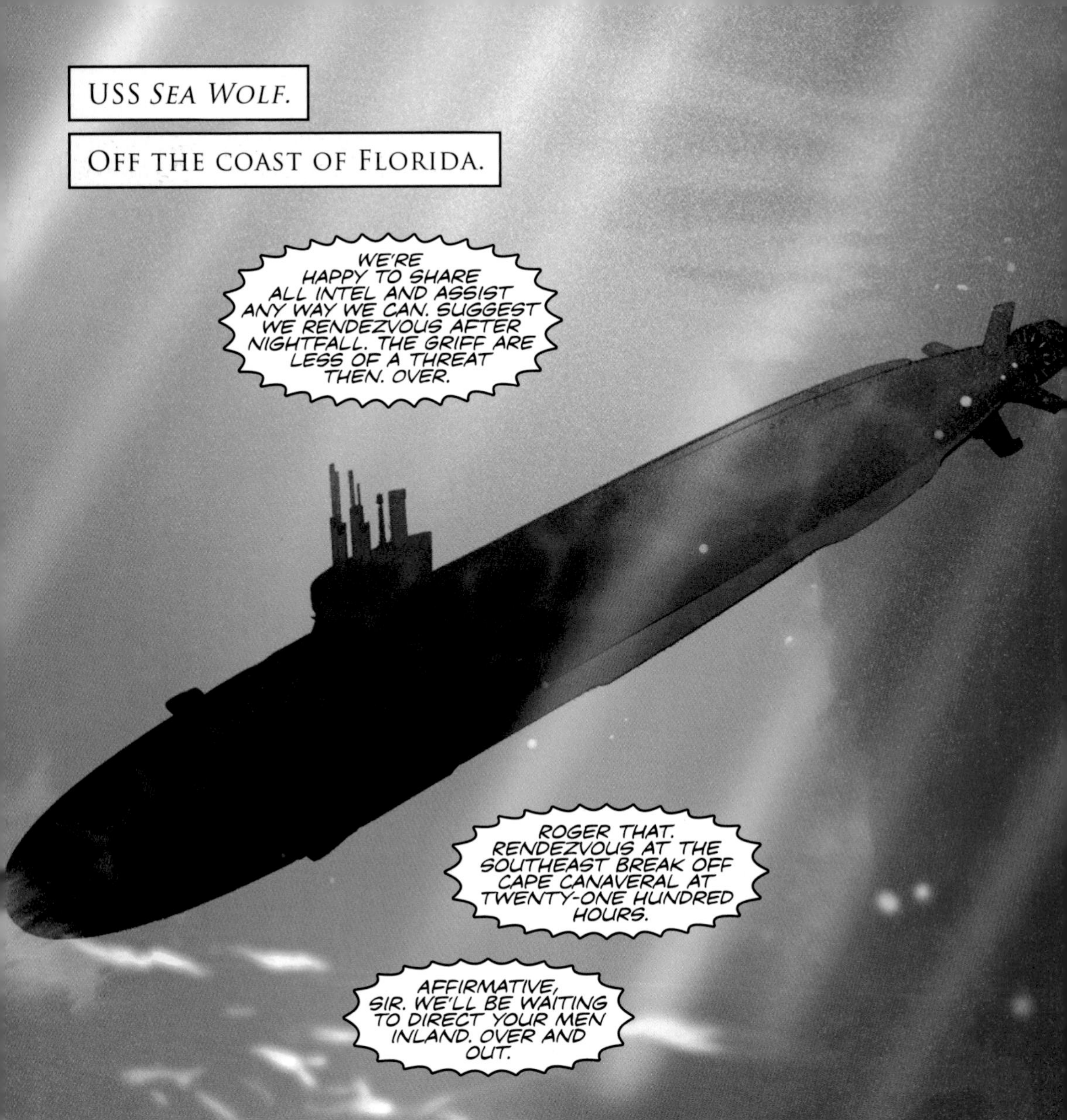
USS *Sea Wolf.*
Off the coast of Florida.
WE'RE HAPPY TO SHARE ALL INTEL AND ASSIST ANY WAY WE CAN. SUGGEST WE RENDEZVOUS AFTER NIGHTFALL. THE GRIFF ARE LESS OF A THREAT THEN. OVER.
ROGER THAT. RENDEZVOUS AT THE SOUTHEAST BREAK OFF CAPE CANAVERAL AT TWENTY-ONE HUNDRED HOURS.
AFFIRMATIVE, SIR. WE'LL BE WAITING TO DIRECT YOUR MEN INLAND. OVER AND OUT.

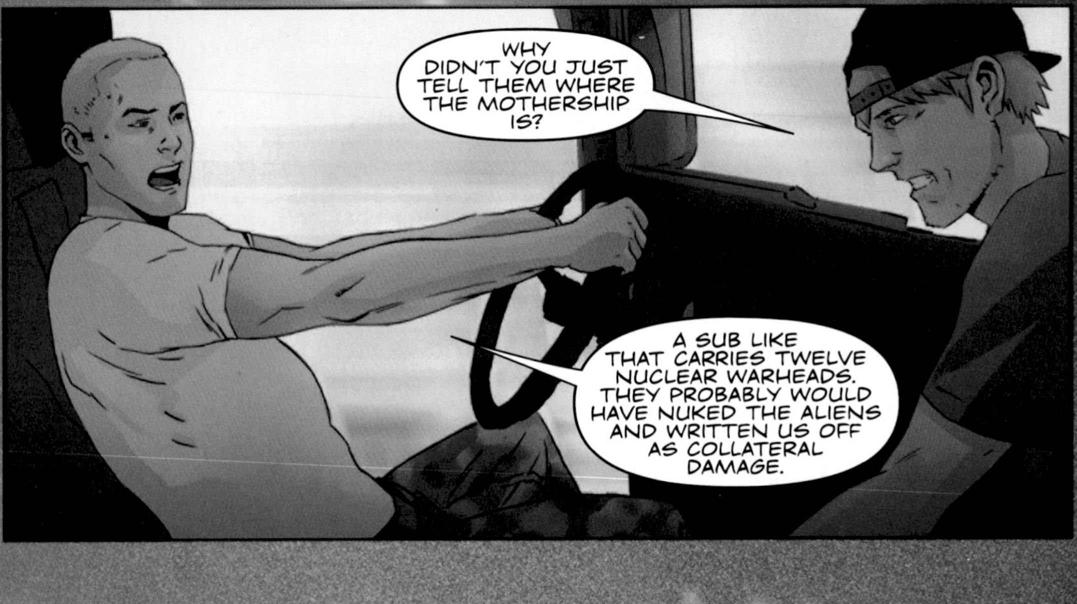
WHY DIDN'T YOU JUST TELL THEM WHERE THE MOTHERSHIP IS?
A SUB LIKE THAT CARRIES TWELVE NUCLEAR WARHEADS. THEY PROBABLY WOULD HAVE NUKED THE ALIENS AND WRITTEN US OFF AS COLLATERAL DAMAGE.

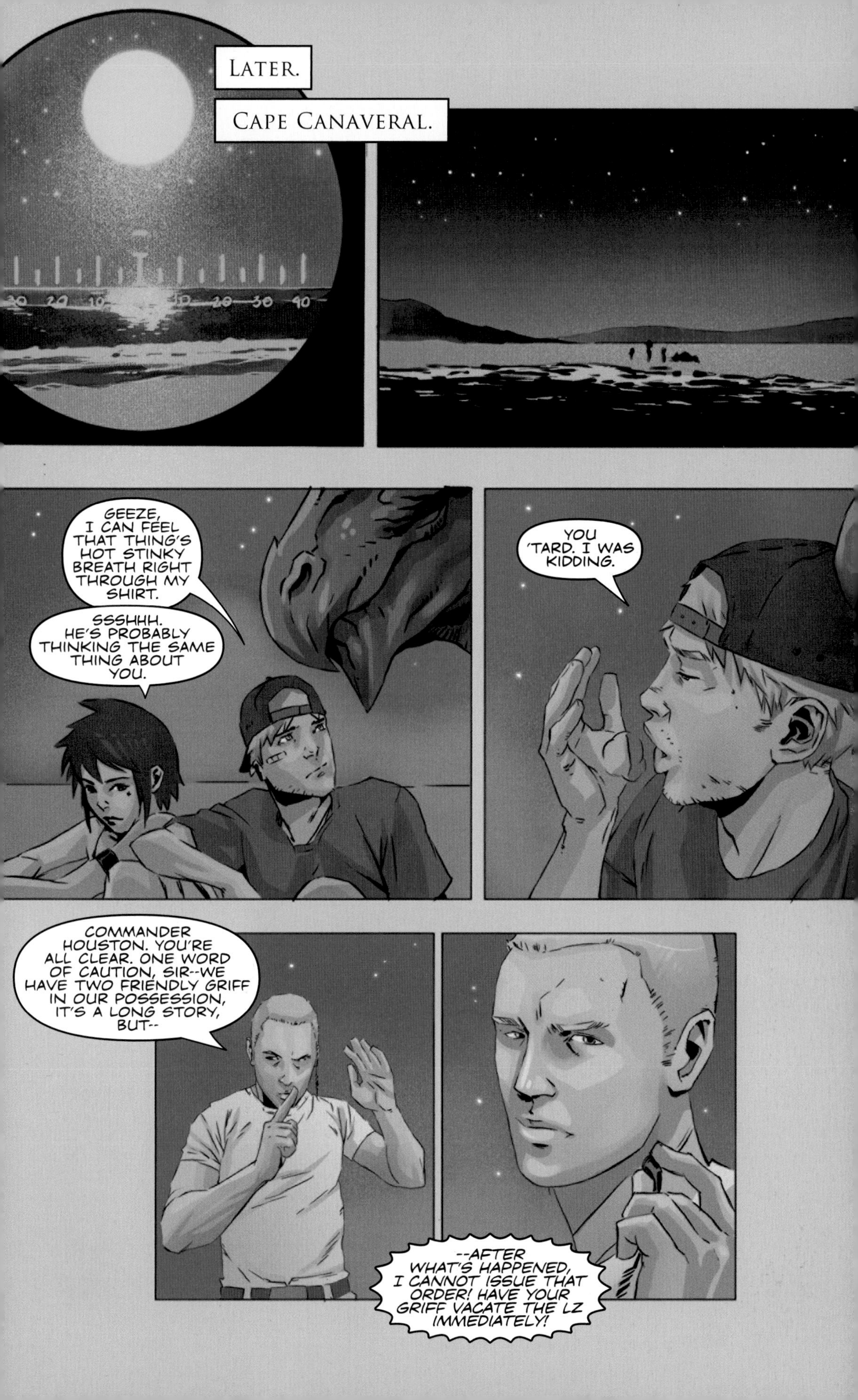

LATER.
CAPE CANAVERAL.
GEEZE, I CAN FEEL THAT THING'S HOT STINKY BREATH RIGHT THROUGH MY SHIRT.
SSSHHH. HE'S PROBABLY THINKING THE SAME THING ABOUT YOU.
YOU 'TARD. I WAS KIDDING.
COMMANDER HOUSTON. YOU'RE ALL CLEAR. ONE WORD OF CAUTION, SIR--WE HAVE TWO FRIENDLY GRIFF IN OUR POSSESSION, IT'S A LONG STORY, BUT--
--AFTER WHAT'S HAPPENED, I CANNOT ISSUE THAT ORDER! HAVE YOUR GRIFF VACATE THE LZ IMMEDIATELY!

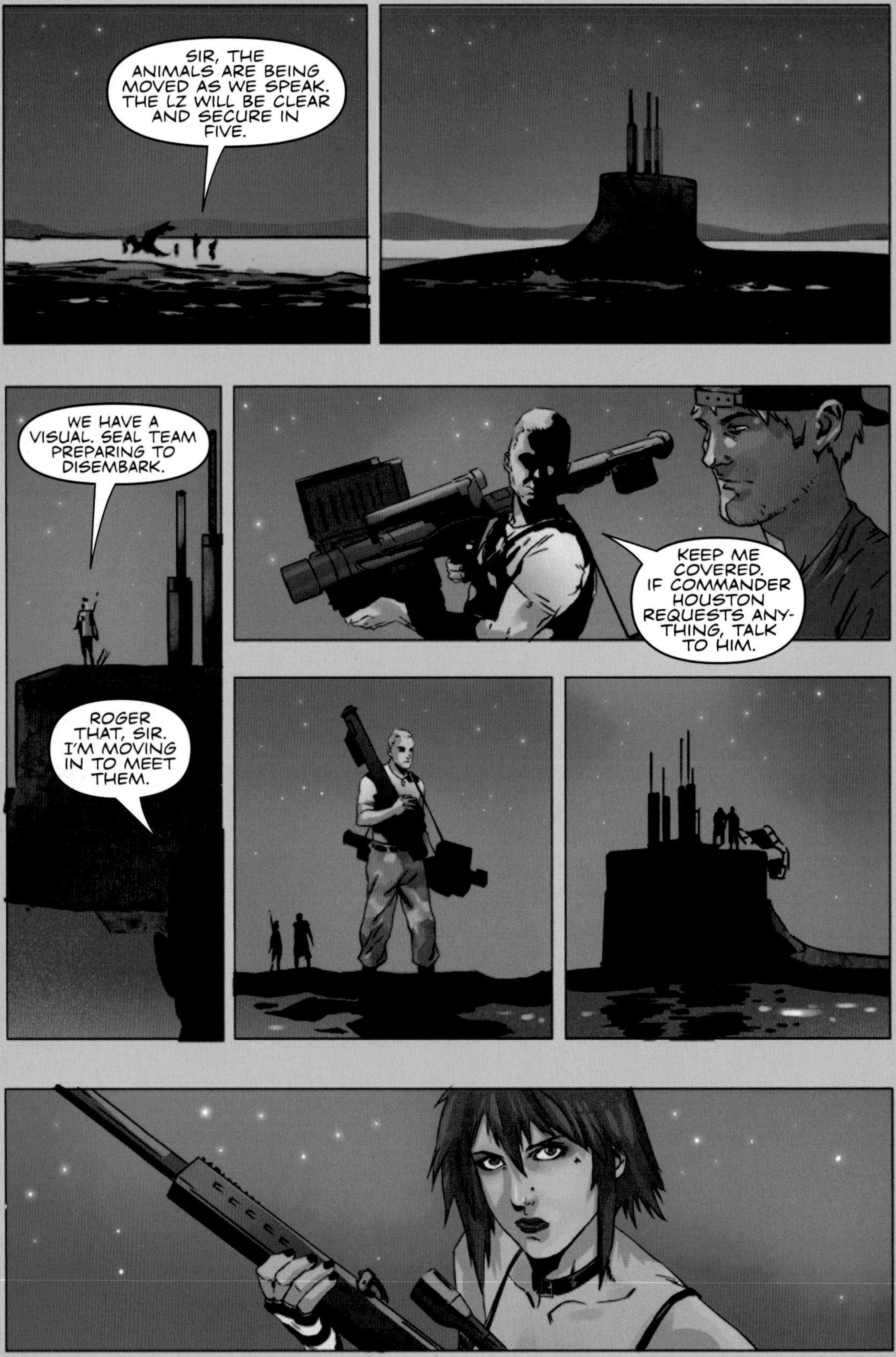
SIR, THE ANIMALS ARE BEING MOVED AS WE SPEAK. THE LZ WILL BE CLEAR AND SECURE IN FIVE.
WE HAVE A VISUAL. SEAL TEAM PREPARING TO DISEMBARK.
KEEP ME COVERED. IF COMMANDER HOUSTON REQUESTS ANY-THING, TALK TO HIM.
ROGER THAT, SIR. I'M MOVING IN TO MEET THEM.

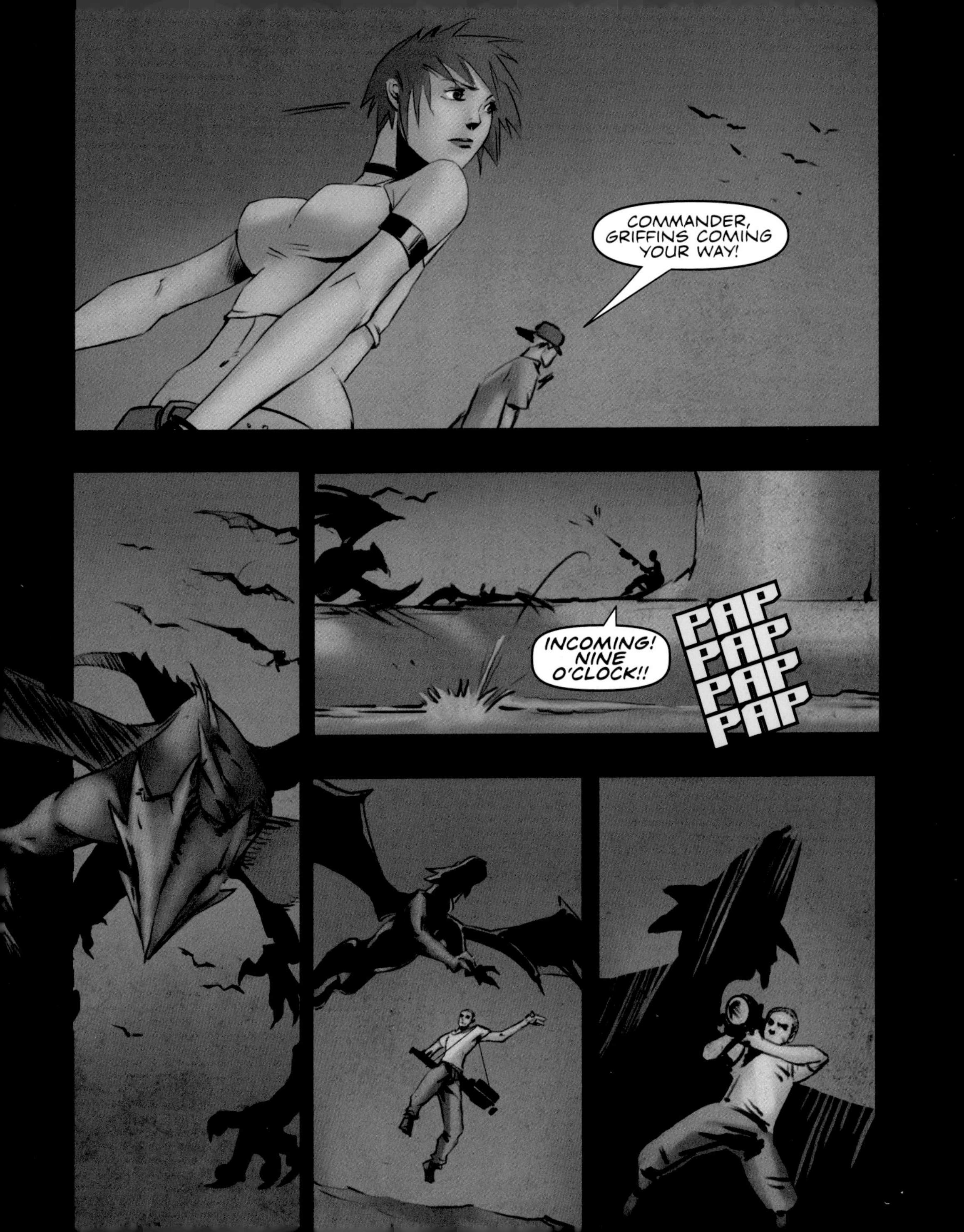
COMMANDER, GRIFFINS COMING YOUR WAY!
INCOMING! NINE O'CLOCK!!
PAP PAP PAP PAP

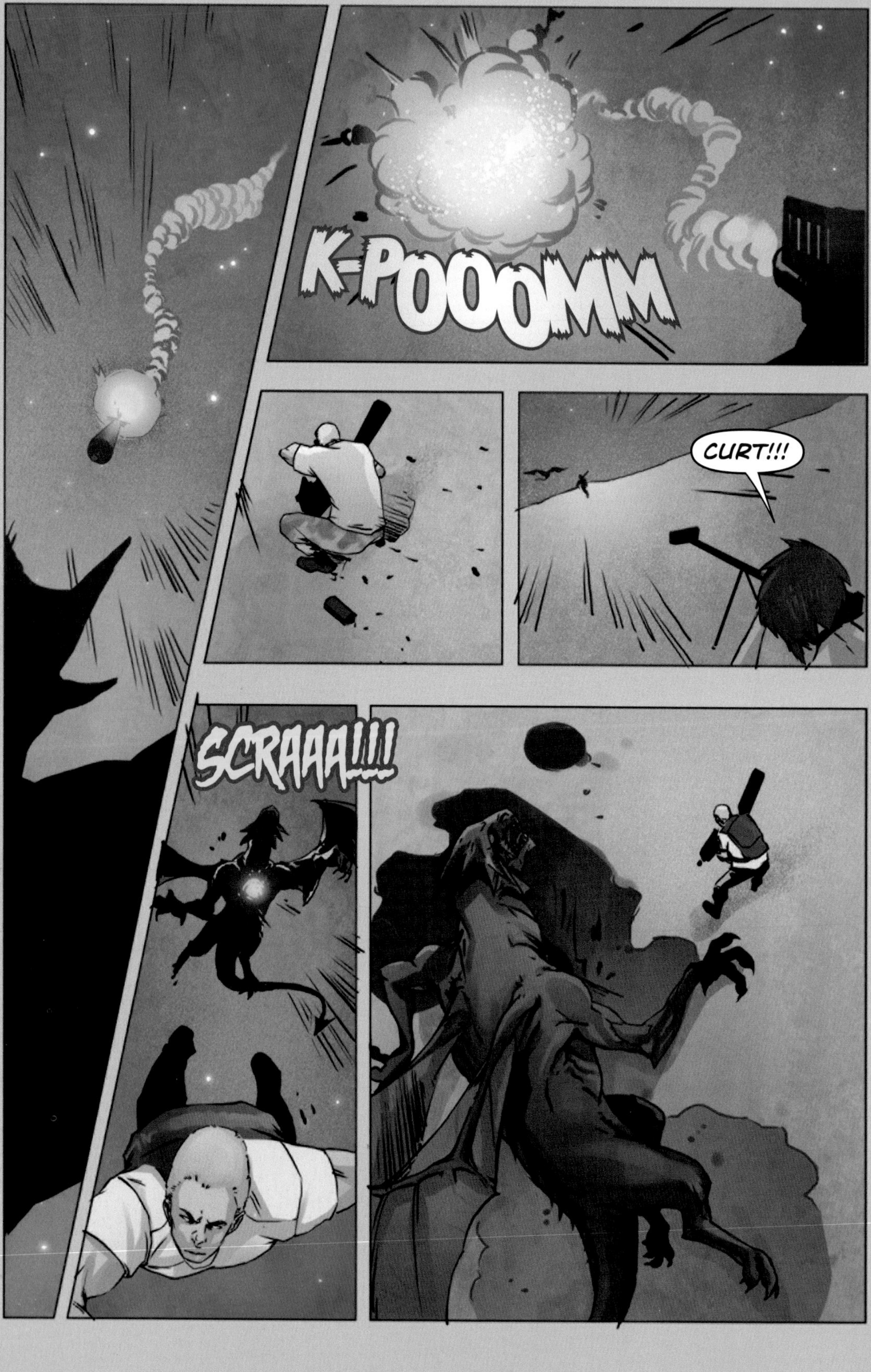
K-POOOMM
CURT!!!
SCRAAA!!!!

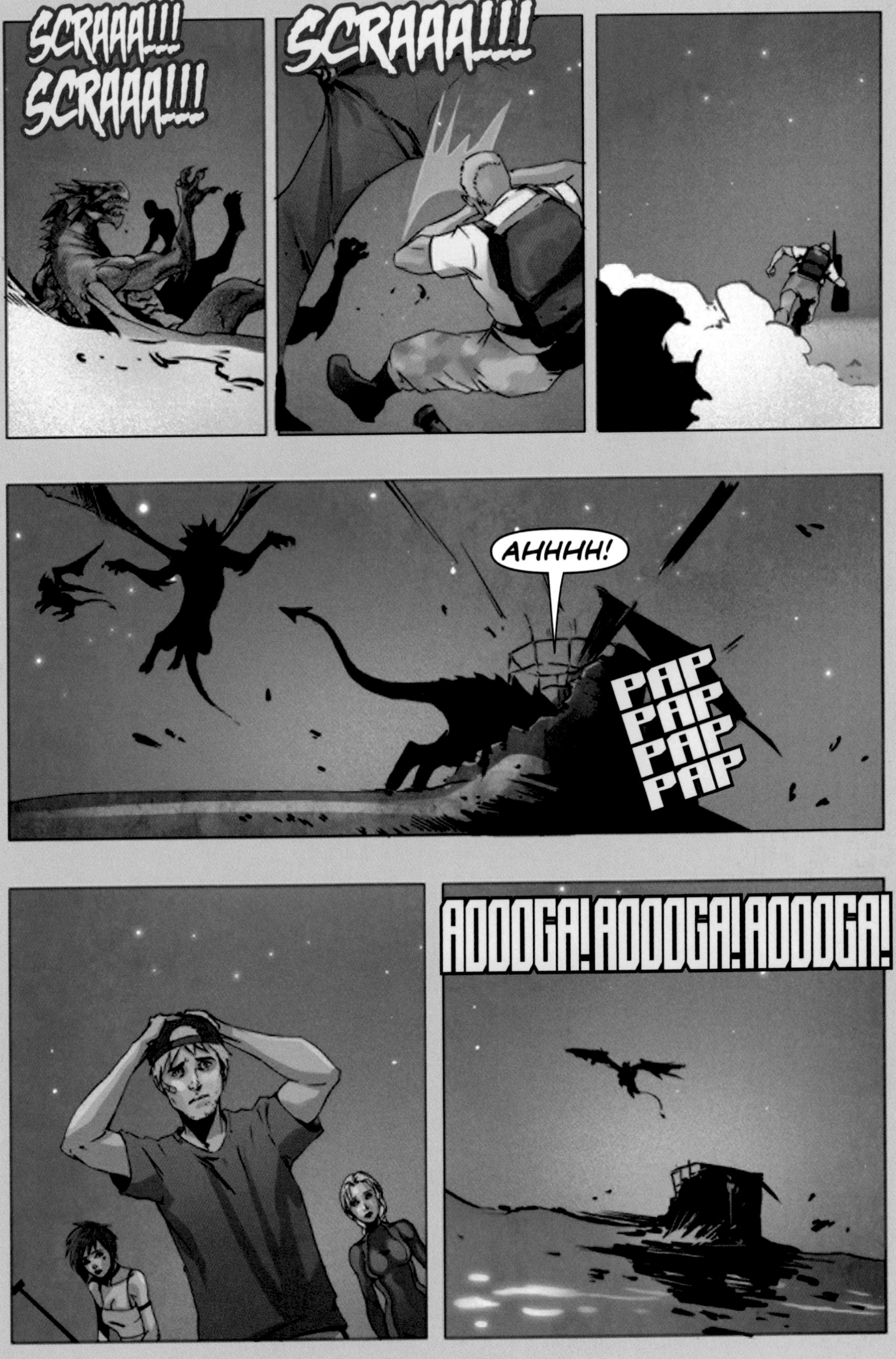
SCRAAA!!!! SCRAAA!!!!
SCRAAA!!!
AHHHH!
PAP PAP PAP PAP
AOOOGA! AOOOGA! AOOOGA!

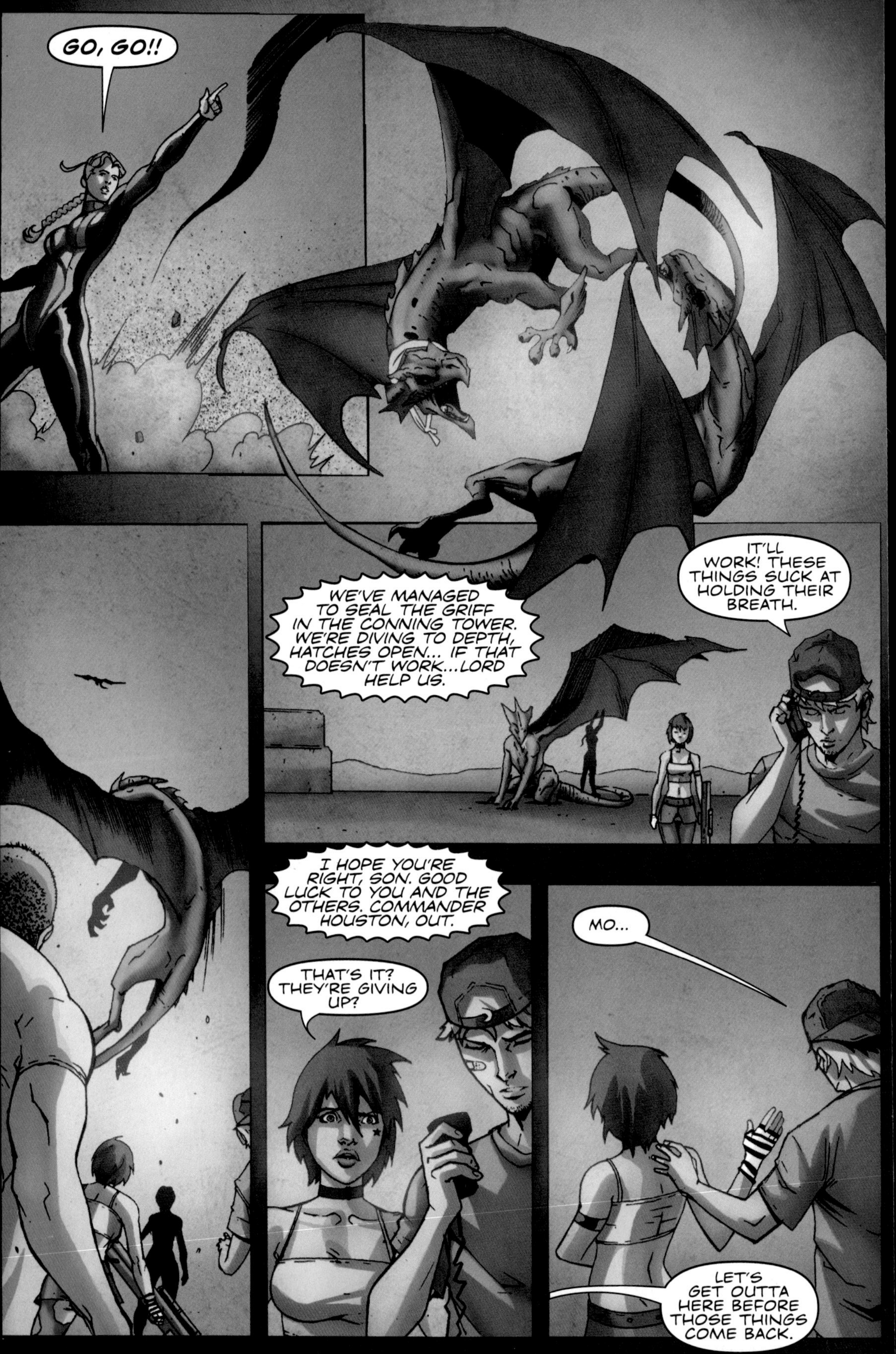
GO, GO!!
WE'VE MANAGED TO SEAL THE GRIFF IN THE CONNING TOWER. WE'RE DIVING TO DEPTH, HATCHES OPEN... IF THAT DOESN'T WORK...LORD HELP US.
IT'LL WORK! THESE THINGS SUCK AT HOLDING THEIR BREATH.
I HOPE YOU'RE RIGHT, SON. GOOD LUCK TO YOU AND THE OTHERS. COMMANDER HOUSTON, OUT.
THAT'S IT? THEY'RE GIVING UP?
MO...
LET'S GET OUTTA HERE BEFORE THOSE THINGS COME BACK.

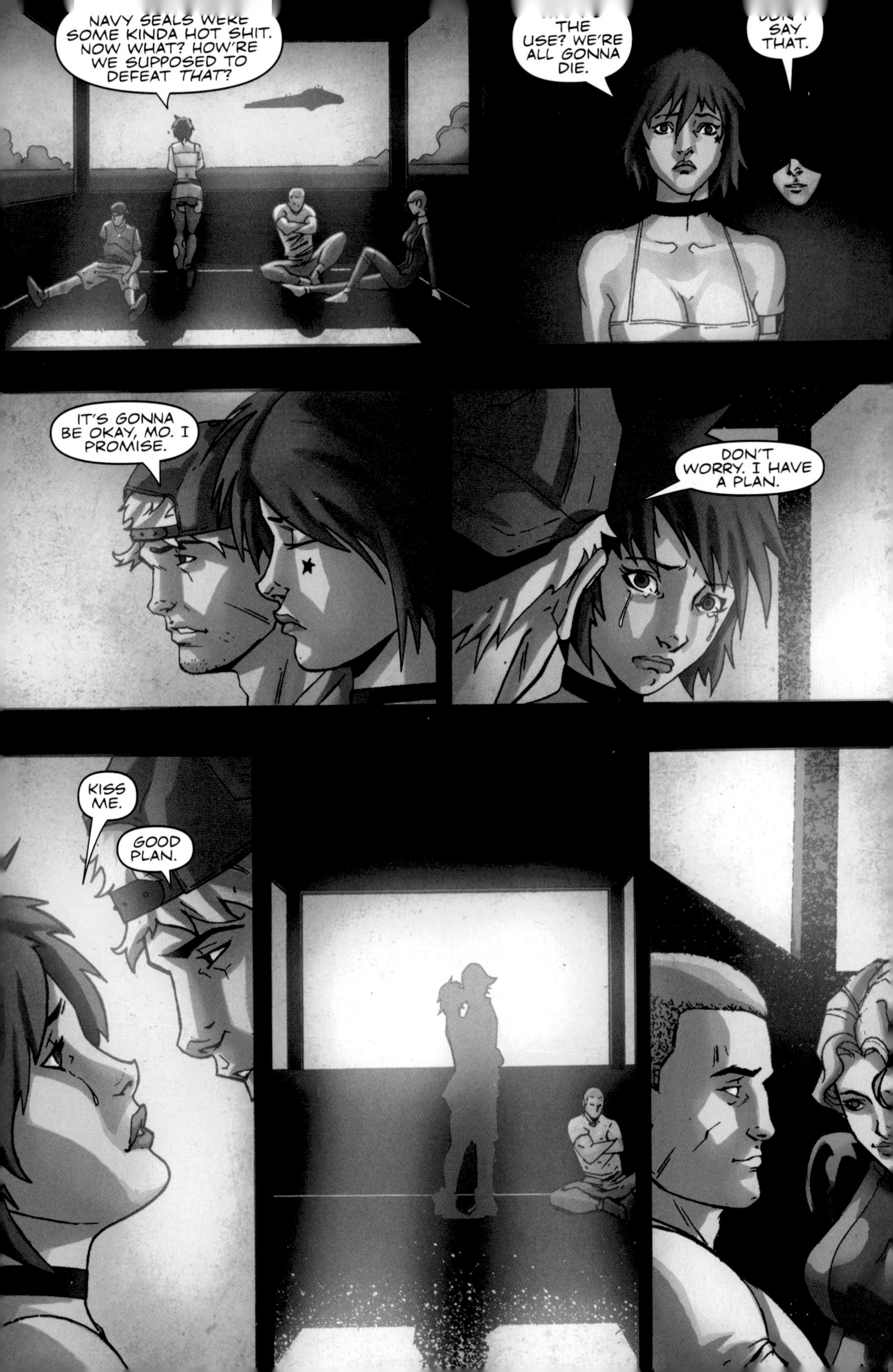
NAVY SEALS WERE SOME KINDA HOT SHIT. NOW WHAT? HOW'RE WE SUPPOSED TO DEFEAT THAT?
THE USE? WE'RE ALL GONNA DIE.
SAY THAT.
IT'S GONNA BE OKAY, MO. I PROMISE.
DON'T WORRY. I HAVE A PLAN.
KISS ME.
GOOD PLAN.

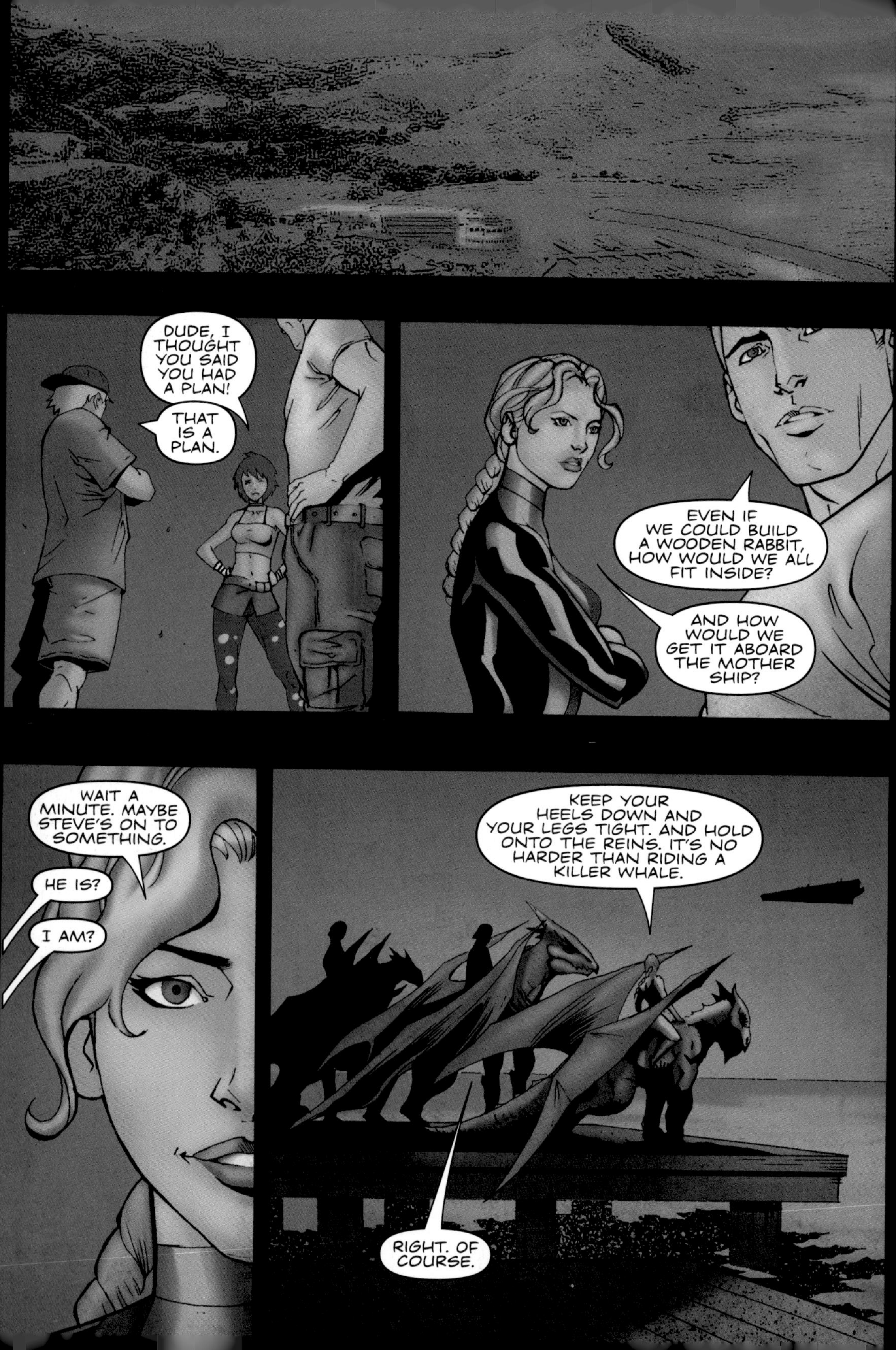
DUDE, I THOUGHT YOU SAID YOU HAD A PLAN!
THAT IS A PLAN.
EVEN IF WE COULD BUILD A WOODEN RABBIT, HOW WOULD WE ALL FIT INSIDE?
AND HOW WOULD WE GET IT ABOARD THE MOTHER SHIP?
WAIT A MINUTE. MAYBE STEVE'S ON TO SOMETHING.
HE IS?
I AM?
KEEP YOUR HEELS DOWN AND YOUR LEGS TIGHT. AND HOLD ONTO THE REINS. IT'S NO HARDER THAN RIDING A KILLER WHALE.
RIGHT. OF COURSE.

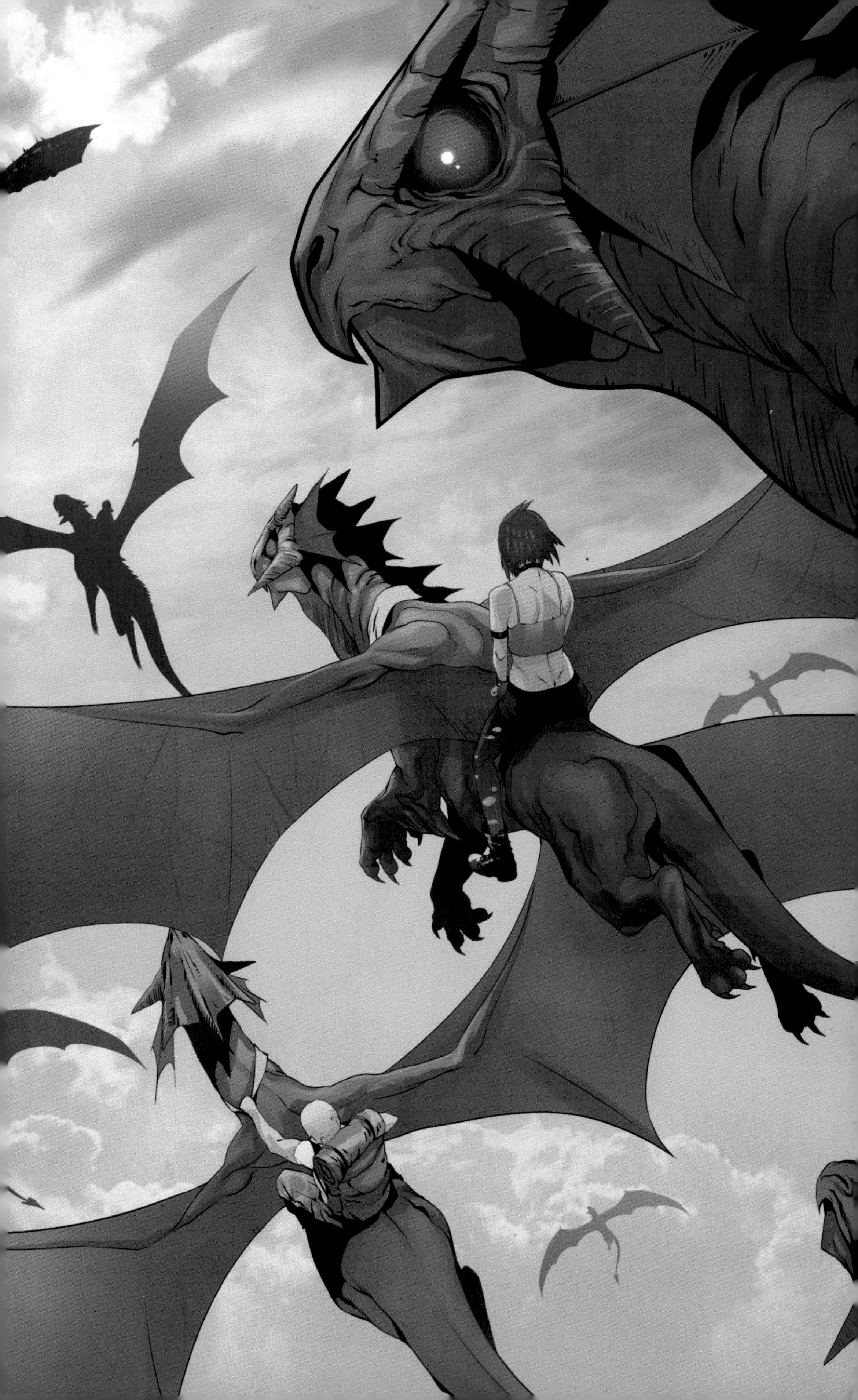

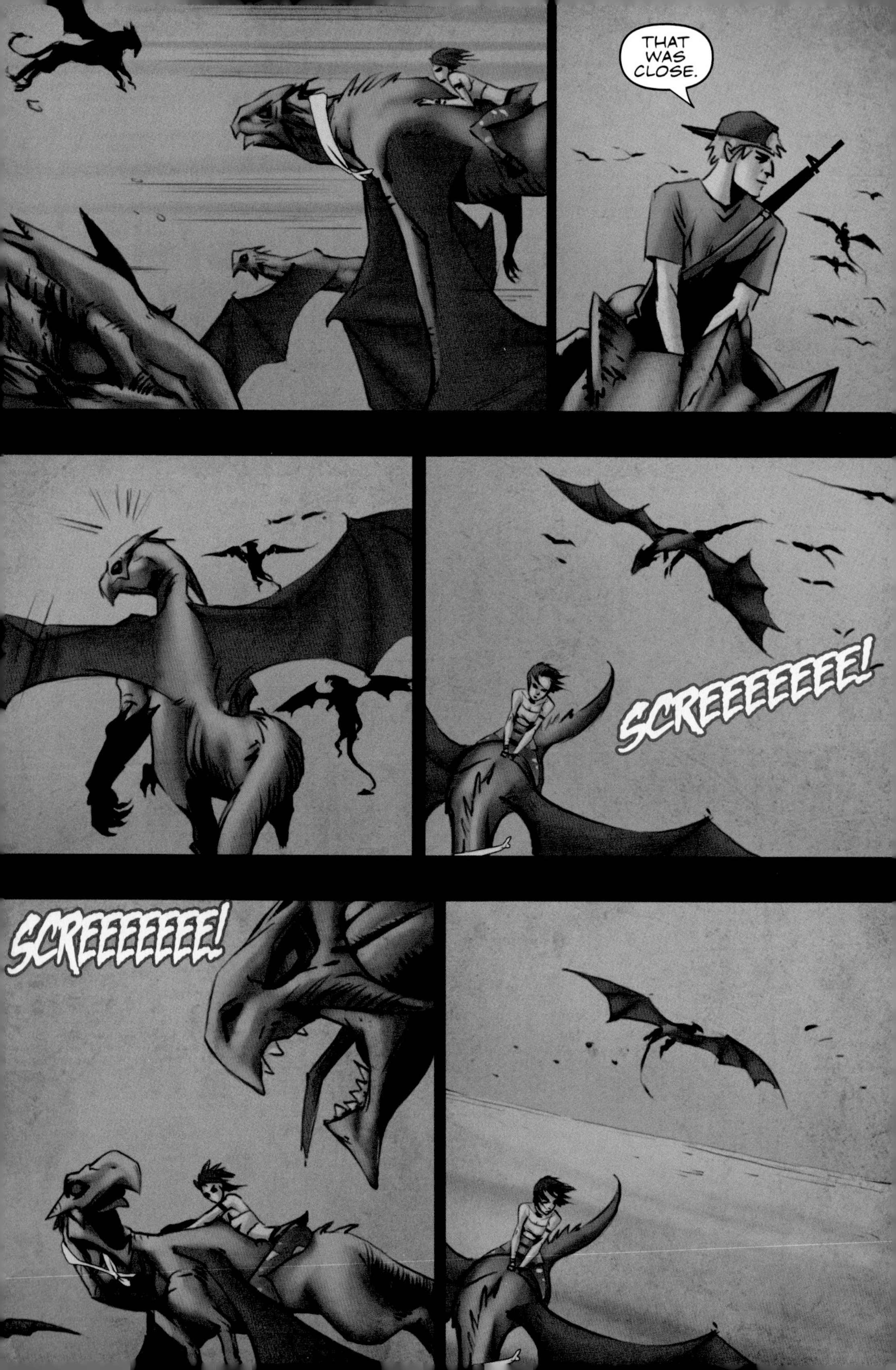
THAT WAS CLOSE.
SCREEEEEEEE!
SCREEEEEEEE!

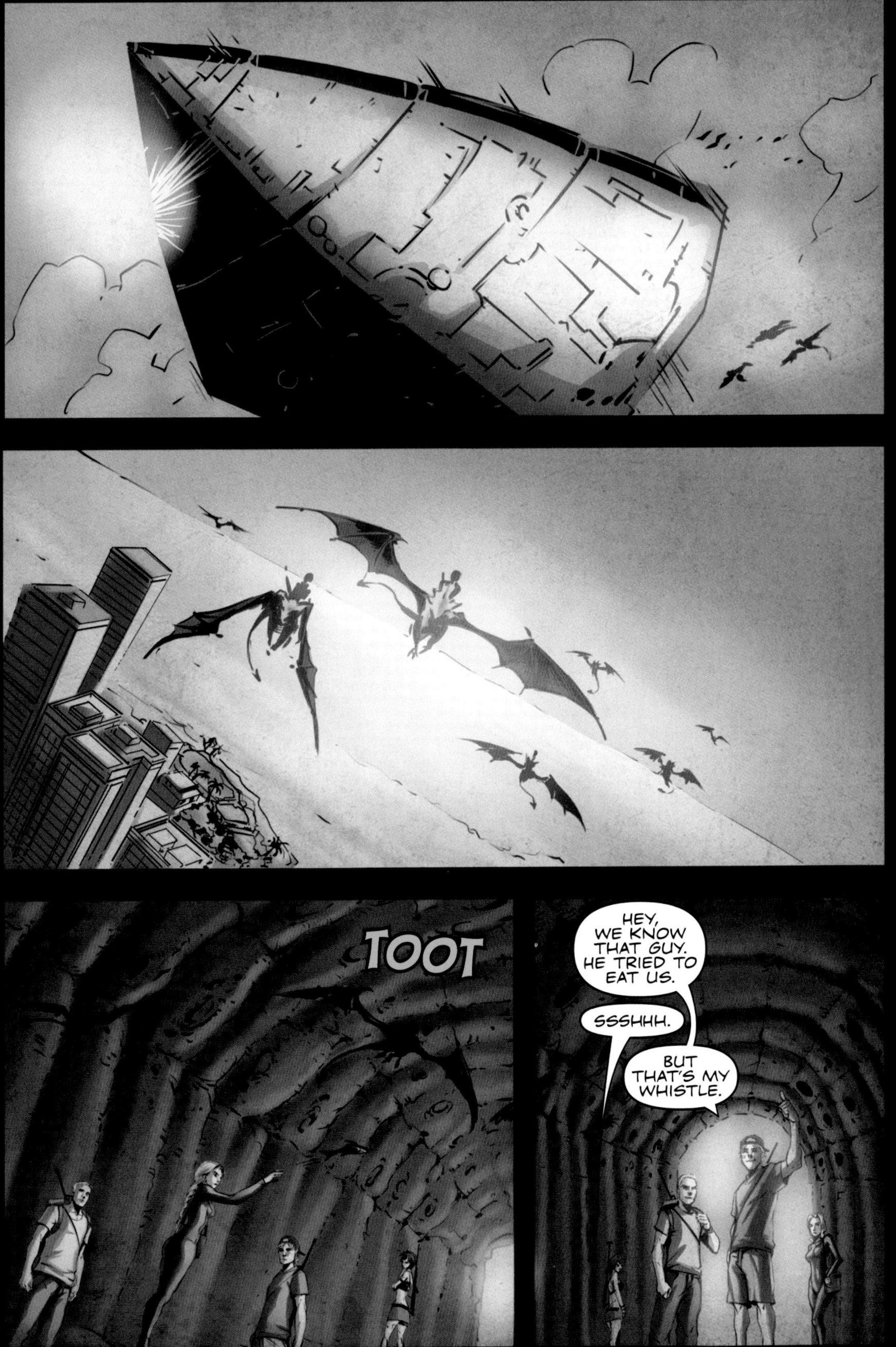
TOOT
HEY, WE KNOW THAT GUY. HE TRIED TO EAT US.
SSSHHH.
BUT THAT'S MY WHISTLE.

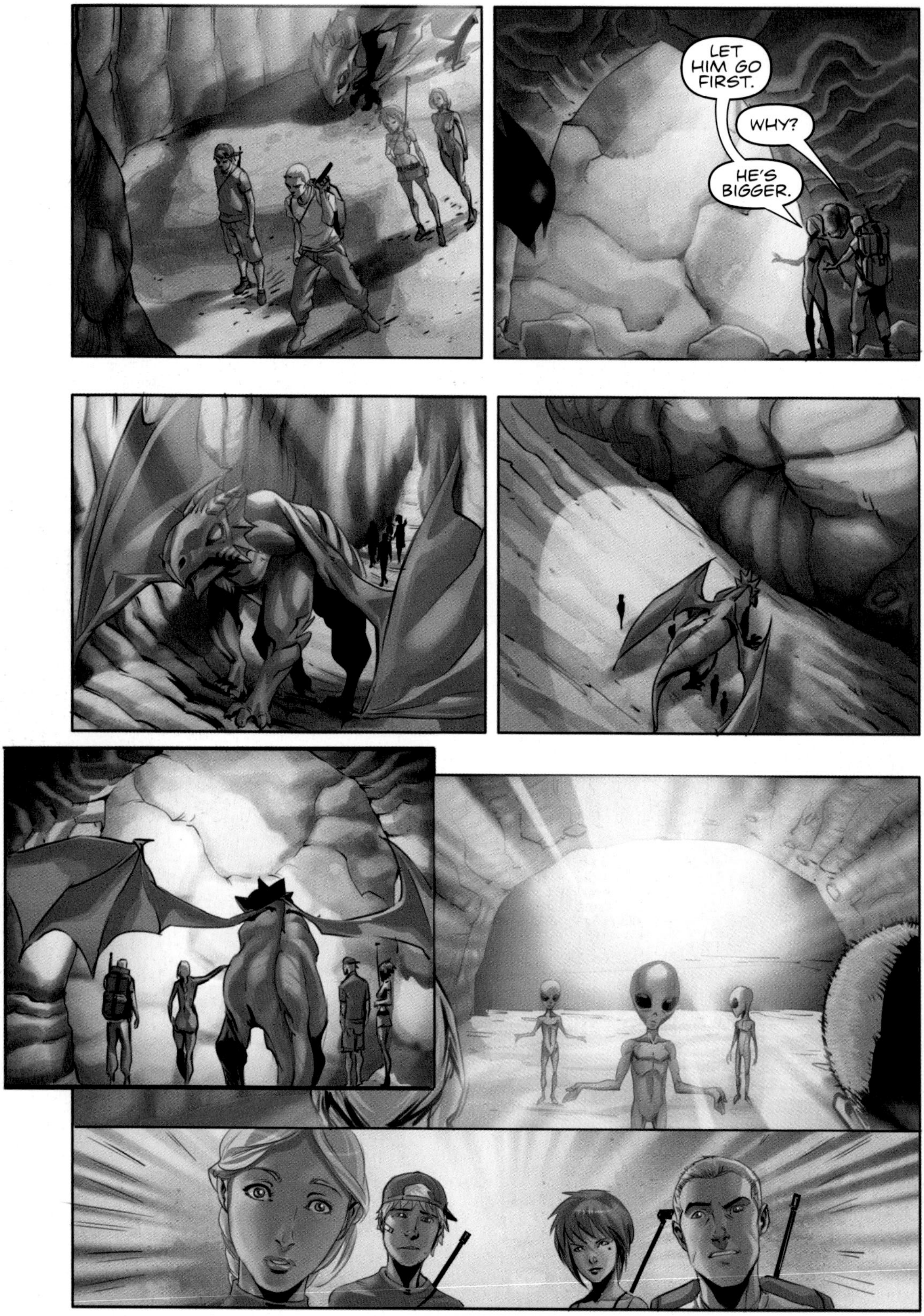
LET HIM GO FIRST.
WHY?
HE'S BIGGER.

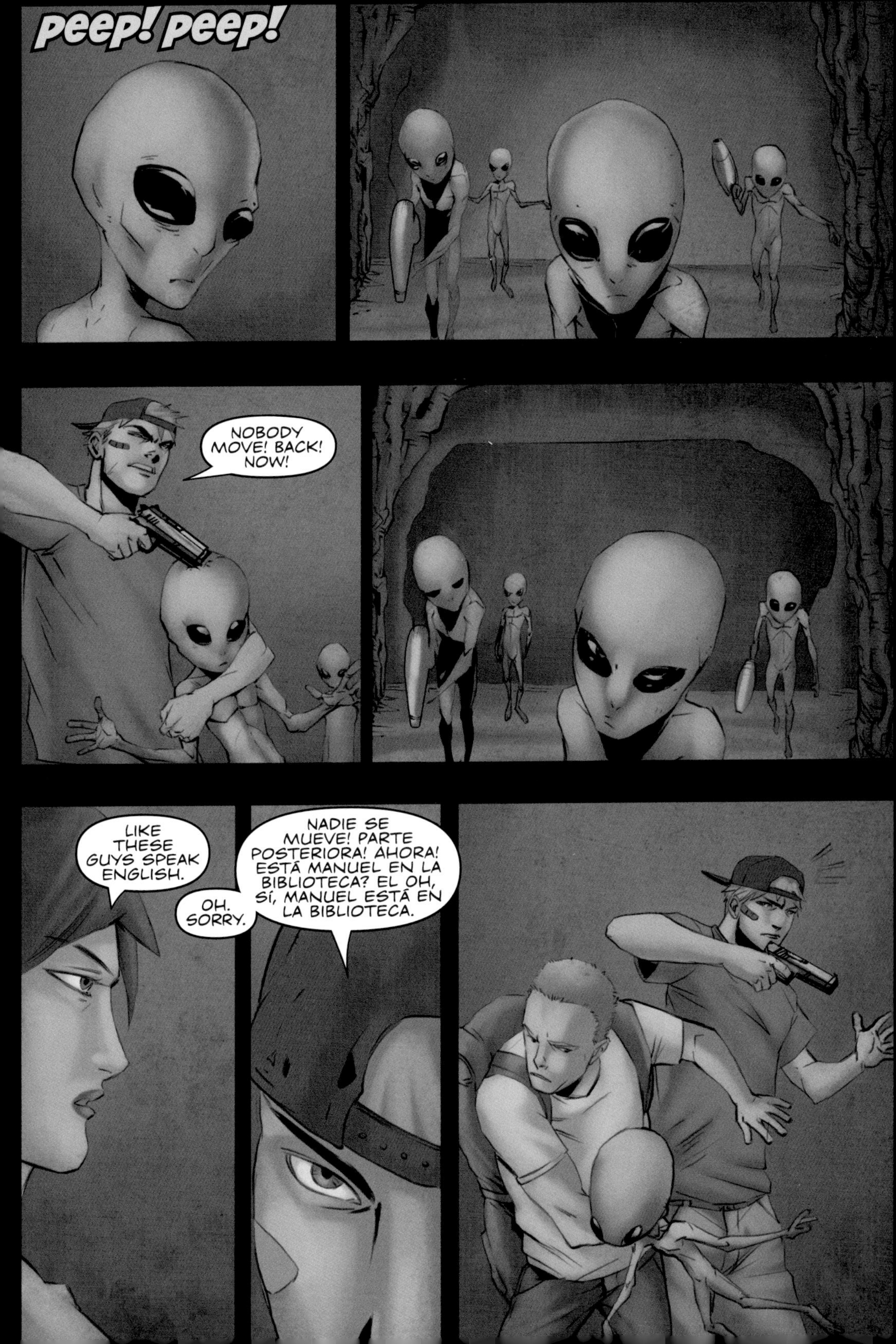
PEEP! PEEP!
NOBODY MOVE! BACK! NOW!
LIKE THESE GUYS SPEAK ENGLISH.
OH. SORRY.
NADIE SE MUEVE! PARTE POSTERIORA! AHORA! ESTÁ MANUEL EN LA BIBLIOTECA? EL OH, SÍ, MANUEL ESTÁ EN LA BIBLIOTECA.

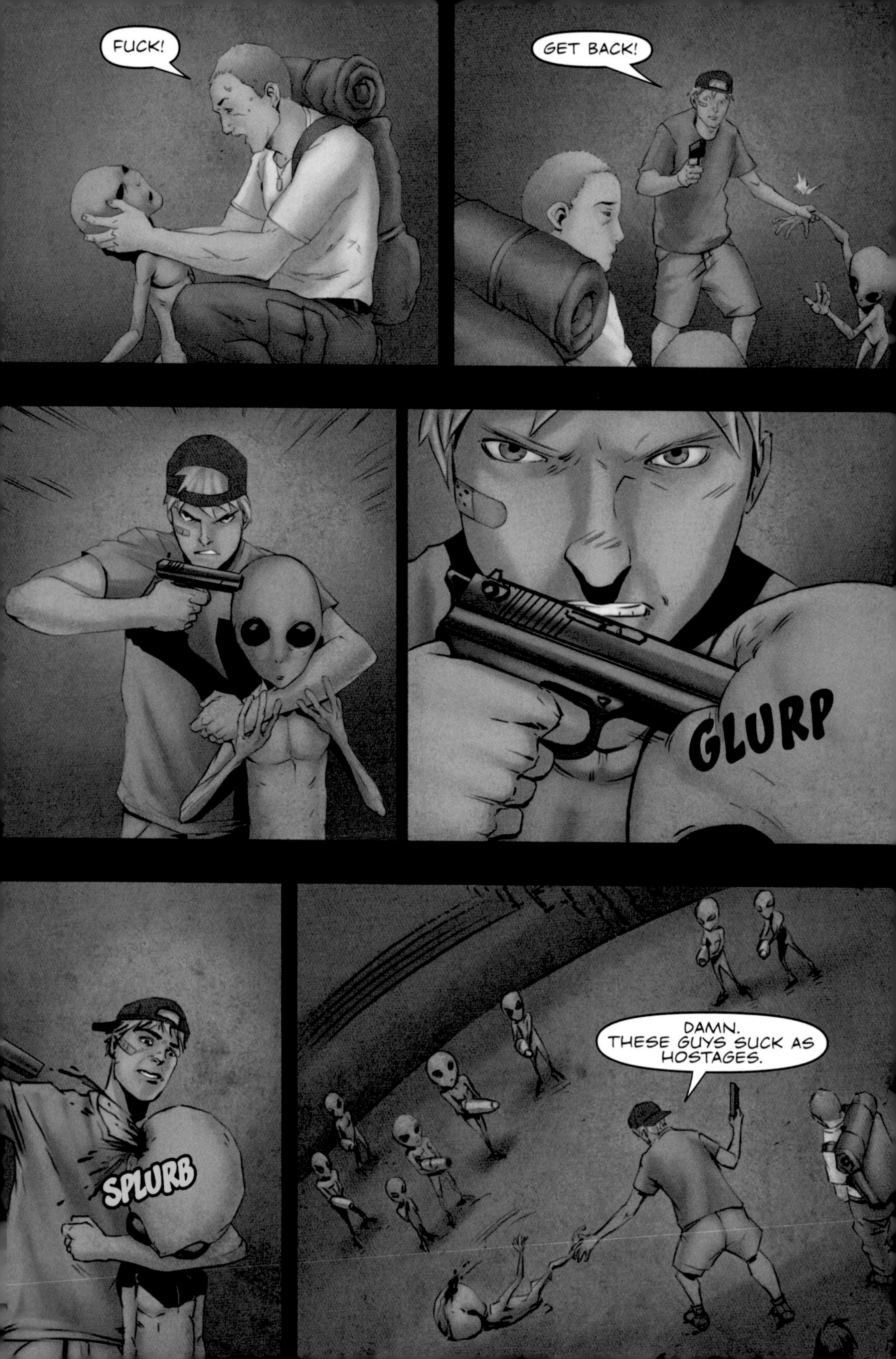
FUCK!
GET BACK!
GLURP
SPLURB
DAMN. THESE GUYS SUCK AS HOSTAGES.

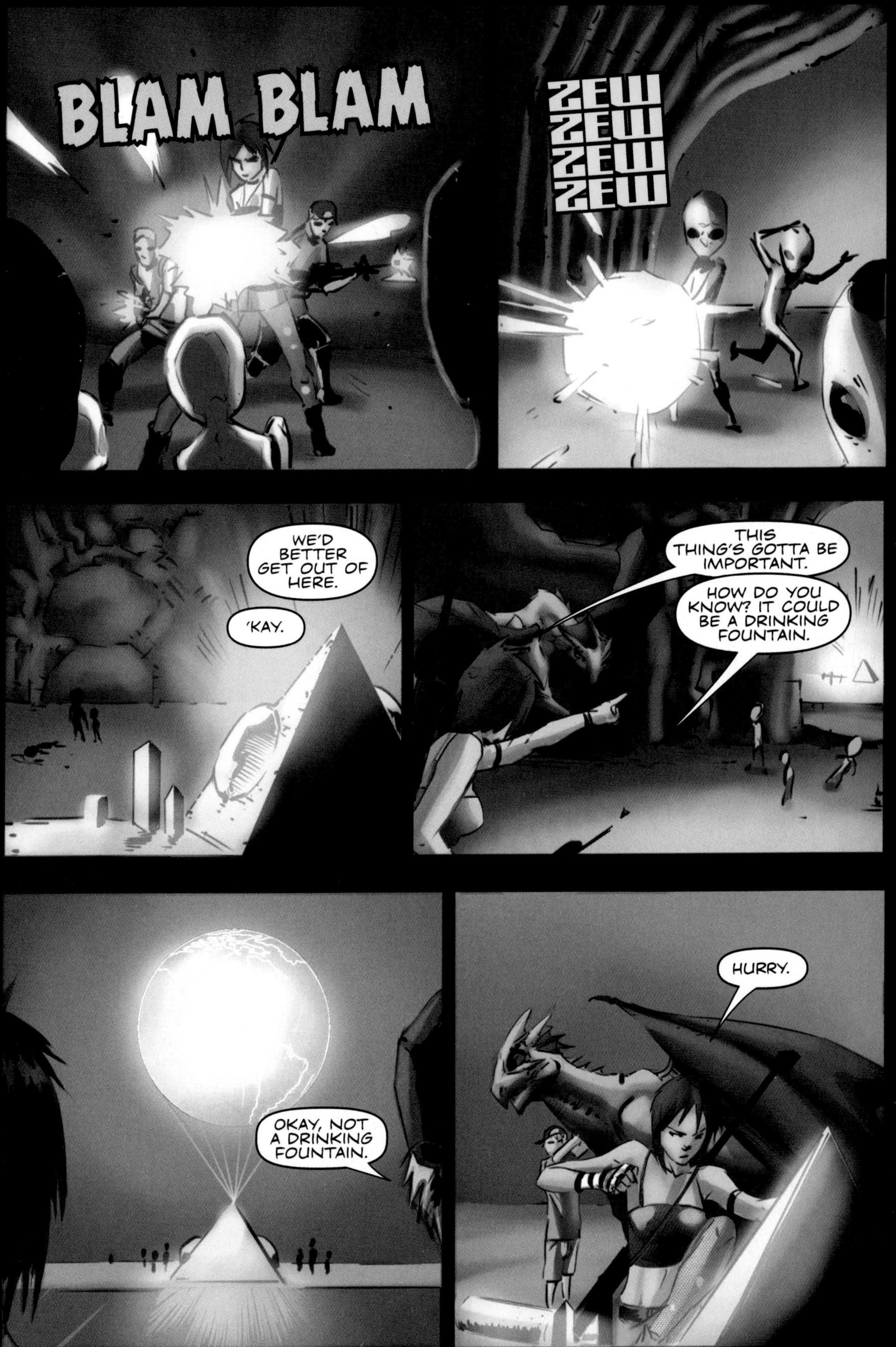
BLAM BLAM
ZEW ZEW ZEW ZEW
WE'D BETTER GET OUT OF HERE.
'KAY.
THIS THING'S GOTTA BE IMPORTANT.
HOW DO YOU KNOW? IT COULD BE A DRINKING FOUNTAIN.
OKAY, NOT A DRINKING FOUNTAIN.
HURRY.

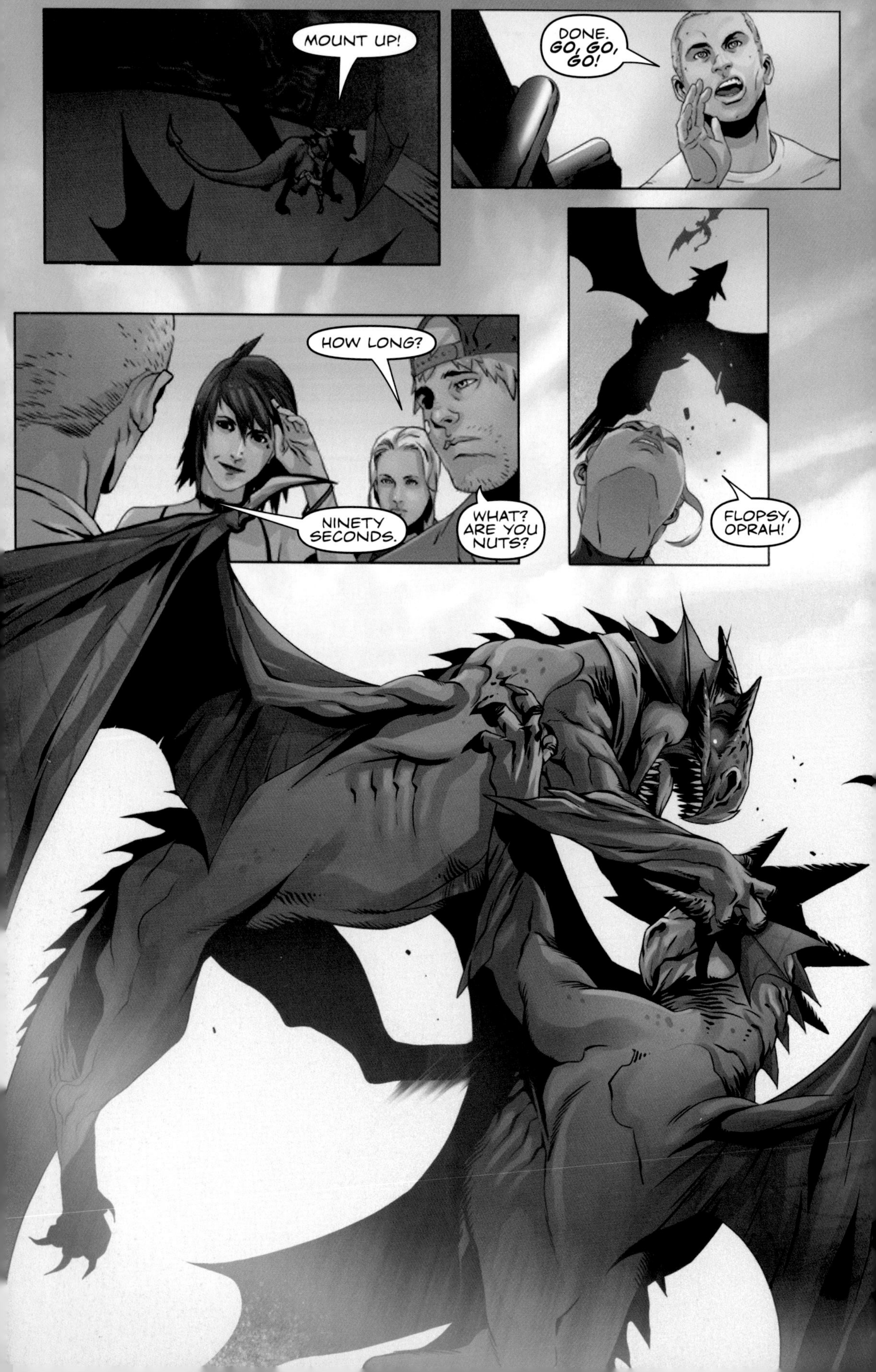
MOUNT UP!
DONE. GO, GO, GO!
HOW LONG?
NINETY SECONDS.
WHAT? ARE YOU NUTS?
FLOPSY, OPRAH!

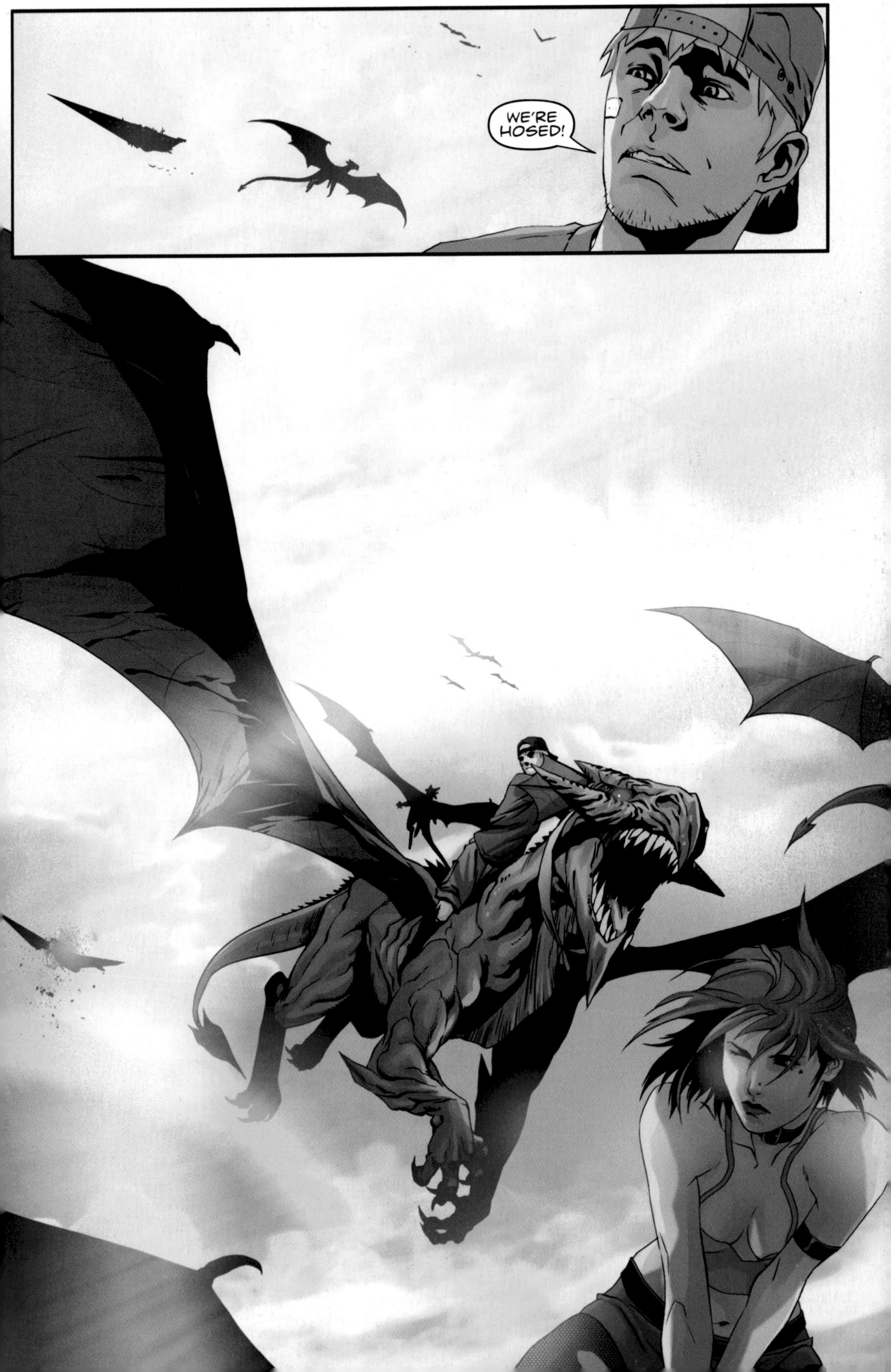
WE'RE HOSED!

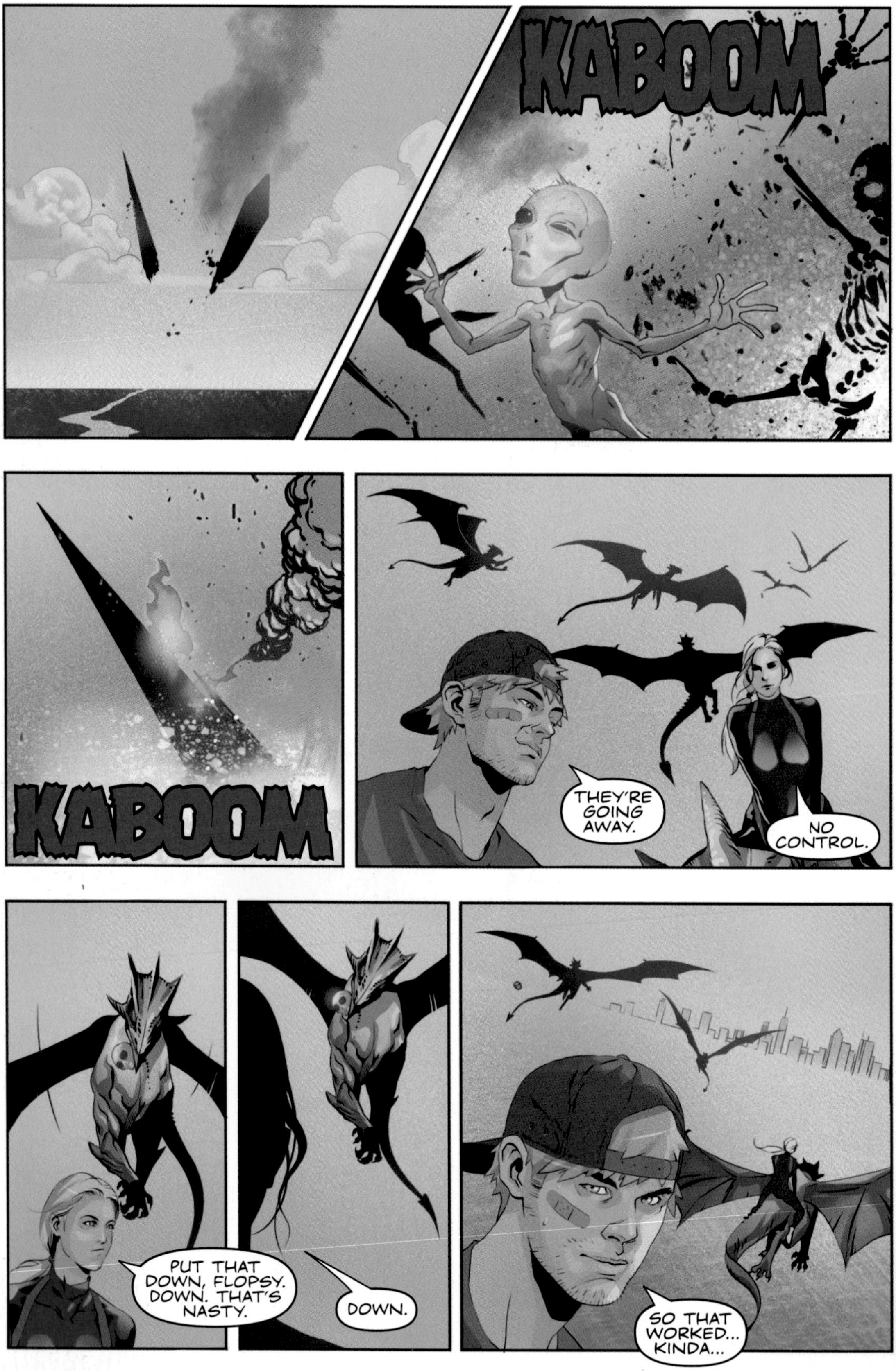
KABOOM
KABOOM
THEY'RE GOING AWAY.
NO CONTROL.
PUT THAT DOWN, FLOPSY. DOWN. THAT'S NASTY.
DOWN.
SO THAT WORKED... KINDA...

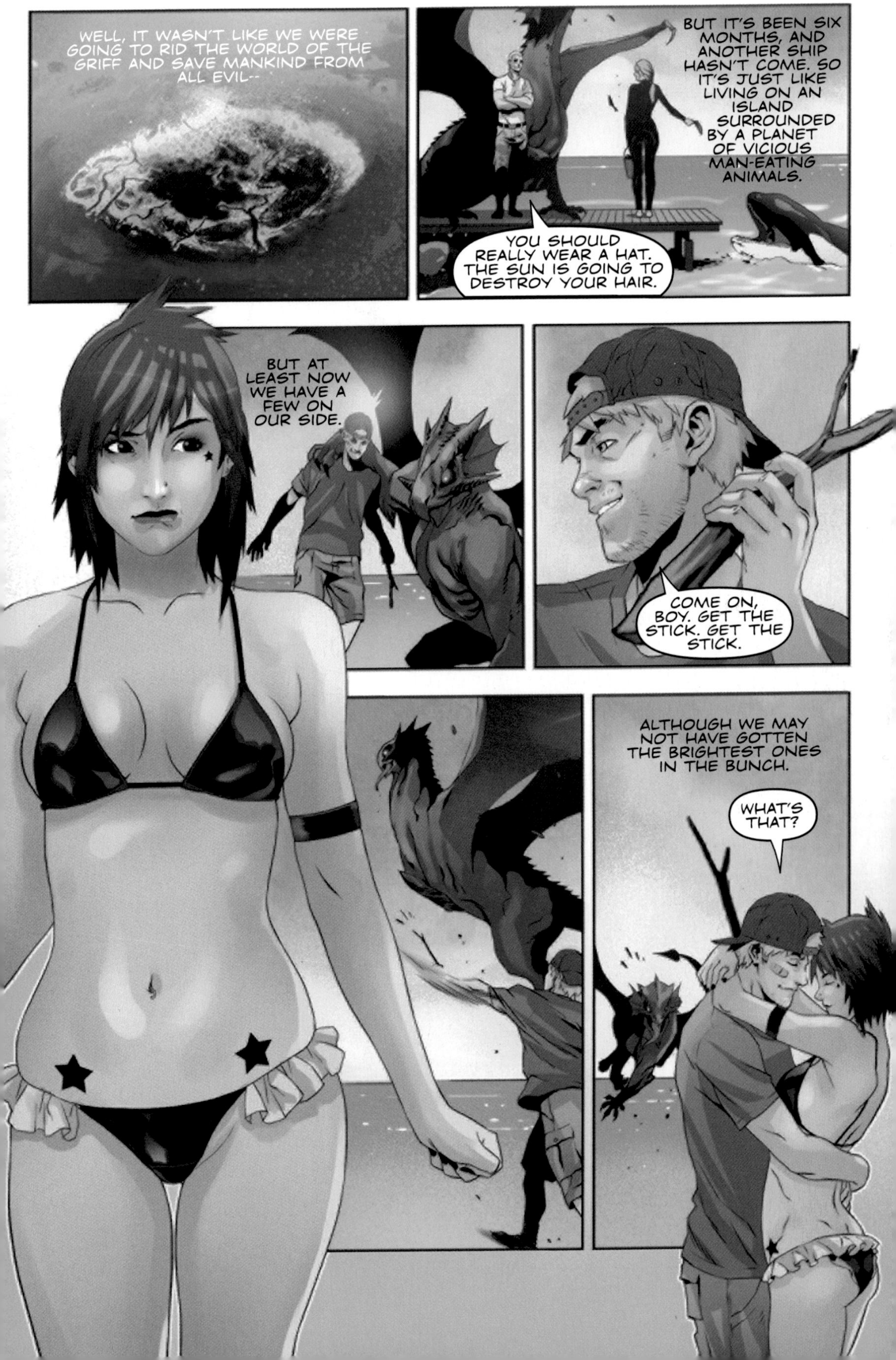
WELL, IT WASN'T LIKE WE WERE GOING TO RID THE WORLD OF THE GRIFF AND SAVE MANKIND FROM ALL EVIL--
BUT IT'S BEEN SIX MONTHS, AND ANOTHER SHIP HASN'T COME. SO IT'S JUST LIKE LIVING ON AN ISLAND SURROUNDED BY A PLANET OF VICIOUS MAN-EATING ANIMALS.
YOU SHOULD REALLY WEAR A HAT. THE SUN IS GOING TO DESTROY YOUR HAIR.
BUT AT LEAST NOW WE HAVE A FEW ON OUR SIDE.
COME ON, BOY. GET THE STICK. GET THE STICK.
ALTHOUGH WE MAY NOT HAVE GOTTEN THE BRIGHTEST ONES IN THE BUNCH.
WHAT'S THAT?

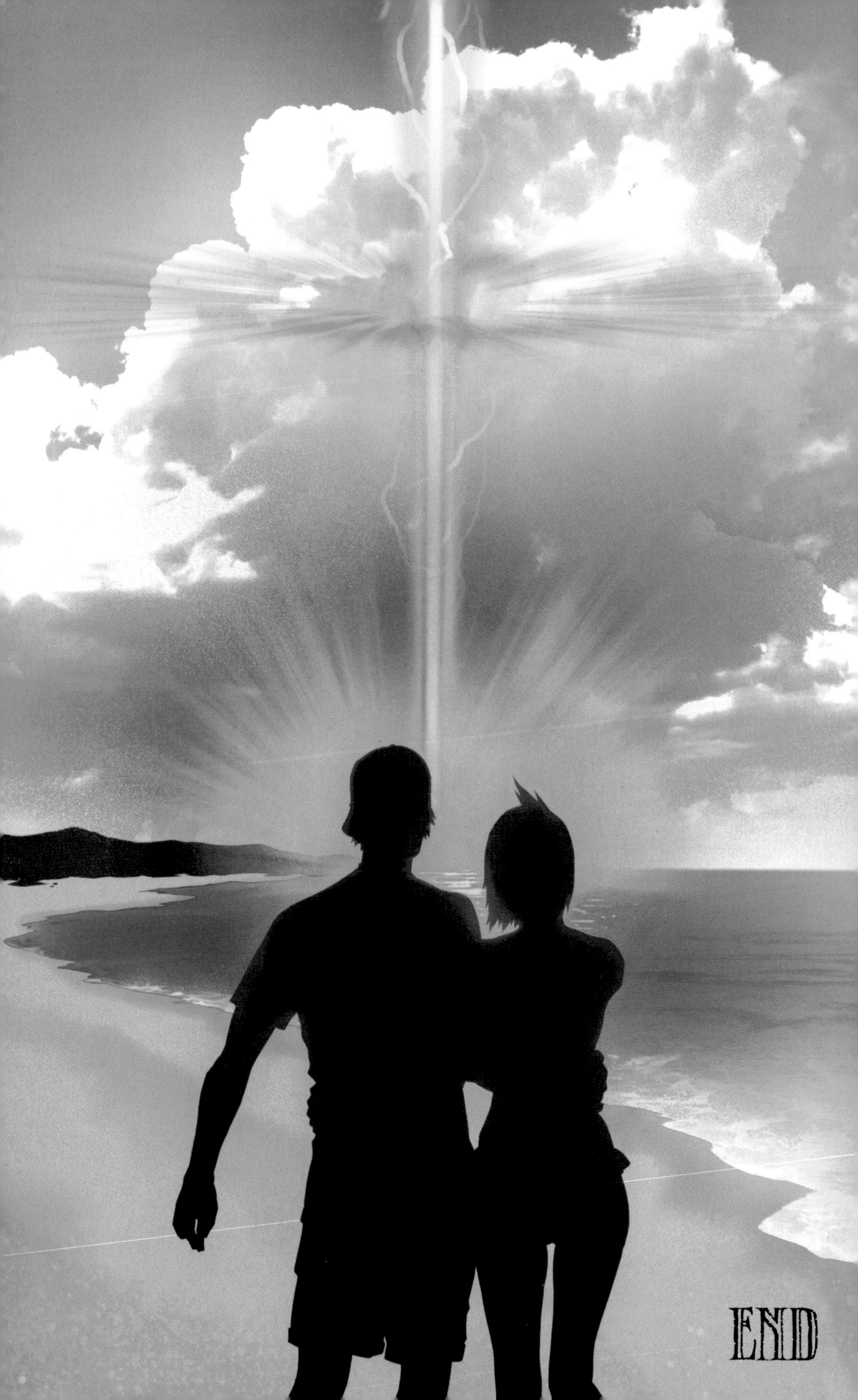
END

Afterword

It all started a long time ago with a book review of *Coyote Blue* in *Men's Journal*. I remember reading it and thinking, Wow, this would make a great movie. Fifteen years, four production companies, and countless screenplay drafts later, I still think so. Unfortunately, no one else does. At least no one with a few million bucks lying around. But that's Hollywood.

The best part of adapting *Coyote Blue* was collaborating with Chris. We became fast friends, eventually traveling to Montana to scout locations for the production. Back then, Chris was a smoker. It wasn't unusual for him to have hourly, hour-long cigarette breaks. Not an easy thing to deal with when you're a nonsmoker.

I remember him lighting up seconds after he finished working out. I was incredulous. Chris assured me it was the best cigarette of the day.

I can still recall the moment he asked to read something I'd written. Naturally I was nervous and told him so. He asked why. I told him, "Showing you my writing is like showing your jump shot to Michael Jordan."

He laughed and I knew it was going to be okay. Writing *The Griff* turned out to be a lot of fun. We spent countless weekends acting out scenes and making each other laugh.

Our biggest challenge came when we tried to decide on a way to end the story. We had the world taken over by huge lizardy flying things, but then what? I remembered something from a college psychology class – possibly the only thing I remember from that class: how a family of baby ducks imprinted with a farmer's rubber boots. I can still see the photo from the textbook: a line of ducklings waddling after the farmer's boots as though the boots were a substitute for their mother.

That became the spark that provided Liz the opportunity to fight back using the same weapon that had wreaked havoc on the planet. Like our characters, we were saved.

—Ian Corson

BONUS

WORLD OCEAN WORLD

MATERIAL

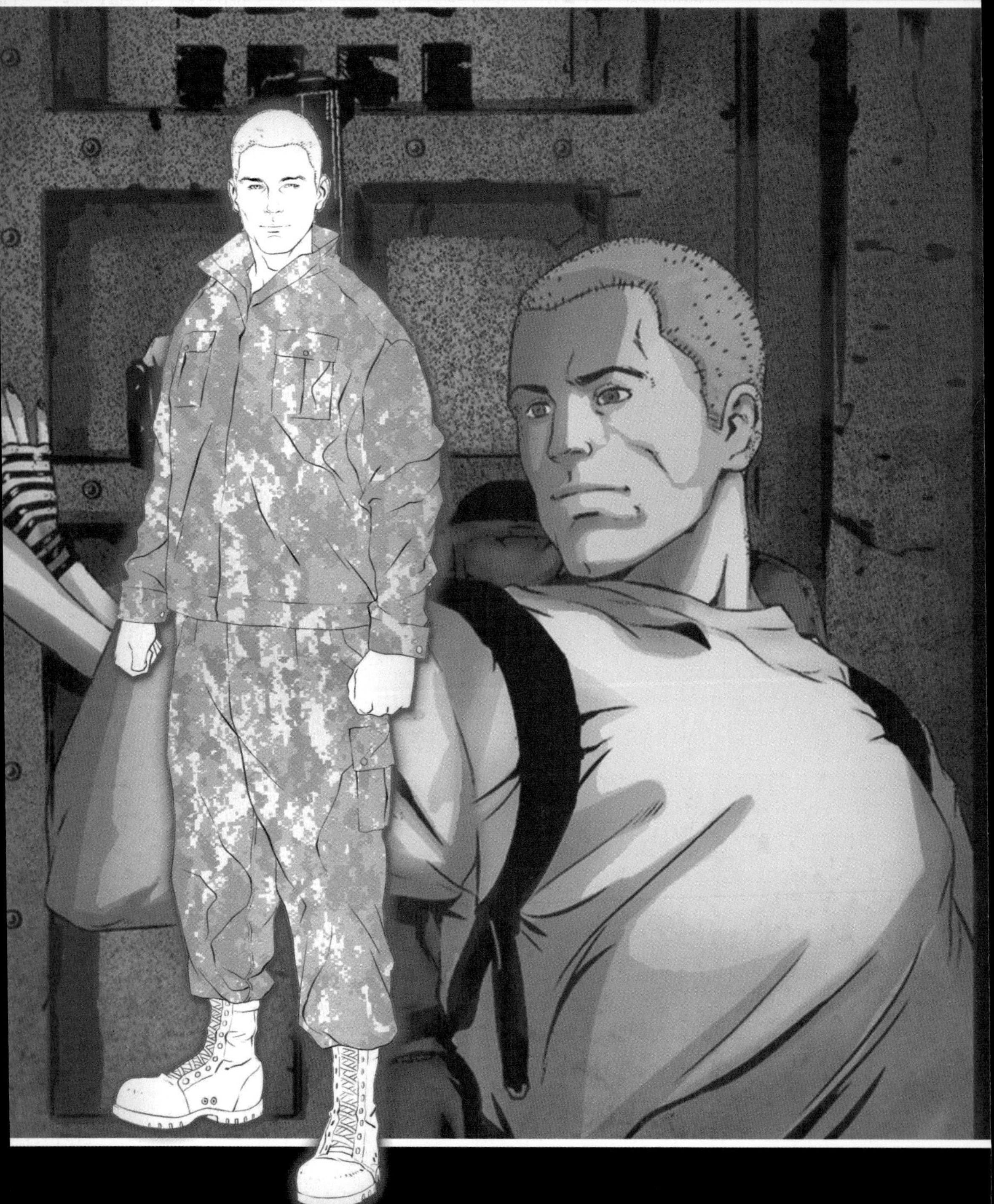

CURT

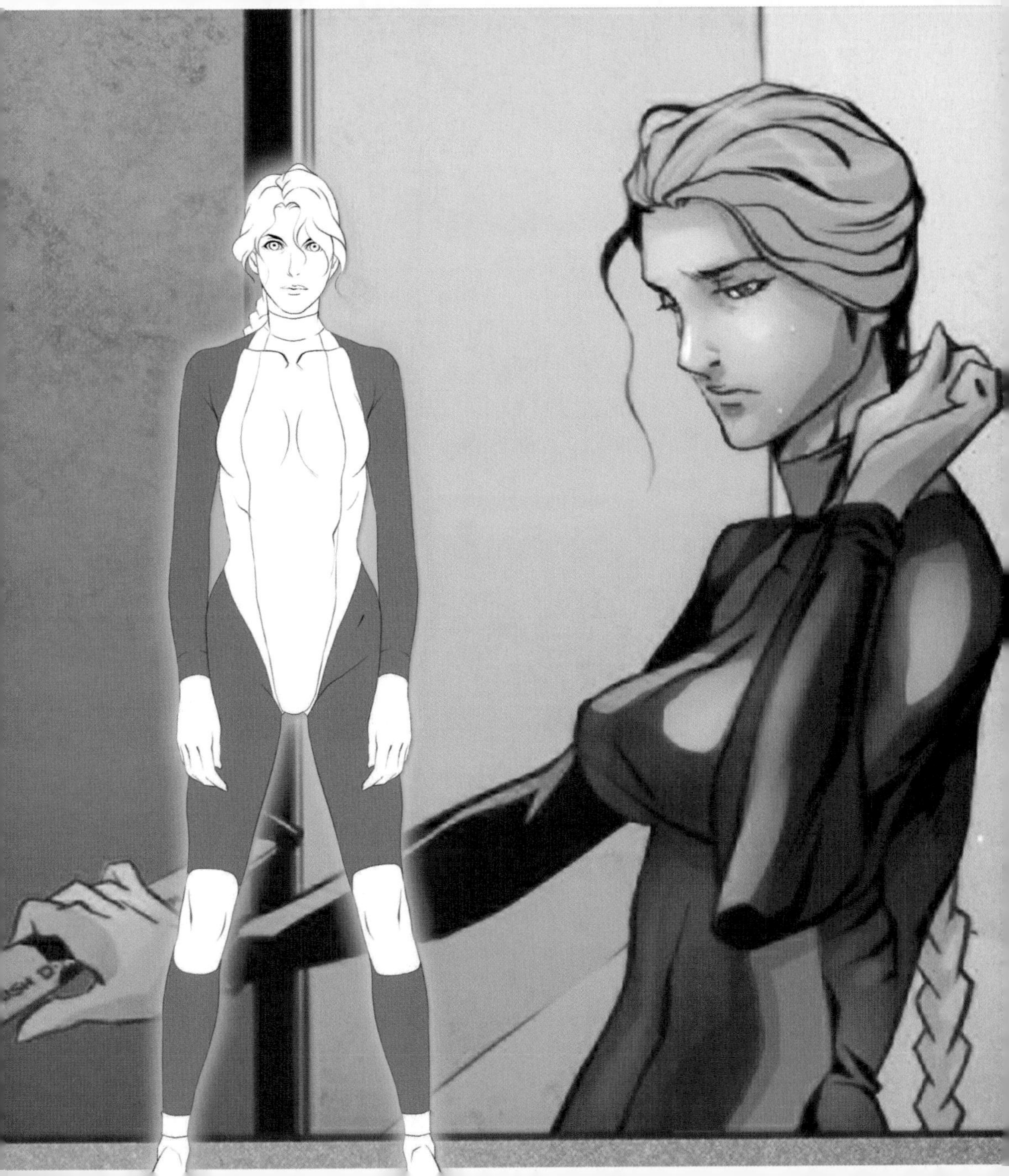

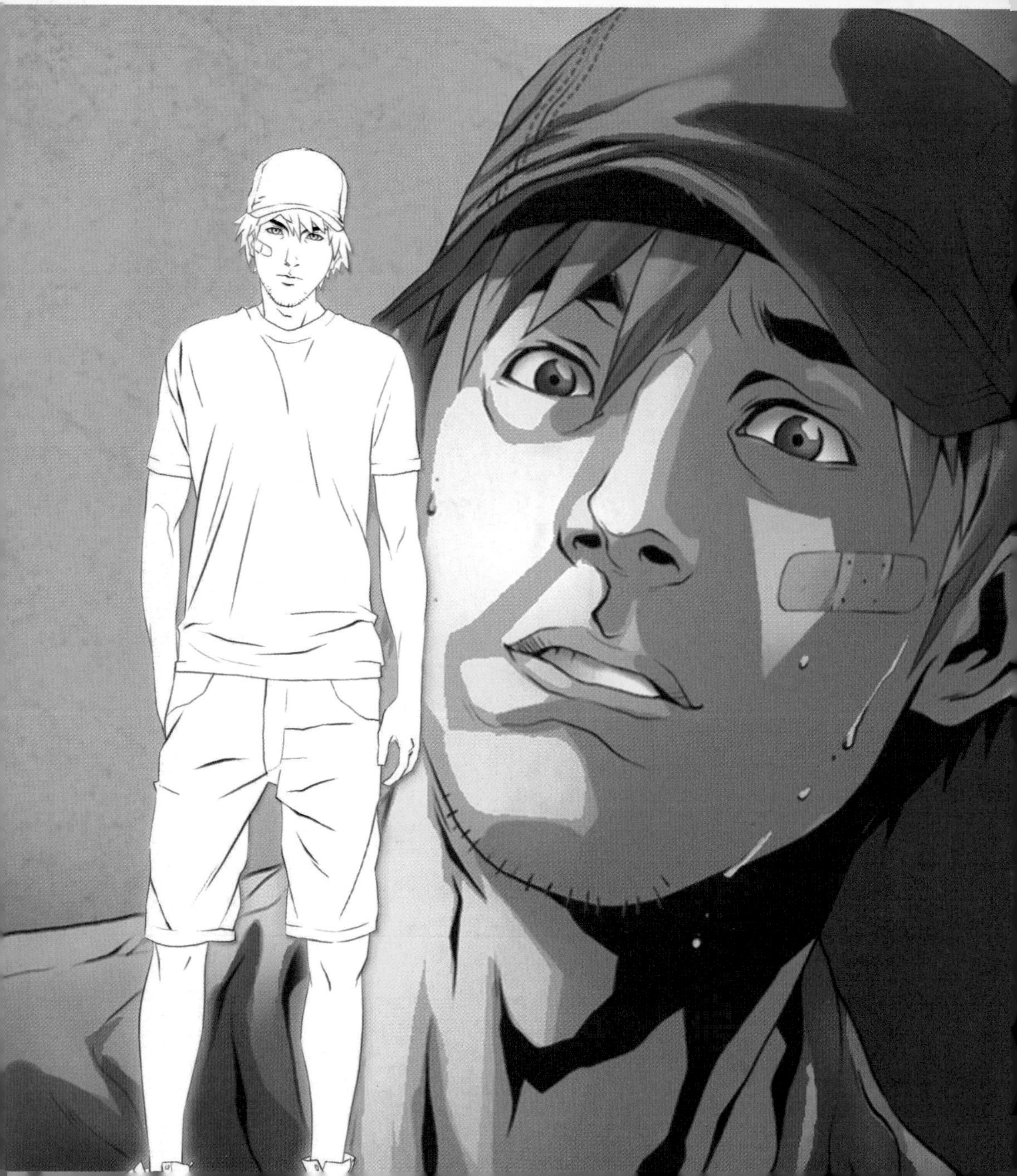

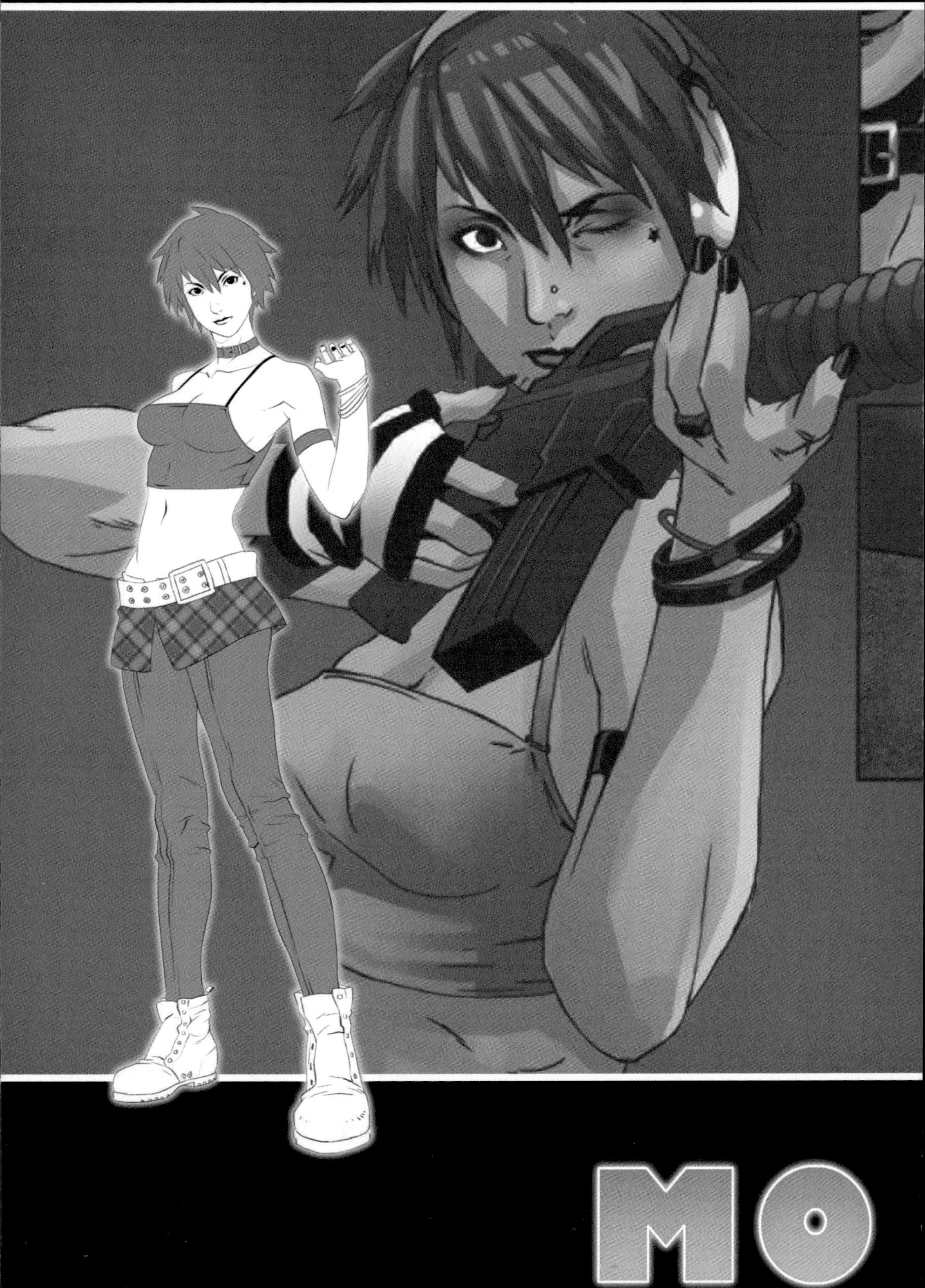
MO

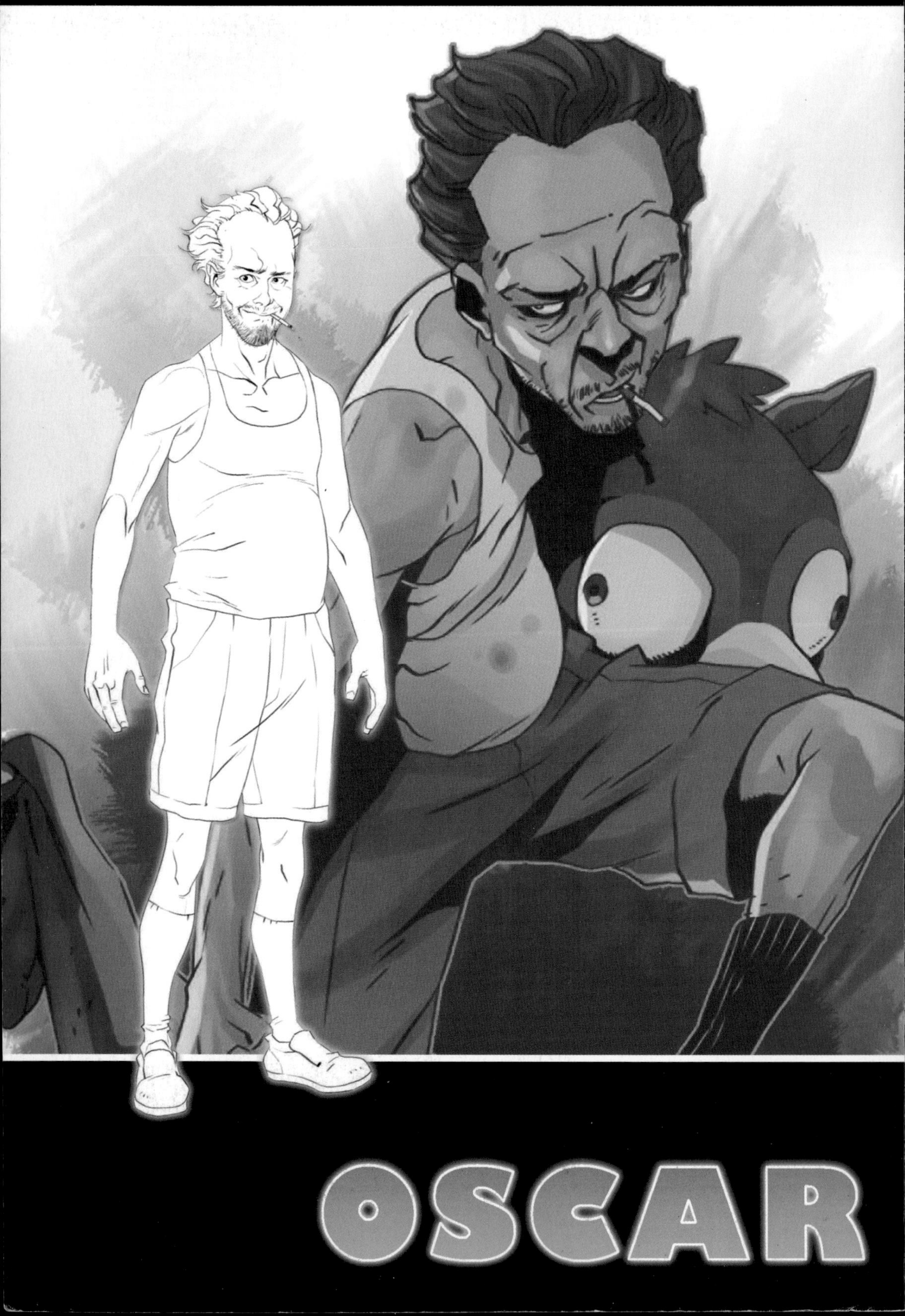
OSCAR

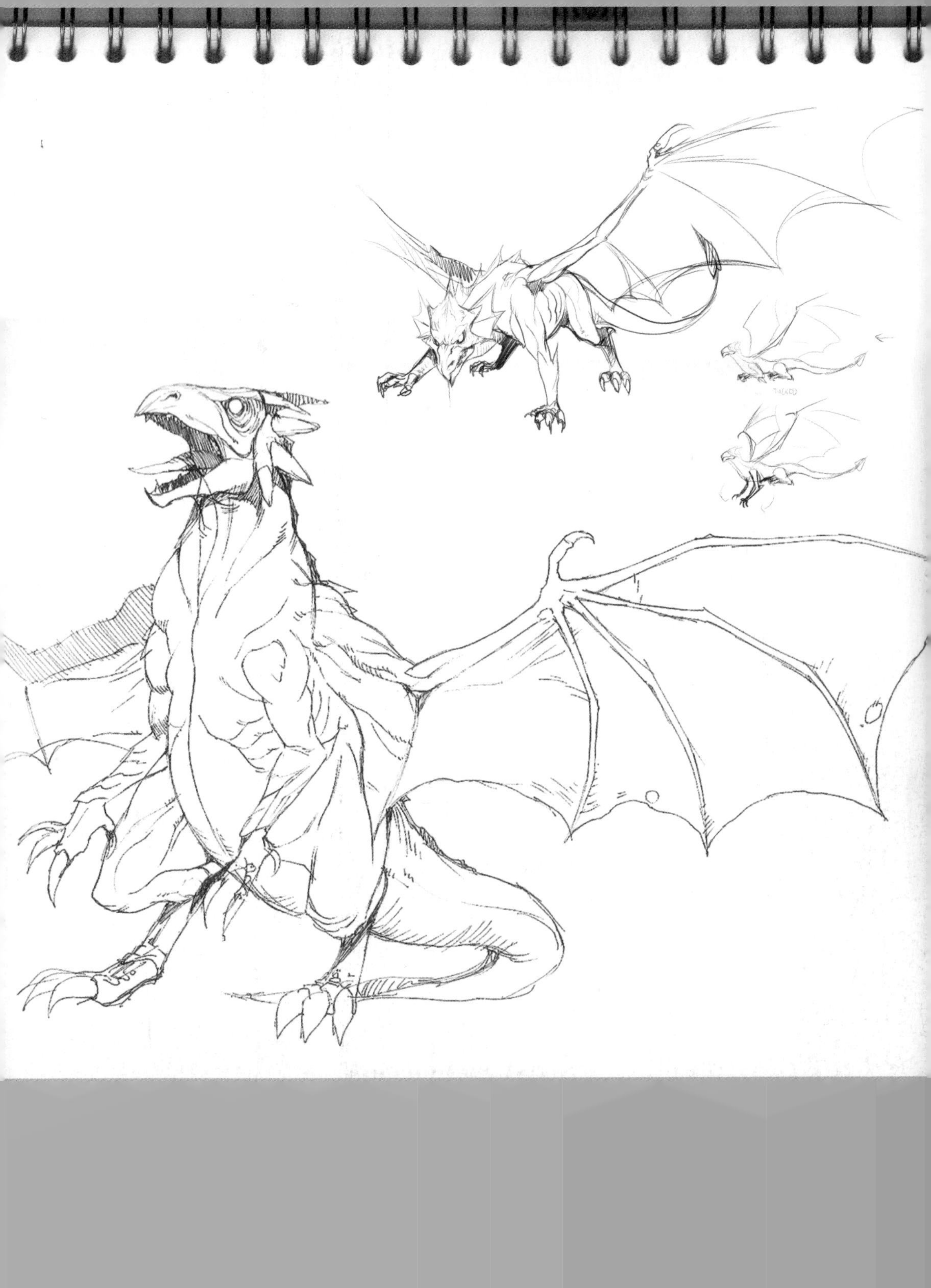
TUCKED

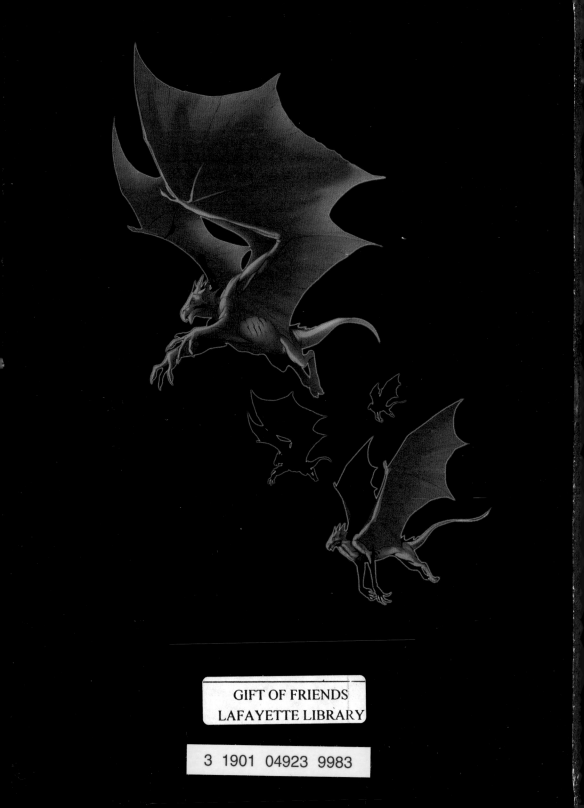